FLIGHT FAILURE

INVESTIGATING THE NUTS AND BOLTS OF AIR DISASTERS AND AVIATION SAFETY

Donald J. Porter

Prometheus Books

Guilford, Connecticut

PB Prometheus Books

An imprint of The Rowman & Littlefield Publishing Group, Inc.
4501 Forbes Boulevard, Suite 200, Lanham, Maryland 20706
www.rowman.com

Distributed by NATIONAL BOOK NETWORK

British Library Cataloguing in Publication Information Available

Library of Congress Cataloging-in-Publication Data

Names: Porter, Donald J., author.
Title: Flight failure : investigating the nuts and bolts of air disasters and aviation safety / Donald J. Porter.
Description: Lanham, MD : Prometheus Books, an imprint of the Rowman & Littlefield Publishing Group, Inc., [2020] | Includes bibliographical references and index. | Summary: "This book chronicles maintenance-related accidents caused by individual, corporate, or governmental negligence and brings the industry's current state of affairs into sharp focus. The author, a former aviation engineer, examines how failures of the smallest of parts have brought down airliners, explaining sometimes esoteric mechanical issues for readers with no technical background."— Provided by publisher.
Identifiers: LCCN 2019054472 (print) | LCCN 2019054473 (ebook) | ISBN 9781633886223 (paperback) | ISBN 9781633886230 (epub)
Subjects: LCSH: Aircraft accidents—Investigation—United States—Case studies. | Airplanes—United States—Maintenance and repair—Case studies. | Aeronautics—United States—Safety measures. | Disasters—United States—Case studies. | LCGFT: Case studies.
Classification: LCC TL553.52 .P67 2020 (print) | LCC TL553.52 (ebook) | DDC 363.12/465—dc23
LC record available at https://lccn.loc.gov/2019054472
LC ebook record available at https://lccn.loc.gov/2019054473

∞™ The paper used in this publication meets the minimum requirements of American National Standard for Information Sciences—Permanence of Paper for Printed Library Materials, ANSI/NISO Z39.48-1992.

To my late mother, Elsie,
who inspired me to pursue writing,
and to my wife, Rita, for nurturing that career

CONTENTS

INTRODUCTION

There is incredible power in the smallest of things. A speeding bullet can kill an elephant. A match can destroy a 100,000-acre forest. In aviation, a cotter pin worth two cents and no larger than a paper clip can bring down a 300,000-pound jetliner, killing hundreds of people.

Consider what happened over Indonesia and Ethiopia. Minutes after taking off in good weather, two Boeing 737 MAX 8 jetliners became victims of malfunctioning sensors. The sensors caused the tails to angle the noses of the planes downward, with the frenzied pilots unable to correct their flight paths. The near-new jets plummeted into earth and sea. A total of 346 people aboard the planes were killed. In March 2019, all MAX airliners were grounded.

60 Minutes aired an investigative report on April 15, 2018, citing safety issues at Allegiant Air, a major low-fare airline. On August 17, 2015, the flight of one of Allegiant Air's MD-83 jetliners, carrying 158 people, was aborted during takeoff from Las Vegas. Gaining speed, the plane had lifted off by itself—before its pilots moved the controls and far too early during the takeoff roll. The startled crew wisely rejected the takeoff and stopped the jet before it careened past the end of the runway. The cause: a missing cotter pin in the elevator control mechanism. A mechanic hadn't taken an extra minute to slip the pin into a nut.

An estimated 20 percent of aircraft accidents are caused by mechanical failure. Over the last fifty years of commercial aviation, the same types of accidents have occurred repeatedly.

On September 1, 1961, a mechanic forgot to install a cotter pin in a linkage that controlled the elevator of a four-engine TWA Constellation departing from Chicago. The plane limped into the air and four minutes later slammed into a cornfield. The fiery crash killed all seventy-eight people aboard, including twenty children. There are dozens of other accidents, some old, some new, many fatal—all caused by missing bolts and pins.

Not unlike searching for a needle in a haystack, investigators sift through the accident scenes of crashes like these in a search for clues. Each investigation turns into a challenging mystery begging for a cause to be found as soon as possible. Once the obvious is ruled out, laying the blame on a nut or bolt calls for painstaking detective work—even more so when it involves targeting a person or organization responsible for a deadly maintenance error.

How and why such accidents continue to happen is a seldom-discussed, dark side of commercial aviation.

The comfort and amenities of air travel are no more. But surely airline maintenance is better than ever. Ask a group of passengers and be prepared for a quizzical look. They may assume that it's better.

When *60 Minutes* presented its investigation of Allegiant Air, there were revelations concerning maintenance oversights, an improper firing, poor recordkeeping, and weak Federal Aviation Administration (FAA) enforcement. One of the incidents mentioned had to do with the missing cotter pin. Although an investigation by the media should interest anyone who flies, most passengers don't rank safety high on their list of concerns. Cheap fares are what matter. It has been reported that more than 10 million viewers watch *60 Minutes* on Sunday nights. This specific broadcast resulted in unfavorable publicity for the airline and for the aviation industry as a whole, but a fast-moving news cycle soon eclipsed the story of the takeoff mishap. Within days, the stock for Allegiant had recovered. And just as many people as before the broadcast continued to buy tickets from the carrier.

Accidents often result from a safety culture at the airlines that allows mistakes to flourish. The FAA is caught in a middle role, regulating safety on one hand and assuring the fiscal stability of airlines on the other. It's a difficult balancing act.

Whether an airline is large or small, whether it flies older planes or newer ones, maintenance errors creep in regularly. This happens especially when there is a corporate culture that does not make passenger safety its primary concern.

The passengers aboard the Lion Air and Ethiopian Airlines MAX 8s didn't have a chance. In 2015, the Allegiant Air MD-83 never left Las Vegas, and the passengers suffered no more inconvenience than an extra night in a hotel (in 2000 an Emery Worldwide Airlines DC-8-71 had been the victim of a similar event, although that turned out to be fatal). These are not obscure incidents. Beginning with the advent of modern aviation, missing hardware has often been responsible for accidents, regardless of whether the plane is a Cessna 152 or Boeing 747.

On September 11, 1991, a mechanic forgot to install dozens of screws that secured part of the tail of a Brasilia airliner flown by Continental Express. The plane broke apart in midair, killing everyone aboard. The outcome: regulators made a big push to improve safety with the goal of not repeating such a horrific accident. In 1998, another Brasilia barely made it back to the airport. Screws holding the same part of the tail were missing—exactly what had happened earlier. Lessons can be forgotten and mistakes repeated.

An Airbus A320 operated by Jetstar Airways in Australia suffered a thrust reverser failure during landing on December 18, 2017. The cause was unusual: a pin was required to be inserted in the mechanism *only* during maintenance. However, a mechanic forgot to remove the pin prior to the plane's return to service. Fortunately, there were no injuries.

On the flip side, considering the thousands of planes flying over the United States at any given time, the chance of these accidents occurring is statistically remote. However, they have happened and likely will again. There are no clear-cut safeguards in place to prevent their recurrence.

Unlike in years past, much maintenance at the major airlines is outsourced to independent overhaul bases. Some of the facilities are overseas and poorly supervised. Regardless of where the work is performed, stress, inadequate training, poor communication between work shifts, and other issues continue to result in deadly outcomes. What you are about to read are accurate accounts of why accidents occur for the smallest of reasons, quite literally. This book presents information gleaned from thousands of pages of accident reports combined with first-hand knowledge accumulated during my years in the aviation industry. Demystifying technical issues behind these accidents, and understanding how they might be prevented in the future, is my interest.

Aviation is unforgiving. It always will be. When it comes to maintaining airplanes properly, a zero-tolerance standard is imperative. Unfortunately, that lofty goal has not been attained.

1

WHO'S MINDING THE STORE?

It's a rare day when a mishap at the airlines doesn't find its way into the evening news. What viewers usually see is outrageous passenger behavior or poor service on the part of employees. However, a more solemn story occasionally gets their attention: a plane crashes, and people die.

The headlines on October 29, 2018, reported such a disaster. A Boeing 737 MAX 8 jetliner crashed in Indonesia, killing 189 people. Then on March 10, 2019, another MAX 8 crashed, this time in Ethiopia, and 157 passengers and crew died. The accidents had something in common: two identical, near-new jetliners crashing minutes after takeoff, within five months of each other.

As the words for this chapter are being written, there are no final conclusions on why these jets met their horrific fate. And there's no absence of stories in the media concerning Boeing Commercial Airplanes, the manufacturer that designed and built the planes.

Theories concerning the baffling accidents are easy to find. Some pilots point to inexperienced flight crews of foreign airlines incapable of handling major emergencies. Others rake Boeing over the coals for selling planes with design defects. Still others suspect sloppy maintenance or poor workmanship. Even the airlines are blamed for not recognizing the risk in operating the unproven planes they have bought. Ultimately, the cause may involve a combination of design, pilot training, maintenance, and mistakes on the part of industry and government for approving a plane that wasn't safe.

For now, one bit of evidence has emerged as the impetus that brought on a string of failures contributing to both accidents. Sensors designed to measure the angle of attack (AOA) of the wings apparently malfunctioned. The AOA is the angle formed between the chord (width) of a wing and the direction of air flowing past the wing. Collins Aerospace manufactures these two-pound, high-tech sensors. One of them, improperly repaired by Xtra Aerospace in South Florida, is suspected of starting the cascade of events that resulted in the deaths of the air travelers in Indonesia.

Accidents caused by aircraft design deficiencies seldom warrant headlines—unless people die. A well-known airliner of the 1960s that experienced several horrific accidents due to design flaws was the turboprop-powered Lockheed Electra. Another string of accidents involved the McDonnell Douglas DC-10 jumbo jet of the 1970s. Today, the public's attention is riveted on the troubled 737 MAX.

Having dominated the world of aircraft production for over one hundred years, Boeing remains the only U.S. maker of airline transports. Lockheed and McDonnell Douglas, Boeing's longtime competitors, exited the airliner manufacturing business decades ago.

The MAX is likely to become the final iteration of Boeing's long-standing single-aisle jetliner; the original 737-100 first flew on April 9, 1967. A series of MAX models is available in four sizes, each of their fuselages "stretched" to seat anywhere from 138 to 204 passengers in two classes.[1] The MAX 8 is the medium-size variant of this series. The program had been lauded as highly successful, and by January 2019, Boeing had received more than five thousand firm orders for the MAX series, including 201 planes committed to Lion Air in Indonesia. International air carriers ordered more MAXs than domestic carriers, but Alaska, American, Southwest, and United committed to buying 549 of the jets, including those already delivered.

The distinguishing feature of all MAXs is their pair of engines: CFM International LEAP-1B turbofans capable of providing 29,000 pounds of thrust each.[2] These fuel-stingy engines, combined with split-tip winglets and other aerodynamic enhancements, allow the MAX to consume considerably less fuel than the 737 Next Generation (NG) model it replaces. If it weren't for fuel-efficient engines, the airlines would have no reason to buy such hundred-million-dollar jetliners. Pilot salaries and the cost of fuel rank high on the list of items to worry about for chief financial officers at the airlines. Their priorities are saving fuel and moving ahead to automate more of the functions that employees now handle.

The LEAP's fan diameter of sixty-nine inches compares with the sixty-one-inch diameter of the CFM56-7BE engine powering the NG. This may not seem like much of a difference, but adapting an engine with a larger diameter fan to an airframe designed one-half century ago presented a problem for the engineers at Boeing. The 737-100 featured slender, 14,000-pound-thrust Pratt & Whitney

JT8D turbofan engines mounted under its wings and not the large-diameter, $14.5-million fanjet masterpieces powering the MAX. The design challenge centered on providing enough clearance between the bottom of the rotund LEAP engine nacelles and the pavement. If the clearance were insufficient, a pilot could accidentally hit a light fixture along a taxiway. Aware of this possibility, the engineers lengthened the MAX nose landing gear by eight inches. To gain additional clearance and move the plane's center of gravity more toward the nose, they also cantilevered the three-ton engines forward and slightly higher than the leading edges of the wing. A cursory look reveals that the engines on the original 737 appear to have 80 percent of their length carried under the wings, while the MAX's LEAP engines seem to have 80 percent of their length *ahead* of the wings. (A DIFFERENCE IN SAFETY)

The executives at Boeing elected to pursue an evolutionary design approach to develop the MAX by making the plane a variant of the 737NG, rather than embarking on the riskier course the company took in developing its 787 Dreamliner by certificating the MAX as an all-new plane. This short-cut for the MAX avoided the requirement that the FAA certificate the MAX as a new plane, but Boeing soon discovered that integrating today's technology and a dated airframe brought unexpected roadblocks.

The handling characteristics of the MAX 8 differ from those of the NG because the heavier LEAP engines are mounted further ahead of the plane's center of gravity. This created stability and control problems. If a pilot maneuvered the MAX to generate "an angle of attack close to the stall angle of around fourteen degrees, the previously neutral nacelle generates lift," observed Bjorn Fehrm, an aeronautical engineering analyst.[3] If lift is developed ahead of the center of gravity, a plane will have a tendency to pitch upward. The curved surfaces of the LEAP nacelles created that kind of lift. During testing, this became apparent during steep AOA and high-airspeed flying. To counter this characteristic, a software-activated control system was developed, the MAX becoming the first model of a 737 so equipped. Boeing had another reason for incorporating the system: without it, spending time and money on a new FAA type certificate would be required—instead of an amended certificate based on the NG.

On a parallel path with the MAX engineers in Seattle, Boeing's competitors at Airbus SE in Europe pushed ahead to develop the A320neo. At first glance, the A320neo's overall look is similar to that of the MAX, both of them single-aisle, twin-engine jets. "Neo" is an abbreviation for "new engine option," referring to the LEAP engines and other high-efficiency engines compatible with the A320neo airframe. Seven months after the A320neo was introduced, Airbus had received more than one thousand orders and commitments for the plane. Meanwhile at Boeing, development work for the MAX lagged more than eighteen months behind that of the A320neo. In 2011, Boeing hoped to launch the program and corner the market with large orders from several airlines. It was fortunate in doing so, but in competing with Airbus for additional orders, the company found itself neck and neck in a race with its European competitor. The MAX and A320neo would have to fight for a substantial share in the global market for single-aisle jetliners. "They weren't going to stand by and let Airbus steal market share," said Mike Renzelmann, a retired Boeing 737 MAX flight controls engineer.[4]

The intense race that developed to scoop up orders and develop the MAX took a human toll at the Boeing plant in Seattle. Extended workdays and weeks became the norm. Employees who worked well under pressure stayed; those who couldn't cope with the stressful environment retired or moved to other companies. "This program was a much more intense pressure cooker than I've ever been in," said Rick Ludtke, a MAX cockpit design engineer. "They wanted the minimum change to simplify the training differences, minimum change to reduce costs, and to get it done quickly."[5]

The first flight of a MAX took place on January 29, 2016. On May 22, 2017, passenger service was inaugurated with Malindo Air in Malaysia.

As dawn arrived over the coast of Indonesia at 6:20 a.m. on October 29, 2018, the pilots of Lion Air Flight 610, after taking off from Soekarno-Hatta International Airport in Jakarta for Depati Amir Airport in Pangkal Pinang, Indonesia, lost control of their three-month-old MAX 8.

As the plane's nose landing gear lifted off from runway 25L, the captain's yoke[6] began shaking, normally warning the crew of an impending stall. Throttles pushed forward, the engines continued to develop almost 58,000 pounds of thrust. The captain didn't reduce power, and the plane gained airspeed rapidly. Two minutes after takeoff, while climbing, the flaps were retracted. Within seconds, the nose began angling down, the jet dropping rapidly. In an attempt to counter the dive, the captain moved the flaps back down but then retracted them again. Pulling back on the yoke, he also clicked a thumb switch that controlled the horizontal stabilizer trim. It raised the nose—but five seconds later the nose-down travel resumed. The switch was repeatedly pressed and then released to bring the nose up, but the pitch angle dropped again after each five-second reprieve. The crew then climbed to 5,000 feet. Over six minutes, more than twenty-five of the frightening down-and-up cycles took place. Then there was a final, mystifying, automatically controlled nose-down trajectory that the pilots were unable to counter, and the plane entered a screaming high-speed dive exceeding 10,000 feet per minute.

Ten minutes into the eleven-minute flight, thirty-one-year-old Captain Bhavye Suneja, a citizen of India, told his copilot, Harvino, a forty-one-year-old Indonesian having a single name, to take over the controls. Seemingly overwhelmed, Harvino hesitated. By now, the stabilizer had reached its maximum nose-down angle. While Suneja struggled with the controls, Harvino flipped through the pages of a "quick reference handbook." But there wasn't time. Its nose pointing down sharply, the plane had already lost thousands of feet of life-saving airspace. The plane was stuck in a steep, downward trajectory not far above the sea. Adjusting the trim wheels next to their seats to manually change the stabilizer angle became their last hope. But the high airspeed of the jet meant that the extreme aerodynamic forces the speed created prevented them from turning the wheels.

The MAX 8 plummeted nose first into the Java Sea at a reported 500 mph, its airframe disintegrating on impact. Suneja, Harvino, and the 187 other souls aboard were killed instantly.

In the days following the crash, Indonesian accident investigators suspected that when the flaps were retracted after takeoff, an unknown force had moved the nose down. Suneja and Harvino tried to counter that force by clicking on the thumb switches. While they fought the nose-down force, the captain's yoke continued to shake, warning them of a stall that didn't exist. The distraction continued for the entire duration of the short flight.

What neither pilot knew was that an automatic system had taken over control of the jet without their knowledge. They didn't understand why the apparently erratic downward movements began and continued, or how to stop them. Whatever actions they took proved mostly ineffective. There was no mention of this predicament in the handbook that Harvino held in his hand. And nothing had been discussed with the pilots during flight simulator training sessions. "To expect someone at a moment of high pressure to do everything exactly right is really tough," said Alvin Lie, an Indonesian aviation expert and the country's ombudsman. "That's why you don't want to ever put a pilot in that situation if there's anything you can do to stop it."[7]

Another Lion Air crew had reported a series of problems with this particular MAX 8 the day before its final flight. They included AOA, altitude, and airspeed mismatches between the pilot and copilot instruments. One of the Collins AOA sensors was replaced, and ground tests indicated that the plane was safe to again transport passengers. It was not. During the course of the accident investigation, it was reported that Boeing had voiced concerns about the quality of Lion Air's maintenance practices, asserting that the logs for the accident plane indicated "ineffective troubleshooting in the days before the accident" as a possible cause.[8] The manufacturer also questioned why the crew was ineffective in stopping the diving. Rusdi Kirana, the founder of Lion Air and one of Boeing's biggest MAX customers, was upset by the unproven allegations. He interpreted the comments as meant to shift blame from Boeing to the airline and its pilots.

The investigation continued to focus on an AOA sensor on the left side of the fuselage that had malfunctioned. Its signal was thought to be the reason why the horizontal stabilizer continually changed its angle and forced the plane's nose down. The sensor's output signal was indicative of the nose being dangerously high and creating a stall condition whereas in fact, the nose was in a dangerously low position. Adding to their mental confusion, the pilots were being warned of an impending stall by the continuously shaking yoke, even though the plane was not stalling. What was going on? In the background, unknown to the pilots or likely to *anyone* other than Boeing engineers and managers, the sensor's false signal had activated something called the Maneuvering Characteristics Augmentation System (MCAS).

Aviation Daily, an authoritative publication covering the airline industry, reported, "The MCAS was needed for certification purposes to enhance pitch stability with slats and flaps retracted at very light weights and full aft center of gravity, ensuring the MAX handles like the NG."[9]

An AOA sensor consists of a vane protruding from a sealed housing into the airstream. Small enough to fit in a person's hand, it has only one job: to measure the angle of the air flowing across the surface of a wing. If a plane's nose rises too steeply while the plane is flying too slowly, a stall can result. It's a condition where the AOA becomes so high that the air flowing over the wing is heavily disrupted. This results in not enough lift being developed to overcome the weight of the plane. To prevent this from happening, the MAX was equipped with MCAS, which was not a feature of the NG or earlier versions of the 737. Upon receiving an AOA signal from a sensor, MCAS would command the nose to drop for ten seconds and then repeat the action at five-second intervals if the same condition were sensed. There was no limit to the number of times the system could activate.

To recover from a dive, pilots are trained early in their careers to pull a yoke, stick, or control wheel backward to reposition the angle of the plane's elevator. In the MAX, this action proved meaningless. The aerodynamic force created by MCAS, which resulted from significantly changing the angle of the horizontal stabilizer, was far greater than any opposing force produced by the elevator. "After a period of time, the elevator is going to lose, and the stabilizer is going to win," said Pat Anderson, a professor of aerospace engineering at Embry-Riddle Aeronautical University.[10]

Combining sophisticated flight control automation with an older but proven airframe required an innovative approach for the system design engineers at Boeing. The computer-aided assistance of MCAS would ensure that the tactile feel of the MAX flight controls closely replicated that of the NG flight controls. Boeing's reputation among pilots (especially those flying for U.S.-based airlines) has been founded on providing them with direct control of its planes without interference from behind-the-scenes automation. So strong is this view that pilots have often routinely asserted, "If it's not Boeing, I'm not going."[11] Airbus adopted a far different philosophy, turning heavily to digital technology for taming or limiting pilot actions, particularly those considered risky. For younger, more computer-literate groups of pilots, increased Airbus automation is welcomed, particularly by crews working for international air carriers. It's especially true for pilots who have logged relatively few flight hours.

Whenever groups of seasoned pilots gather, discussions often revolve around whether or not automated flight control systems have eroded basic "stick and rudder" flying skills. "You get a lot of takeoffs and landings, but no one gets much flying practice," said Keith Mackey, a safety consultant and former airline pilot speaking about newer generations of airline pilots. "They know which buttons to push and when to push them. [But] when something begins to fail, it becomes a puzzlement."[12]

On November 6, 2018, Boeing alerted the airlines and their pilots via a company bulletin about how to save the day should the nose drop unexpectedly. It noted that faulty AOA sensor data could trigger ten-second increments of nose-down stabilizer movement. A thumb switch on the yoke could temporarily stop the movements, but they would restart five seconds after the switch was released. The bulletin stressed that crews follow an existing "runaway stabilizer checklist" to stop the cycling. Published a day after the Boeing bulletin, here's what the FAA told all operators of MAXs in an emergency airworthiness directive (AD):

> This emergency AD was prompted by analysis performed by the manufacturer [Boeing] showing that if an erroneously high single angle of attack (AOA) sensor input is received by the flight control system, that is a potential for repeated nose-down trim commands of the horizontal stabilizer. This condition, if not addressed, could cause the flight crew to have difficulty controlling the airplane, and lead to excessive nose-down attitude, significant altitude loss, and possible impact with terrain.[13]

The AD required Boeing to include in the plane's flight manual the information it published in the bulletin about runaway horizontal stabilizer trim. The AD did not call for the manufacturer to modify the airplane in any way. And it did not mention MCAS by name.

The investigators in Jakarta knew that the AOA sensor on the left side had produced a higher signal than the one on the right. The signal triggered the flight control computer that activated MCAS to drop the nose. Data downloaded from the accident plane's digital flight data recorder (DFDR) revealed that the readings from the plane's two sensors differed by 20 degrees, even when the plane was sitting on the ground.

During Flight 610's brief time in the air, MCAS began a relentless tug of war with the pilots. The system pushed the nose lower while the crew wrestled with the controls in a vain attempt to raise the nose. It seems likely that Boeing's engineers and the FAA hadn't taken into account the stressful conditions that pilots face during emergencies. These conditions can be stupefying even though the situation demands an instantaneous response. There's no time to read a manual, radio a maintenance specialist, or fumble with seldom-used controls or switches. Any action must be embedded in a pilot's memory and performed without delay. But in the situation facing the Lion Air crew, it was impossible to perform by memory something they had never heard of or done before.

If a plane does something unexpected in flight, pilots consult abbreviated emergency checklists. In this case, it wasn't that simple: they weren't familiar with what might be causing the excursions. Boeing had told pilots who flew 737s, including those flying the MAX, to follow its procedure for recovering from a runaway horizontal stabilizer condition. The procedure stressed the need to turn off a pair of cutoff switches on the center console to cut the power that energized a motor-driven jackscrew moving the stabilizer. This would also disable MCAS. With the thumb switches on the yokes now disabled, the pilots would need to adjust the plane's stabilizer angle manually by turning one of the cockpit trim wheels. However, if a plane were flying at speeds as fast as Flight 610 was, aerodynamic forces would make it difficult, if not impossible, for the pilots to turn the wheel. Even more importantly, what happened to Flight 610 didn't resemble a runaway stabilizer; that is, the trim wheels weren't rotating in one direction continuously. If they had been, the pilots should have known what to do.

The MAX lacked a feature existing on the 737NG. On that earlier plane, pulling back on the yoke activated a "column control switch," interrupting unwanted movement of the stabilizer. But MCAS bypassed that switch, eliminating this way to recover from a dive.

Not only was MCAS omitted from pilot training materials, it wasn't discussed during meetings with customer airlines and the FAA. Boeing's rationale for not publicizing the system was to prevent overloading pilots with technical details it deemed irrelevant. The saying "No need to know" was in full force in Seattle. "I don't need to know about every rivet, but I do need to know about something that's going to take over my airplane," said Dennis Tajer, a 737 captain at Southwest Airlines.[14]

Boeing had marketed the MAX by assuring its customers there was no need for pilots to undergo time-consuming flight simulator training beyond that required for the NG. This kept things simple: a single FAA type rating allowed any pilot trained to fly one model of the 737 to fly *any* model 737, including the MAX.

In late 2017, the FAA finalized a report that served as the basis for training MAX pilots about the jet's differences. But it didn't mention MCAS. "It's pretty asinine for them to put a system on an airplane and not tell the pilots who are operating the airplane, especially when it comes to flight controls," said Mike Michaelis, chairman of the safety committee for the Allied Pilots Association.[15]

Pilots assigned to the MAX would discover their transition training amounted to an hour-long session conducted on an iPad. Its purpose was to explore what differences existed compared to the NG. But here again, no information was provided about MCAS or what to do if the system failed. By not requiring training in dedicated MAX flight simulators, the airlines were saving tens of millions of dollars, and those savings served as a prime selling point for the MAX. This was something that Boeing and the airlines didn't wish to change. "The FAA said nothing about this technology at a critical time—when pilots were learning how to fly the plane," said Mary Schiavo, a former Transportation Department inspector general. "It makes you ask the question: How much did the FAA actually know about the technology, especially given the history of delegating to industry?"[16]

On March 10, 2019, a very similar kind of accident happened in Africa. At 8:38 a.m., Ethiopian Airlines Flight 302 departed from 7,624-foot-high Addis Ababa Bole International Airport in Ethiopia for Jomo Kenyatta International Airport in Nairobi, Kenya. The four-month-old MAX 8 found itself in trouble immediately.

Six seconds after liftoff, the yoke in front of the pilot began shaking just as it had in Jakarta, signaling a stall that didn't exist. Instinctively, Captain Yared Getachew and copilot Ahmed Nur Mohammod Nur pushed their yokes forward expecting to counteract what appeared to be an approaching stall. Reaching level flight, the MAX accelerated rapidly, pushed along by the same level of thrust the crew had set for takeoff. Upon the pilots retracting the flaps, the stabilizer moved twice, ten seconds each time, pushing the nose of the plane incrementally lower. Getachew pressed the thumb switch on his yoke to raise the nose. Five seconds elapsed and the timing circuit in MCAS reset. The plane's flight control computer again activated MCAS, triggered by a bad signal from an AOA sensor. Once again, the nose moved down. Getachew responded by flicking the switch again. Nur then turned the power off for the stabilizer motor by moving the two cutoff switches near the throttles, which also de-energized MCAS. The pilots tried to adjust the pitch attitude manually by turning the trim wheels. Because of the plane's high speed, the wheels wouldn't budge. At 8:43, unable to move the wheels, the pilots flipped the cutout switches back on. It would prove to be a fatal move. The nose-down movements of the plane resumed. Clicking their thumb switches as before, the crew was able to complete two rapid nose-up movements. But MCAS simply reset and then triggered a third nose-down activation. This pushed the plane into a steep nose-down attitude, causing a rapid descent from 6,000 feet. Pulling back on their yokes and attempting to move the trim wheels proved useless, and with time running out, the crew became overwhelmed.

Much like what happened to Lion Air Flight 610, MCAS had commanded the plane to dive. And because the plane's engines were producing maximum thrust throughout the flight, the plane picked up tremendous speed as it dove. Also in common with the Jakarta accident, the aerodynamic force created by this speed made it impossible for the pilots to manually turn the trim wheels and return to level flight.

Cleared by air traffic control for an emergency return to Addis Ababa, Getachew managed to turn the jet around, but six minutes after taking off, it disappeared from radar. At 8:44 a.m., Flight 302 crashed in a farm field about forty miles from Addis Ababa, snuffing out the lives of 157 passengers and crewmembers aboard. Slamming into the earth at a near supersonic 575 mph, the plane dug a thirty-two-foot-deep crater ninety-two feet wide and more than a hundred feet long. On impact, the airframe disintegrated into thousands of pieces.

A preliminary accident report issued by Ethiopian authorities didn't provide a probable cause but did cite technical discrepancies with one of the AOA sensors.

> Shortly after takeoff, the angle of attack sensor recorded value became erroneous and the left stick shaker [the system that shakes the pilot's yoke, warning of a stall condition] activated. The left and right recorded AOA values deviated. Left AOA decreased to 11.1° then increased to 35.7° while value on right AOA indicated

19.94°. Then after the left AOA value reached 74.5° in 3/4 seconds while the right AOA reached a maximum value of 15.3°.[17]

The DFDR readings confirmed that a sensor or the technology associated with MCAS was problematic. The investigators determined that the vane of the sensor had pivoted to an extreme nose-high position, possibly damaged by striking a bird.

Flight 610 had been airborne for eleven minutes before crashing. Flight 302 only made it to six minutes. But the similarities between the accidents began to add up. In both accidents, the crews countered the unwanted stabilizer movement using electric trim. This caused MCAS to reset and then repeat cycling because of faulty data from a sensor. If the crews had turned off the cutout switches, kept them off, and resorted to manually turning the trim wheels, MCAS would not have kicked in repeatedly. However, because the throttles were set to develop nearly full thrust, the extremely high speed attained during both flights precluded moving the trim wheels.

On March 14, 2019, the Ethiopian Civil Aviation Authority grounded all MAXs. China and Indonesia followed suit, parking their planes. Other countries did the same. The groundings rattled the executives at Boeing Commercial Airplanes in Seattle. There was plenty of anxiety in the plane maker's corporate headquarters in Chicago too. The airlines in China accounted for about 20 percent of all MAX sales.

FAA officials remained quiet about a possible grounding until a growing number of countries had stopped flying the planes. President Donald Trump took an unusual step on March 13, 2019: he declared that the FAA would ground all MAXs. January 2013 was the last time the FAA had grounded any jetliner, following the discovery of battery overheating problems with the newly introduced Boeing 787 Dreamliner.

Daniel Elwell, acting administrator of the 45,000-employee FAA, cited imagery from newly acquired satellite tracking and physical evidence recovered at the crash site outside of Addis Ababa as the reason why the agency finally grounded the MAX. A jackscrew that moved the horizontal stabilizer of the MAX became the clue that would reveal what happened to both airplanes. The actuator for the plane's horizontal stabilizer was uncovered amid the rubble in the crater. Its jackscrew was stuck in a full nose-down position, indicative of a steep dive, and closely resembled what had occurred in Indonesia.

The FAA issued the following Emergency Order of Prohibition:

Effective immediately, this Order prohibits the operation of Boeing Company Model 737-8 and Boeing Company Model 737-9 airplanes by U.S. certificated operators. On March 13, 2019, the investigation of the ET302 crash developed new information from the wreckage concerning the aircraft's configuration just after takeoff that, taken together with newly refined data from satellite-based tracking of the aircraft's flight path, indicates some similarities between the ET302 and JT610 accidents that warrant further investigation of the possibility of a shared cause for the two incidents that needs to be better understood and addressed. Accordingly, the Acting Administrator is ordering all Boeing 737 MAX airplanes to be grounded pending further investigation.[18]

More than 370 MAXs were operational when the grounding order took effect. "It is a step that should have been taken directly by the federal agency responsible for aviation safety," said former National Transportation Safety Board (NTSB) chairman Jim Hall. "That it came from the White House instead speaks to a profound crisis of public confidence in the F.A.A."[19]

The terrorist hijacking of four jetliners on September 11, 2001, and their subsequent crashing into the World Trade Center, the Pentagon, and a field in Pennsylvania forever intensified the public's concern with aviation security. The U.S. government was forced to conduct background checks for baggage handlers, assign air marshals to planes, tighten airport security, have sturdy cockpit doors installed, and increase passenger screening in terminals. Saddled with a tight budget and dozens of programs to fund, some of these programs were destined for a reduction in scope, The FAA decided to stretch out the certification process for new aircraft. Predictably, frustrated executives from the nation's airframe manufacturers began complaining to members of Congress about the delays. In 2003, in order to expedite the certification process, the lawmakers ordered the FAA to delegate more of its compliance work to the manufacturers.

When the FAA came into existence in 1967, it stationed representatives in the plants of airframe manufacturers to assure that each new aircraft undergoing certification complied with federal safety standards. The FAA, working from a list of employees submitted by the manufacturers, selected technical experts called designees. Managers from the FAA supervised them. This routine was established even though the manufacturers were actually the organizations issuing paychecks to the designees. Then, in 2005, the FAA changed the process for selecting designees to something more to the liking of manufacturers. Known as an Organization Designation Authorization (ODA), it allows the *manufacturer* to choose which employees will approve design work for the FAA. This represented the beginning of what's been referred to by the media as "self-certification" (a term considered misleading by the agency). By 2009, the FAA had delegated much of its inspection authority to Boeing Commercial Airplanes. In 2018, Boeing lobbyists made sure that a few short paragraphs buried in the FAA Reauthorization Act of 2018 ceded still more authority over ODA to a manufacturer.

How did this work? In a testing laboratory, an engineer at Boeing would conduct the test of a system undergoing certification. Meanwhile, a Boeing fellow employee would act as a representative of the FAA to make sure the test complied with federal regulations. During certification work for the MAX, managers at the FAA decided what tasks the FAA's employees would handle and which ones would be delegated to Boeing employees.

The MAX development schedule remained months behind that of the A320neo as rival Airbus continued to breathe down Boeing's neck in the marketplace. The engineers and managers at Boeing, working with a sparse number of FAA engineers, were pushed to extremes. Exacerbating the situation, the FAA fell behind on its certification tasks and more work was shifted to Boeing under the ODA program. The development schedule was pushed to its limits, and on March 8, 2017, the MAX gained amended type certification from the FAA.

The preparation of a functional hazard analysis (FHA) for MCAS was one of the tasks the FAA delegated to Boeing. It would establish the statistical probability of a system failure. Whether MCAS should rely on the output of a single sensor or require two of them would be decided by a "failure classification" resulting from an analysis of the system.

If MCAS should fail and move the stabilizer fully down, it would be classified as a "major failure." This meant that passengers could suffer injuries but not death. However, in the event of an extreme maneuver, such as the plane ending up in an uncontrollable dive due to MCAS activating, the classification would change to "hazardous" because there would be the expectation of serious injury or death for an unknown number of people. This is one level below a "catastrophic" classification, which means the plane will crash and all or most of the passengers die. Although a more detailed failure modes and effects analysis (FMEA) could classify a failure of the system as "hazardous," Boeing stayed with "major" and decided to rely on a single sensor and not two.[20] There was no requirement to prepare an FMEA at that time.

The analysis also specified how far the system would be permitted to shift the position of the horizontal stabilizer. The figure stated was 0.6 degrees. However, after a series of MAX 8 flight tests conducted by Boeing revealed that additional stabilizer movement had been needed to prevent a stall at lower speeds, the original 0.6 value was increased dramatically. In November 2018,

Boeing told the airlines, albeit reluctantly, how MCAS functioned and its possible failure modes. It published a bulletin stating that the stabilizer's movement had been upped to 2.5 degrees. The increased 2.5-degree value meant that MCAS could move the stabilizer more than four times further than was stated in the analysis.[21] The system "had full authority to move the stabilizer the full amount," said Peter Lemme, a former Boeing flight controls engineer. "There was no need for that."[22]

The safety analysis was troubling: a single malfunctioning AOA sensor could trigger MCAS and kill people. And although each MAX was equipped with two Collins AOA sensors, the system's computer received signals from only one sensor during each flight. MCAS was configured to use the signal from one sensor at a time, alternating sensors between flights. Boeing could have configured the system to compare the readings from each sensor to detect a fault. Or the system might have enabled the pilots to check a sensor with the plane on the ground. It would read 0 if working properly.

It's common for critical control and instrument systems to be duplicated or even triplicated in modern aircraft. MCAS escaped such redundancy. "They could have designed a two-channel system," said Lemme. "I don't know why they didn't."[23] But even a duplicate system could prove problematic. If the reading from one sensor differed from the other, deciding which of them was correct would call for additional system complexity. It could take a third sensor to determine which one was accurate. Alternately, a modification of the processor architecture to emulate what the AOA should be during various flight regimes could have been provided. But all of these approaches would have entailed millions of dollars in development costs. Boeing would have had a difficult time passing along such costs to its customers, and the A320neo, rapidly gaining customers for Airbus, coupled with a cost increase for the increased complexity of MCAS, could have cancelled MAX orders.

After the crashes, opinions began to swirl about Boeing's attention to safety. One pilot posted on a forum frequented by airline pilots, "It is rather astounding that MCAS, if it works as described with only a single sensor input, no cross-check for implausibility, and full authority to render the plane difficult or unable to control, even passed a fundamental engineering safety review, much less made it into a certified jetliner."[24]

When Boeing launched the MAX program in 2011, until the first plane rolled out of its plant in 2016, the inspector general for the U.S. Transportation Department criticized the FAA's handling of the jet's ODA process. In 2011, the federal watchdog reported that the process for deciding what systems carried the highest safety risk was ineffective. It was noted that the FAA had not adequately trained employees of the manufacturer to spot violations of the agency's certification criteria. The FAA defended the ODA process in response to the inspector general's concerns.

Unusual for a bureaucracy, a number of current and former employees of the FAA began to recognize that the ODA process, originally believed to be safe for certificating new airplanes, was not foolproof.

"It makes sense because FAA can't be everywhere," said Michael Dreikorn, a former FAA official. "But the reality is it is flawed; you have the fox watching the henhouse."[25] However, in the wake of the September 11 terrorist attacks, the agency's leadership rationalized that it made sense to go this route, stretch its budget, and save taxpayer money. But the previous safeguards had faded away. "They were a nation unto themselves, and basically they treated themselves as independent," said Schiavo, concerning the way the FAA developed a close relationship with Boeing.[26]

"Our current system of aircraft design and certification has failed us," testified Chesley "Sully" Sullenberger in a Congressional hearing. Sullenberger was the US Airways captain whose skillful ditching in the Hudson River in 2009 saved the lives of all 155 people aboard.[27]

Several years after ODA was established, the FAA grounded all 787 Dreamliners for unexplained battery fires. There were questions about whether the ODA process had degraded the thoroughness of FAA oversight. An NTSB investigation determined that inadequate FAA and Boeing oversight of the manufacturing process was to blame.[28]

The battery problems occurred fourteen months after the 787 first entered passenger service in November 2011. The FAA had allowed Boeing to write the safety standards for the batteries, develop testing protocols, and perform their testing. In 2008, the standards for the battery system had been approved with special conditions, and stricter guidelines were released. However, the FAA didn't require Boeing to meet those guidelines.[29]

The battery system wasn't the only issue rattling the 787 program. To assemble the jet, Boeing Commercial Airplanes had built a 1.2 million sq. ft. facility in North Charleston, the third-largest city in South Carolina. It then moved the assembly work from Everett, Washington, after unionized workers there threatened to strike, thereby, taking advantage of South Carolina's miniscule unionization rate, the lowest in the nation. The company trained thousands of semi-skilled workers and conveyed to them on an informal basis that joining a union would not be the best move for their careers.

It didn't take long for quality-control problems to spiral out of control at the plant. Debris and hand tools were found wedged in different areas of the airframes. Ladders were reportedly found stuffed in the tails of planes undergoing flight testing. Metal shavings were scattered on electrical wiring under cabin floor panels. When the company didn't satisfactorily correct these and other safety issues, the FAA was pushed into taking action. From June 2013 to October 2014, the agency discontinued the use of Boeing employees serving in an ODA capacity. It assigned federal employees to oversee and sign off on the work. When the company assured the FAA that its quality standards were finally up to par, Boeing employees were reassigned to the ODA role.

Some of the quality problems were resolved but others later cropped up. On May 22, 2019, the *New York Times* reported that the executive in charge of all 787 operations in North Charleston had left the company abruptly. His dismissal came about a month after the newspaper published an investigative report detailing "shoddy production practices and weak oversight at the factory."[30] A safety culture dedicated to producing quality products was lacking. "The Federal Aviation Administration and the industry it regulates share a cozy relationship that sometimes takes a front seat to safety," said Jim Hall, recognizing the hazardous scenarios that characterized Boeing's assembly work.[31]

FAA oversight of aircraft certification had been questioned long before ODA or the current problems with the MAX, however. Fifty years ago, the FAA certificated planes that later killed people. The McDonnell Douglas DC-10 jetliner sailed through certification without a hiccup—with a system that moved pins in place to lock the plane's cargo doors designed incorrectly. The MAX 8 accidents offer a startling resemblance to what happened with the DC-10.

The DC-10 was powered by two turbofan engines mounted on the wings, with a third located below the vertical stabilizer. A successor to the company's DC-8, it offered a far wider fuselage for seating up to 380 passengers. Lockheed, the only McDonnell Douglas competitor building a comparable airplane, entered the same market with its L-1011 TriStar. Although the L-1011 was more technologically advanced, the DC-10 outsold the Lockheed plane by a wide margin because of its lower price and earlier introduction. The first DC-10 rolled from the company's plant in Long Beach, California, on July 23, 1970. McDonnell Douglas Corporation had invested $1 billion to develop the jumbo jet. Much of the company's future success depended on it.

To beat Lockheed, the design work at McDonnell Douglas was rushed, as was the DC-10's production. Even its flight-testing was hurried. In the process of doing so, details that later escalated into major safety issues were overlooked. "In the late sixties, there was a race going to see who could get the first jumbo out," said John Nance, aviation analyst and author. "One of the things they could not suffer was too many delays based on some problem with the design."[32]

Taking delivery of new DC-10s, the airlines began scheduling flights throughout the world. One of them was American Airlines Flight 96, departing Detroit Metro Airport for Buffalo, New York, on June 12, 1972. Five minutes after takeoff, as the plane climbed through 11,750 feet above Windsor, Ontario, the plane's aft cargo door blew open and fell off. Before departure, although the outward opening door had been difficult to close, it appeared to be secured tightly according to baggage handlers and a mechanic at the airline. When the door blew off in flight, instantaneous decompression caused the cabin floor to collapse, damaging steel control cables that operated flight control actuators, including one for the rudder. Faced with no control of the rudder or thrust of the center engine, it was a miracle the crew was able to nurse the plane back to Detroit for an emergency landing. Fortunately, there were no major injuries among the fifty-six passengers and eleven crewmembers aboard.

Completing a lengthy investigation, the NTSB announced a probable cause for the accident. "The design characteristics of the door latching mechanism permitted the door to be apparently closed when, in fact, the latches were not fully engaged, and the latch lockpins were not in place."[33]

The FAA studied a list of recommendations from the NTSB to prevent a similar accident but it refused to issue a mandatory airworthiness directive to modify the door latch. FAA Administrator John Shaffer, a Nixon administration appointee, telephoned Jackson McGowen, head of the aircraft division at McDonnell Douglas, concerning the door issue. They concocted what was termed a "gentlemen's agreement." McGowen would order that a small observation window be installed in the cargo doors to make sure that baggage handlers could visually check the pins for proper latching. But the design of the locking mechanism would stay the same. Shaffer, not wishing to rock the boat with his coveted contacts in the aviation industry, went along with McGowen's suggestion. The "peepholes" were installed in all DC-10s, but the unreliable latching mechanism remained untouched.[34]

Protecting its public image, the company had, in effect, shifted blame for the unsecured door to the baggage handlers in Detroit.

All went smoothly for the DC-10 program until March 3, 1974. Turkish Airlines Flight 981 fell out of the sky on that day and crashed in a forest outside Paris, France. All 346 people aboard were killed. The plane's cargo door had failed as it did over Windsor, but this time it sucked the floor farther down than before, forced by the enormous volume of pressurized air exiting the cabin. The sunken floor severed vital control cables and hydraulic lines. In an instant, the jet became uncontrollable, and less than a minute later it augered into the ground. The tremendous loss of life resulted in an unprecedented public outcry over the safety of all DC-10s. The FAA then mandated a complete redesign of the door actuating mechanism—specifically, the pins that had never been designed to lock properly.[35]

The crash in France became an embarrassment for the FAA. It appeared to the public that the agency had failed to make the manufacturer fix something as basic as door latches for almost two years. McDonnell Douglas began losing credibility as well. The manufacturer, with the government's blessing, had settled on installing inadequate inspection windows and didn't develop a permanent fix. As a result of that decision, 346 people died.

The DC-10's problems weren't over. On May 25, 1979, American Airlines Flight 191 crashed upon departure from O'Hare International Airport in Chicago. All 271 people aboard died. This time, the plane's left engine had separated from its wing on takeoff, destroying critical flight control systems and rendering the plane uncontrollable. NTSB investigators determined that the design of the engine pylons and wing slats, along with poor airline maintenance practices, were to blame. Faced with little choice in the matter, the FAA grounded all DC-10s for one month. The probable cause of the accident, published in the NTSB's investigative report, vilified the plane's design and the FAA's poor oversight of McDonnell Douglas:

> Contributing to the cause of the accident were the vulnerability of the design of the pylon attach points to maintenance damage; the vulnerability of the design of the leading edge slat system to the damage which produced asymmetry; deficiencies in Federal Aviation Administration surveillance and reporting systems which failed to detect and prevent the use of improper maintenance procedures.[36]

The widespread reluctance of travelers to fly on DC-10s resulted in ulcers for airline executives. It also continued to sour the time-honored reputation of McDonnell Douglas. The company had made serious mistakes during the DC-10 program. It rushed the plane into production. At the same time, its executives played down questionable design practices related to the door latches, engine pylons, and flight control systems to save time and money. All this took place as the FAA stayed largely in the background. The agency could have demanded that the troublesome systems be redesigned and retrofitted to all DC-10s in service. To this day, Flight 191 holds the unenviable distinction of being the deadliest aviation accident in United States history.

McDonnell Douglas and Lockheed had discovered that splitting a finite market for two competitive airliners would cause one of the programs to fail. This resulted in only 250 TriStars being sold compared to about 400 DC-10s, and Lockheed needed to sell 500 of the jets to break even. In 1981, Lockheed announced that TriStar production would end. Lockheed never manufactured an airliner again.

Both Lockheed and McDonnell Douglas had run headlong into competition from Airbus, which sold new fuel-efficient A300s and A310s. At Boeing, wide-body 767s were also available. Lockheed Aircraft Corporation had manufactured airliners since 1927; Douglas Aircraft Company had produced them since 1934. During the twentieth century, these two companies manufactured most of the airliners in the world, but that prominence didn't last. Douglas, beset with poor leadership, was lucky to be acquired by McDonnell Aircraft Corporation in 1967. Too many ongoing aircraft programs and too little cash had brought it to the brink of bankruptcy, and the company never regained its leadership status. Boeing and Airbus now dominated the market. Picking up the bones, Boeing acquired struggling McDonnell Douglas Corporation in 1997. The move consolidated America's remaining airliner manufacturing capability into one publicly owned corporation.

Beginning soon after the MAX accident in Indonesia, some pilots placed blame on the relatively inexperienced crews flying for airlines overseas. They felt that the Lion Air pilots should have reduced the engine thrust, responded instantly to the nose dropping, and attempted to correct it by turning off the cutout switches. Concurring, other pilots believed that the less-experienced Ethiopian crew should have also pulled back the thrust for reducing the air-speed to manually control the trim—and never turned the cutout switches back on. There was no shortage of these and other opinions about what the dead pilots should have done but didn't.

In May 2019, pilots operating a 737 flight simulator replicated the final moments of Flight 302. The sessions were flown voluntarily as part of an anonymous airline's periodic training. The purpose was to practice recovering from a stuck trim wheel condition while flying fast and rapidly losing altitude. The scenario was similar to what the crew of Flight 302 had faced after cutting off power to the stabilizer motor and MCAS. Based on pilot experiences in the simulator, it was reported that they felt the Ethiopian crew "faced a near-impossible task of getting their 737 MAX 8 back under control."[37] The simulator pilots described it as "eye-opening."[38]

Faced with a stuck stabilizer, the simulator pilots had to hold significant backpressure against the yokes to maintain level flight. But doing so created a force pressing against the elevators that prevented them from turning the trim wheels. They reverted to an unorthodox, three-step technique called "the roller-coaster." First, they released all backpressure on the yokes to allow the nose to drop; this reduced air pressure on the elevators. Next, they moved the previously immovable trim wheels to bring the nose up. Finally, they pulled back on the yokes to raise the nose gradually and slow the descent. The process was then repeated: release backpressure, manually trim the stabilizer, resume backpressure.

It was reported in *Aviation Daily* that "neither the current 737 flight manual nor any MCAS-related guidance issued by Boeing discuss the roller-coaster procedure for recovering from severe out-of-trim conditions."[39]

The FAA didn't require Boeing to ensure that MCAS would function properly if a sensor malfunctioned. If the airlines purchasing the jets wanted the system to have a redundant, self-check capability, they had to buy AOA indicators as optional equipment, and most of them passed on the offer.[40] Tewolde GebreMariam, CEO of Ethiopian Airlines, told Reuters, "The angle of attack indicator was on the option list, along with the inflight entertainment system."[41]

On May 5, 2019, Boeing dropped a bombshell in the media's lap, again reluctantly. It did nothing to prop up the company's credibility.

When MAXs began flying for the airlines in 2017, the engineers at Boeing had assumed that a "sensor-disagree" warning light was operational in every MAX the company delivered. The light's purpose was significant: it notified the flight crew of mismatched readings between the two AOA sensors. A few months after the jet began passenger service, it was discovered that the lights functioned *only* on planes equipped with extra-cost AOA indicators. Only 20 percent of MAX customers had bought these indicators. The remaining customers assumed that the warning system was operational on their more sparsely equipped MAXs.

By way of a safety review board convened by Boeing in the months following the Lion Air accident, the AOA sensor-disagree light issue was discussed. The participants reaffirmed a previous decision at the company that its absence *did not* constitute a safety of flight risk. The FAA concurred, considering the light's inclusion as primarily a "maintenance" troubleshooting aid. "The software delivered to Boeing linked the AOA disagree alert to the AOA indicator," a brief statement from the company explained. "Accordingly, the software activated the AOA disagree alert only if an airline opted for the AOA indicator."[42]

While rows of MAX 8s gathered dust in the desert at a sprawling airport in Victorville, California, and ninety-three other locations scattered around the world, a Senate commerce subcommittee convened a hearing on March 27, 2019. Its purpose was to provide FAA officials with an opportunity to explain how the plane was certificated using the ODA process. Prior to the hearing, Rep. Peter DeFazio, chairman of the House Committee on Transportation and

Infrastructure, called for keeping the airplanes grounded until expert third parties approved their airworthiness. This amounted to a slap in the face for FAA officials. "The traveling public need assurances that the FAA will only recertify the aircraft for flights if and when the FAA, outside safety and technical experts, and pilots agree the aircraft is safe to fly," DeFazio said. Referring to the ODA, he added, "Someone's writing your paycheck but you're going to be there as 'I'm representing the FAA' and you're going to be totally immune to pressure from the company."[43] Former NTSB chairman Jim Hall concurred that more should be done. "Congress needs to take a closer look at the FAA's practices and procedures to make sure that safety is the top priority," he said, "and should overhaul the agency to provide more direct government oversight."[44]

As the lengthy hearing droned on, Acting Administrator Daniel Elwell defended the FAA's process for certificating aircraft and overseeing manufacturers. Regarding MCAS, he repeatedly stressed, "It made the MAX feel exactly like the [737] NG to fly. MCAS is not actually an anti-stall system; it is a supplement to the speed trim system."[45] To clarify, although MCAS is part of the trim system and is intended to alter the "feel" of the controls to match the feel of NG controls, it can prevent stalling.

On May 15, 2019, during the next scheduled hearing for the MAX, Earl Lawrence, executive director for aircraft certification at the FAA, joined Elwell. Responding to a question about why MCAS was integrated into the plane's flight control system, Lawrence replied,

> The MCAS system was installed to make sure it [the MAX] was in compliance with a specific regulation concerning handling characteristics. That was the method Boeing chose to meet that requirement. If they didn't do it through MCAS, they would have had to meet the requirement through some other means, which could have been a *structural* change.[46]

Lawrence's statement shed light on the reason why Boeing selected MCAS to satisfy the FAA certification requirements. It decided to make software changes in the plane's flight control computer rather than develop expensive modifications of the NG's airframe. Without MCAS, those modifications could have resulted in the FAA mandating an all-new type certificate for the jet rather than an amended one, dramatically raising costs and increasing development time. "We shouldn't expect pilots to have to compensate for a flawed design," Sullenberger testified during a House Transportation and Infrastructure Committee hearing on June 19.[47]

For well over a half-century, airplanes have relied on AOA sensors shaped like weather vanes to warn pilots of an approaching stall. But the devices are far from foolproof. FAA Service Difficulty Reports submitted since 2004 document that 216 sensors have failed. This includes sensors damaged on the ground or from striking birds in flight. In 2008, a fatal accident involved two AOA sensors failing on an Airbus A320. The plane crashed off the coast of France, and everyone aboard was killed. The sensors' vanes had frozen, upsetting the jet's flight control automation and causing the accident. In August 2019, responding to increased concern over AOA sensor malfunctioning, the FAA issued a safety bulletin that stressed the need to protect the delicate devices from accidental damage.

To remedy the safety shortcomings involving MCAS, the engineers at Boeing kept up a frenzied pace to enhance the system's functionality. The media was advised of the fixes in August 2019. One of the changes reportedly involved the use of both MAX flight control computers to activate MCAS, rather than the single one used previously. Each computer would now receive input from the two AOA sensors. The revised software has the ability to compare the outputs from the computers. If the AOA outputs disagree with each other by more than 5.5 degrees, the stabilizer will not be activated automatically and the pilots will fly the plane manually without the support of MCAS. The intent is to provide protection from differing sensor outputs and errors introduced by the computers. One reason why the previous single computer concept was abandoned was because a false output from it could trigger MCAS even if both AOA sensors functioned correctly.

Also important to pilots flying the MAX, there had been no requirement to provide training in dedicated MAX flight simulators. Complicating the issue in North America was that only Air Canada had such a simulator. At the time of this writing, airlines operating MAXs in the United States have none. To better understand the influence of pilot skill levels, the FAA brought in both seasoned and low-time pilots to observe their actions in a flight simulator that replicated flight conditions during the two MAX accidents.

Buying new jetliners is a high-stakes business deal for airline CEOs. Gone is the era when personal relationships swayed such purchases. Deals were sealed with a handshake then. In today's cutthroat world of negotiating billion-dollar purchase contracts, a plane's price, fuel economy, and availability mean far more than relationships—and, not surprisingly, comfortable passenger seating. Much like buying a new car, price and fast delivery are what close the sale. Nowhere was this more evident than in 2011 when American Airlines prepared to buy hundreds of new jets from two competing manufacturers.

In July, the airline announced an order of unprecedented size: it would buy 460 single-aisle jets from Airbus and Boeing. Of the 260 Airbus planes on order, 130 of them would be A320neo models. Overall, the deals were reported to be worth more than $38 billion. However, the contract with Airbus scuttled a long-standing monopoly that Boeing had nurtured with American Airlines. The sales team in Seattle needed to scramble to prevent Airbus from getting the entire order. That competitive pressure caused Boeing to convert the 737NG to LEAP engines rather than develop an all-new airplane. If Boeing couldn't deliver on time, the airline would buy additional planes from Airbus. As for Airbus SE, their marketing department executives were ecstatic. The manufacturer hadn't sold a plane to American Airlines for more than two decades. "Not only have they sold jets to American, but they have forced Boeing's hand into pushing for a re-engined 737," commented Saj Ahmad, an analyst at FBE Aerospace in London.[48] The massive order got the wheels spinning in Seattle and Boeing's luck improved: an order for 201 MAXs arrived from Lion Air. The cascade of sales turned the MAX into a banner program in terms of its multi-billion-dollar potential. Long-term, the MAX could evolve as the most profitable product line in Boeing's history. Or be forgotten.

On October 25, 2019, the FAA revoked the repair station certificate for Xtra Aerospace LLC in Miramar, Florida. Its doors were closed forever. Indonesian, FAA, and NTSB investigators asserted that the company had incorrectly calibrated the AOA sensor fitted to Lion Air's ill-fated MAX. A required check to validate the correct setting had not been made. It was in error by 21 degrees. According to the FAA, Xtra "did not substantiate that it had adequate facilities, tools, test equipment, technical publications, and trained and qualified employees to repair parts."[49] The FAA didn't escape blame either. The Lion Air accident report charged that its oversight of Xtra was "inadequate."

The result: 189 people aboard Lion Air Flight 610 became victims of a worker in Florida who misaligned a tiny electrical resolver inside the sensor.

The worldwide fleet of MAXs transported in excess of 10 million passengers between May 2016 and the jet's grounding in March 2019. There were no reported accidents. It took failed AOA sensors to trigger the fatal crash sequences. The accidents made the world aware of the existence and insidious flaws of MCAS.

The malfunctioning AOA sensors triggered the chain of events that resulted in the planes crashing. But they also unleashed a Pandora's box of shocking revelations that soured the reputations of Boeing and the FAA.

Boeing executives thought they could control messages about the MAX and handle matters with the FAA and airlines discreetly, without alerting the public.

They were wrong, underestimating how fast bad news travels. In today's digital world, social media places everyone and everything on a world stage to be judged, favorably or unfavorably.

Many of today's concerns about the MAX may fade from the public's memory a year from now. A Reuters/IPSOS poll released on May 15, 2019, indicated that half of the adults in the United States did not know about the two accidents. And of those who did, only 43 percent could identify the MAX 8 as the type of plane involved. Only 3 percent said that the make and model of a plane they board was important to them. By contrast, 57 percent responded that ticket prices were most important. Should these numbers hold for the foreseeable future, it will be good news for Boeing and the airlines that continue to buy and fly the MAX. But the future fate of the MAX, as well as that of Boeing and how the FAA governs aviation, remains a matter of conjecture.

Note: Many of the details presented in this chapter were derived from Komite Nasional Keselamatan Transportasi Republic of Indonesia, "KNKT Aircraft Accident Investigation Report, PT. Lion Mentari Airlines, Boeing 737-8 (MAX); PK-LQP, Tanjung Karawang, West Java, Republic of Indonesia, 29 October 2018."

2

LEAVING LAS VEGAS

The gambling mecca that sprouted up on the sands of the southern Nevada desert in 1931 is now a fun getaway destination for over 40 million visitors each year. They come to Las Vegas to relax, to try their luck at gaming tables, and to soak up dazzling entertainment in resorts lining the four-mile-long Las Vegas Strip.

In 1976, when casino-style gaming was legalized in Atlantic City, New Jersey, the worried casino bosses in Nevada were forced to update what they offered customers. It spawned a new era of constructing immense resort hotels featuring amusement parks, casinos spanning a city block, mega-theaters hosting superstars, and plenty of empty guest rooms to fill.

By 2015, the once dusty railroad town had grown into a major metropolis and home to most of the world's largest hotels. More than 149,000 guest rooms were ready to accommodate the mass of tourists. Day and night, they arrived by plane, bus, and car.

For decades, city officials sought to attract an airline dedicated to transporting tourists into town to fill the rooms. Several undercapitalized air carriers tried and failed. At last, a startup called Allegiant Air rose to the occasion, gained momentum, and parlayed its surprising early success into a twenty-first-century money machine. It became the unofficial hometown airline of Las Vegas. Its parent company, Allegiant Travel Company, peddled vacation packages to customers at the same time it sold tickets for its airline subsidiary.

Allegiant Air's beginnings stretch back to 1997 when its planes began flying hops between Fresno and Las Vegas. A year later, the carrier received government approval to make scheduled flights throughout the United States.

It soon flew charters to Mexico and Canada as well, adding more cities on a regular basis.

The expansion continued, but rising fuel costs caused the carrier to file for Chapter 11 bankruptcy protection in December 2000. Watching the action unfold from the sidelines, Maurice J. Gallagher Jr., a crafty, aggressive entrepreneur, would pull it out of the financial swamp and become its savior.

Gallagher worked his way into the aviation industry after earning an MBA from the University of California, Berkeley, in 1974. He went on to run a struggling California-based airline in the 1980s and then joined two investors in 1992 to put together a $1 million deal to launch ValuJet Airlines in Florida. Cashing in his ValuJet stock after the airline suffered a well-publicized, fatal accident, he returned to California to seek still another aviation investment.

Soon to become the major creditor of Allegiant, Gallagher gained control of the debt-ridden company in 2001 by loaning it $2 million. He restructured its operations using the low-cost model pioneered at ValuJet, focusing on serving smaller markets that didn't interest major carriers. As CEO and chairman, he moved the corporate headquarters from California to Summerlin, an upscale community in the desert west of Las Vegas. At the time Gallagher and his hand-picked team of executives assumed control, the airline operated a total of four previously owned McDonnell Douglas DC-9 jetliners.

By March 2002, Gallagher had helped raise Allegiant out of bankruptcy, and he began negotiating contracts with Nevada casinos to fly their guests into town. He also bought the airline's first MD-80 series jetliner. From 2002 through 2004, his executives fine-tuned the carrier's scheduled service, now serving thirteen smaller cities. In 2002 Allegiant flew 80,000 passengers. By 2006 the number had hit 1.9 million. The key to the airline's resurgence and profitability involved bundling tickets with hotel packages, a business concept that exploded into a major profit center.

Two dozen more MD-80s were added to the fleet. In November 2006, Allegiant Travel Company successfully floated an initial public offering of its stock. The airline itself was structured as a subsidiary of the company.

Allegiant Air succeeded in the travel marketplace by advertising rock-bottom fares. Flying its fleet of secondhand MD-80 jets, it eventually mushroomed into the nation's ninth-largest air carrier. To keep ticket prices low, the airline doesn't offer common amenities like frequent flyer points or onboard entertainment. Passengers pay to get a seat and little else. Many customers don't care about the extras because they seldom fly anywhere unless they find cheap fares. The airline is especially popular with older couples bored with retirement and families living on limited incomes.

Allegiant Air's headquarters and principal hub in Nevada has been augmented by a growing number of bases spread around the country. It boards passengers from little-used airports a few miles outside major cities and jets them to tourist meccas or regional airports located away from well-traveled paths. The planes fly into some places that most people wouldn't have a reason to visit. But tickets are priced low enough to entice passengers to trek out of town and fill the seats of Allegiant's jets.[1]

The airline offers nonstop flights from dozens of small cities like Duluth, Allentown, and Idaho Falls to popular vacation spots. During the freezing winter months, packed Allegiant planes fly to cities where there's plenty of sunshine.

Allegiant Air owes much of its success to the Internet, where people searching for cheap fares end up buying tickets. To keep costs down, it rents ticket counters at airports on an hourly basis, offers flights only through its website, has no toll-free phone number for reservations, and doesn't cooperate with travel agents. It prides itself on keeping things simple—and increasingly profitable. Much like anything else that may seem to be too good of a deal, ticket holders discover that fact upon boarding. They had better be prepared to pull out their wallet to pay for a bottle of water, changing seats, or even stowing a bag.[2]

Based on thousands of posts appearing on traveler websites from verified Allegiant Air customers, a considerable number of them aren't happy. They cite delays due to mechanical problems and tardy pilots, cramped seating, dirty cabins, rude employees, and being nickel-and-dimed to pay extra for things that are gratis at other airlines. But in spite of a deluge of negative reviews, coupled with an abundance of publicity questioning the reliability of Allegiant Air planes, waves of budget-minded customers eagerly buy tickets through Allegiant's website. Fares available on the website appear to be the lowest fares of any airline, but the final price can be much higher once customers select add-ons. The charges for everything from seat assignment, boarding pass printing, and taking a cherished poodle along add up rapidly. Conversely, there's no doubt that many of Allegiant's passengers are return customers. They enjoy paying economical fares, and because they don't need to make timely connections with other flights, delays don't faze them.

The signage on Allegiant Air jets stresses the fact that the airline is a full-service travel company that serves economy-minded customers. The slogan painted in large letters along the fuselage of each Allegiant jet stresses the point: *Travel is our deal.* The colorful livery adorning its planes features a bright sunburst design on the tail that symbolizes the airline's "sunny" destinations. But Allegiant prides itself on being a travel company first and foremost—not an airline. The planes are incidental to its hospitality business. Not surprisingly, it's been reported that commissions on hotel and rental car packages contribute up to one-third of the company's revenue.[3]

How Allegiant Air grew into one of the nation's most profitable airlines is no secret. It buys mostly older jets and flies to and from airports where it can avoid head-to-head competition with competitive carriers. Because it employs one shift of pilots and flight attendants to fly to a destination and return during a single day, a change of crews isn't needed. Its jets usually fly to cities located not more than four hours' flying time from its base. This means that each of the planes returns to its base each night. Many of the cities see Allegiant Air flights only twice a week. The airline picks up passengers there and brings them back a few days later. Unlike major airlines that need their expensive jetliners to remain in the air almost continuously to make a profit, Allegiant Air's largely depreciated fleet can spend time parked without impacting profitability. And because Allegiant's jets aren't flying around-the-clock, the probability of delays is minimized. Theoretically at least, less use translates into fewer mechanical problems.[4]

In Illinois, Peoria is one of the cities that Allegiant Air serves. In 2015, Greater Peoria Regional Airport (today the General Wayne A. Downing Peoria International Airport) reported that planes headed for Las Vegas were always packed. Allegiant Air offered only a few flights a week at the most but succeeded in putting a passenger in every seat.

The early Monday morning hours of August 17, 2015, found 158 men, women, and children from Peoria winding up their stays at hotels along the Las Vegas Strip. They had arrived a few days earlier. Peoria is the polar opposite of raucous Las Vegas, providing a vivid contrast between a go-go entertainment paradise and a Midwestern city's staid culture. The mini vacations had been long enough to recharge their spirits and sedate lifestyles, if not their wallets. For the tired group toting suitcases, it was time to fly home. Their reservations called for returning to Peoria aboard Allegiant Air Flight 436 in the mid-afternoon.

Stuffed shoulder-to-shoulder in cabs, shoved into tightly packed hotel courtesy vans, and putting up with 100-degree summer heat, they began arriving at McCarran International Airport around noon. After checking in their luggage, they navigated through mammoth TSA security lines at a crawl. Lugging overstuffed carry-ons, they arrived at their assigned gate in Terminal 1, ready to board a nonstop to Peoria. The scheduled departure time was 2:20 p.m. Exhausted from struggling with crowds and the blazing heat outside, some picked up magazines and treats at Hudson News, plopped into seats near the gate, and savored the air-conditioned comfort.

An announcement bellowed forth from the public address system: the departure time for Flight 436 had been moved to 6:15 p.m. A four-hour delay did nothing to perk up anyone's disposition: they wouldn't get home until well past midnight.

Because the plane scheduled for their flight had been sidelined for undisclosed mechanical problems, the passengers were told to pick up their belongings and walk to another gate. No plane was there, however. They would need to wait for it to arrive. To endure the seemingly endless hours ahead, some grabbed a cheeseburger at Burger King or a Frappuccino from Starbucks. Others indulged in adult beverages. Finding it irresistible to escape the allure of slot machines, several of them decided to try their luck one last time.

As they killed time, a replacement MD-83 jetliner finally pulled into the gate. It carried FAA registration number N407NV.

The plane they would board was the popular twin-engine version of a series of jetliners manufactured by McDonnell Douglas, a company acquired by Boeing in 1997. As essentially longer versions of DC-9s, the MD-80s served as the workhorses in Allegiant Air's fleet, numbering forty-eight of its seventy-six planes at the time. McDonnell Douglas delivered N407NV to Finnair in 1991. It served with two other airlines until May 2009, when Allegiant Air bought the jet. Although used MD-80s were configured with 150 seats, the airline had converted them to seat 166 passengers. Removing the galleys formerly used for hot meal preparation opened up enough space to squeeze in sixteen additional seats.

When the waiting passengers were told to finally board Flight 436, newspapers and empty paper cups ended up in trashcans. The ticket holders formed a single line to enter the gate's stuffy jetway. The temperature outside the building still hovering well over 100 degrees, it was fortunate that Terminal 1 was air-conditioned. But the plane they were about to board was *not*. "We were delayed and wound up sitting in the desert heat for [about] two hours," said Lori Miller, one of Flight 436's frustrated passengers. "It was ninety-six degrees in the plane."[5]

The sun beating down on the aluminum skin of the fuselage turned the cabin into an oven. The refreshing air they had enjoyed in the terminal was no more though it existed only a hundred feet away from where they were captive. The delays and bone-dry heat stretched their patience.

Following a two-hour delay, Miller and her fellow passengers were escorted off the plane and told to remain near the gate. Understandably angry, they clamored for an iced tea or cold beer to regain their composure or at least prevent dehydration. The airline's customer service representatives, who seldom appeared at the gate, didn't answer questions concerning why the passengers had been sealed in a sizzling aluminum tube for so long, unabashedly conveying the impression that such matters were to be expected. Little known to first-time customers of Allegiant Air, sweltering in a hot cabin for extended periods of time wasn't something unusual.[6]

It's difficult for customer service representatives to pacify irate passengers when flight delays occur. Airline operations require that the arrival and departure times of each flight coincide with a master schedule or chaos can result. As an example of how a situation can turn ugly, consider an incident caused by a "mechanical" that delayed a jet's departure. The carrier was not Allegiant Air, and it was the second delay for the weary souls aboard. The seriousness of the problem was not known, and a representative waited until the last minute to tell the strapped-in passengers that the plane would not be going anywhere for at least two more hours. A near-riot broke out, passengers screaming at and cursing the hapless employee. One man struck a flight attendant before trying to flee through an emergency exit. Airport police tackled him, slipping on handcuffs.

Pilots hate delays as much as passengers. Late departures create extra work for them. Sitting in a cramped cockpit stewing over delays, pilots must coordinate with flight dispatchers to input revised performance and navigation data into their flight management systems. Coordinating with dispatchers, they must determine if enough fuel is aboard and ensure that the toilets are serviced to accommodate a prolonged wait. Worst of all, at least from the perspective of pilots, they don't get paid for such delays. Hourly pay begins when the plane's parking brake is released.

Back at the Allegiant Air gate, another half-hour elapsed before a representative directed the weary passengers to re-board. Again, they grudgingly filed into the plane through the jetway. As they slipped into their seats, the pilot announced that variable weather conditions along the intended route would require deviating from the planned course. More fuel would be consumed, requiring a landing at Wichita for refueling before the flight continued on to Peoria. Seated and strapped in, the fares hoped they wouldn't be herded off a second time. The cold air blowing through the vents was a welcome relief. Bargain prices meant that even small things such as the rush of cool air was appreciated. Pondering the delays, some of the passengers began to conclude that Allegiant Air might be the aerial equivalent of a Greyhound bus.

Outside the terminal, the temperature had hit 109 degrees at mid-afternoon. Even during the evening hours, it wasn't cooling off much, but by 6:30 p.m., everything appeared to be in order. While one of the two flight attendants offered a bit of levity over the PA system in a feeble attempt to ease anxieties, the pilots prepared the MD-83 for departure. After starting its two Pratt & Whitney JT8D turbofan engines and completing perfunctory after-start checklists, they received an all-clear signal from a ramp agent to depart the gate. Releasing the parking brake and contacting McCarran ground control, they taxied to the active runway. Clear of other aircraft parked along the terminal's concourse, they set the plane's flaps then handled a dozen other items on the taxi checklist. One of the checks involved pushing the control yokes fully forward to make sure a warning light lit on an annunciator panel. The test served as verification that N407NV's elevator boost system worked correctly. No problems were noted.

Checklist items completed satisfactorily, the jet commenced a crawl to runway 25R to begin its 1,500-mile journey. A final pre-takeoff checklist was run through as required, while a flight plan was opened with air traffic control. "We finally taxied out to the runway to take off," Miller said, no doubt surprised that her flight had made it this far.[7]

Joseph Yang and fellow pilot Eric Baron knew that the extreme heat radiating off the concrete would require a long takeoff roll.[8] In common with most Allegiant Air flights, N407NV was packed and heavy. Sizzling ambient temperatures don't agree with gas turbine engines such as JT8D fanjets. The thought of not developing sufficient thrust or worse, being faced with an engine exploding during takeoff, was something crews kept in mind. Allegiant Air's MD-80s had established an unpleasant reputation for burning up engines—mostly because they were nearing the end of their operational lives. The hot, thin air typifying the summer months in the desert exacerbated the possibility of such a failure. Keeping the temperature in mind, Yang and Baron were aware that the takeoff roll would consume much of the 14,512-foot length of runway 25R.

After the flight attendants had taken their seats, N407NV was ready to go. A controller in the tower at McCarran cleared Flight 436 for takeoff. The pilot twisted the steering tiller[9] alongside his left leg and jockeyed the slender MD-83 into position on 25R, letting its momentum continue into a takeoff roll. He advanced the throttles fully to develop maximum power—every pound of thrust being needed on the hot evening. The jet began to move, albeit slowly. The combination of a heavy load, blazing runway temperatures, and engines not having many hours remaining before overhaul meant the takeoff roll felt more like a walk than a sprint. The acceleration was laboriously slow. "My husband told me that the plane was not going fast enough to get off the ground," Miller commented later.[10]

As the plane picked up speed, roaring down the runway, distance marker after marker went by but with the plane still earthbound. In seconds, the situation would change—although not for the better.

Less than twenty seconds after releasing the brakes, Yang and Baron sensed that something was terribly wrong. When the plane had reached 138 mph, its nose rose abruptly—without either pilot pulling his yoke rearward. The plane's speed was too slow to take off. But the nose-up attitude persisted.

Training and instinct caused the pilots to immediately reject the takeoff, lowering the nose by pushing forward on their yokes and yanking back the thrust-reverser levers, which caused the engine's clamshell doors to swing open and provide strong deceleration. Simultaneously, ground spoilers were pushed up on the wings while both pilots pressed firmly on the tips of their rudder pedals to maximize braking.

Panic took hold, everyone slammed against non-reclining seat backs by the forceful deceleration. Bodies tensed. Eyes locked. "People were screaming," said Stacie Dalpiaz, a passenger. "The pilots slammed on the brakes, and we all flew forward."[11]

While the pilots found themselves confronted with controlling the MD-83's errant path, the passengers remained helpless—unwilling participants in a heart-pounding drama playing out before their eyes. Dumbstruck, they had no idea where the rampaging plane could be headed. Their worst fear: it might roar off the end of the runway, hit something, and burst into flames. Such thoughts would later turn into recurring nightmares for some of them as they replayed the incident over and over in their minds.

"The nose of the plane was in the air and then suddenly came down hard, and it seemed like the airplane couldn't stop," Miller said of the harrowing experience. "We could smell something hot in the cabin." She stared through a window and noticed the plane had stopped just in time. "We were at the very end of the runway," she said.[12]

A sigh of relief went through the cabin when the eighty-ton jet came to a stop. There was no crash, fire, or emergency evacuation. Competent airmanship, and perhaps a few prayers, had brought the plane to an abrupt halt at the end of runway 25R. Emergency training, gained from years of operating realistic, full-motion flight simulators duplicating emergency conditions, told the pilots that the plane's elevator must have jammed. It had happened before.

Left behind on the runway were shreds of overheated rubber from N407NV's tires, ground into grooves in the blazing concrete. The brakes had overheated, each of them trailing white smoke.

If the pilots had allowed the jet to stagger into the air, it's more than likely that all 158 passengers and six crewmembers would have perished in a fiery crash. With the pilots lacking any way to lower the pitch attitude, the plane could have gained only a few hundred feet of altitude. Its wings would then have stalled, the jet plummeting. The pilots would then have faced a daunting if not impossible task: avoid plowing into the 3,309-room Mandalay Bay Hotel on the Strip, a forty-three-story complex offset not more than 3,500 feet from the departure end of 25R. The death toll from the plane smashing into the megaresort and its adjacent properties could have easily run into the hundreds. "I don't think many people realize [they] were seconds away from their death," posted a pilot on a widely read online forum for airline crews. "This is huge and is indicative of a larger problem. There's no way I'd put myself or my family on an Allegiant flight right now."[13]

Another pilot posted, "Great job abandoning the takeoff, which must have been a split-second decision. The nose came up, and they couldn't lower it. Had the crew waited much longer it might have taken off with no way to recover. This is the kind of hidden maintenance defect that worries me every time I fly. It's crazy how much trust we have in the system."[14]

The plane having been towed from the runway's end to a gate, the frazzled passengers disembarked. There weren't any obvious physical injuries except maybe a few scratches, but it would be a sleepless night. Rattled by the experience, the passengers would need time to deal with thoughts of almost crashing. The psychological trauma involved in surviving a potentially fatal accident can be difficult to process.

Everyone was lucky to be alive and knew it. The airline paid for their hotel rooms that night. At the airport the next day, boarding passes for another flight to Peoria were distributed along with eight-dollar food vouchers. An unknown number of people who survived the near-disaster flew to Peoria on another Allegiant Air MD-80. Others said "Never again" and bought tickets from United Airlines or whatever carrier could get them home as soon as possible.

Most likely unknown to any of the passengers, the pilot's union at Allegiant Air, the Airline Professionals Association, Teamsters Local 1224, had prepared a letter for distribution to the public earlier in 2015. It concerned safety practices at the airline. Reflecting a bitter division existing between pilots and the airline's management, the union's letter didn't pull any punches. The letter was addressed to Allegiant Air passengers.

> We are writing to make you aware of a number of concerns that we, as pilots, have with Allegiant Air. The fact is we are uncomfortable remaining silent about company practices that negatively impact our customers' travel and vacations, including your comfort, and—most importantly—your safety. . . .
>
> If you've had problems with Allegiant, you are not alone. The company's record delays and cancellations have led Allegiant to have the second-highest customer complaint rate out of any U.S. commercial airline. Meanwhile, the fleet is plagued by persistent mechanical problems due to poor equipment and the company's unwillingness to invest in its operation or its workforce, as attested by the numerous FAA safety investigations, aircraft groundings, and training program closures. . . .

In the meantime, we will continue to speak out to protect travelers and our pilots from being taken advantage of by a company consumed with a dangerous approach to its safety standards, customer protection and employees.[15]

In a brief report, the FAA summarized the frightening incident for its files: "The crew reported that the nose wheel lifted off the runway prematurely during the takeoff roll. The captain discontinued the takeoff and returned safely to the gate." The report was to the point but conveyed no details and no sense of urgency about what the FAA would do to prevent future occurrences.

Because the FAA categorized the rejected takeoff as an *incident* rather than as an *accident*, most of the media didn't recognize the gravity of what had occurred. The aborted takeoff was tagged an incident because the plane hadn't been significantly damaged and there were no serious injuries. But its pilot could chime in—on an anonymous incident tracking system:

> Had the aircraft become airborne, a serious accident would have resulted . . . Brake temps were rising, and a tow into the gate was requested and completed. We were met at the gate by the mechanic on duty, along with his colleague. They then did a control check on the empennage, and the mechanics informed us that the left elevator was stuck in the up position.

He wasn't alone in reaching that conclusion about averting a serious accident. "The captain saved the day, but he's one of our most experienced captains," posted a fellow pilot on the airline pilot forum. "We have many new-hire captains on the MD-80. Had there been a lesser MD-80 experienced captain . . . well."[16] Former NTSB board member John Goglia chimed in concerning N407NV's incident. "In a worst-case scenario, they would have been unable to control it. It could have been a disaster," he said.[17] Said another pilot on the forum, "The captain that saved our bacon this time is the same guy that recovered from a landing where an improperly assembled main gear went sideways upon landing. He was actually called on the carpet for a hard landing before maintenance discovered the improper assembly."[18]

The plane was towed to a company maintenance area later that night. Mechanics raised a workstand eighteen feet above the ground to reach the top of the horizontal stabilizer to try to pinpoint the cause of the pitch-up tendency. Upon removal of a small access panel, it became obvious what had gone terribly wrong. A nut had unscrewed from a rod that connected to the elevator control surface on the left side of the jet.[19] It appeared that a mechanic had neglected to install a cotter pin in a slot of the nut, securing the rod that had caused the elevator to move in an unwanted direction.

After installation of another nut and cotter pin, N407NV went on to resume passenger service sixty-two hours after the rejected takeoff. Sitting on the ground, broken planes don't make money for their owners.

Reporters at newspapers and TV stations treated the incident as little more than another cancelled flight at Allegiant Air. There was no fire, no explosion, and no emergency evacuation of passengers to spice up the story. It certainly didn't warrant a big headline. As the next daily news cycle rolled around, the story fell by the wayside. Because no detailed information had been released about how the pilots brought the MD-83 under control, and because the crew was forbidden by the airline to talk about it, reporters would have had to dig deeper. Allegiant Air executives had no interest in talking, and reporters were faced with other stories to pursue.

Allegiant Air was required to report the incident to the NTSB as it involved the failure of a flight control, the report being mandatory because failure of a flight control is a potentially deadly event. However, because an accident by definition had *not* occurred, the NTSB had no further role to play. The responsibility for determining what happened was placed with the FAA.

The MD-80 series of jetliners are growth versions of the original DC-9, a plane first flown in 1965. They have fuselages stretched to seat additional passengers and higher-thrust engines along with upgraded instrument and avionic systems.[20] For more than thirty years, the MD-80 has held the distinction of being the most successful jetliner built by McDonnell Douglas. By 1989, deliveries and orders of the planes had topped one thousand.

Allegiant Air bought and refurbished its used MD-80s for as little as $4 million each, far less than the cost of Boeing 737s. Most of the planes were purchased from foreign airlines. Although they had logged many thousands of hours, this wasn't a concern. Maintenance problems don't necessarily result from the number of hours a plane is flown or its age. Instead, the number of landings and takeoffs made, known as cycles, influences them. Tires slamming onto runways every day play havoc with aging airframes just as a car's mechanical condition depends on whether it spends its life cruising at a steady speed on a highway or creeping along in stop-and-go traffic. It's the short trips and the constant landings that wear out machines. In common with older cars, as planes age, more tweaking is needed to keep their moving parts humming and not missing a beat.

Not long after the incident, "loose nut" problems were discovered in the flight control linkages of two other MD-80 series jets at Allegiant Air. An urgent question needing an answer was now obvious: Did these mistakes result from the negligence of one mechanic or was it a systemic problem permeating the maintenance culture at the airline? "Any failure to properly secure any part of a flight control is a major problem," said NTSB board member Goglia. "More than one occurrence clearly indicates a maintenance organization that is not functioning properly."[21]

3

SMOKING GUN

The 158 passengers aboard Allegiant Air Flight 436 arrived home in Peoria a day late. It's not surprising that some of them vowed never to fly again. They would suffer flashbacks of the rejected takeoff, especially the final agonizing seconds when they felt close to losing their lives. At the airline's headquarters in Summerlin, business went on as usual. The plane hadn't crashed, there were no injuries, and little media coverage resulted. More customers were being booked for future flights than before the incident. The airline's pilots, mechanics, and executives had become accustomed to screw-ups. The FAA didn't get rattled either, but it was required by law to investigate the incident, determine a cause, and prepare a report. And maybe punish the airline.

Three hours after the rejected takeoff, Christian Toro, Allegiant Air's director of quality, contacted the FAA to report the incident. The agency's formal investigation began on August 19, 2015, following a cursory review of the facts by the NTSB. Carlos Flores, a senior safety inspector at the FAA, was assigned to initiate the investigation. Flores had joined the FAA in 1996 following a career at the major airlines where he worked as a mechanic and avionics technician.

Flores contacted Toro, who told him a retaining nut had disconnected from a rod that connected a power boost cylinder to the left elevator of the plane. It caused the rod to rub against the elevator and jam it. Flores also learned about the loose nuts discovered in the other Allegiant Air MD-80s.

Flores's first task was to determine who had been responsible for ensuring that the nut in N407NV's tail had been installed properly. Flores thought it would be premature to blame the mechanics working at Allegiant Air. He suspected there could be another guilty party. Enter AAR Aircraft Services, one of the nation's largest aircraft repair stations—known throughout the industry as MROs (maintenance, repair, and overhaul). AAR specializes in providing outsourced maintenance services for a host of domestic and international airlines. The work performed under contract to Allegiant Air wasn't accomplished in El Salvador or another overseas locale. It had been done in America's heartland, Oklahoma City, Oklahoma. AAR's facility there performed heavy maintenance inspections for primarily Boeing and McDonnell Douglas single-aisle jets. Well-equipped to handle the most complex of tasks, AAR had a 300,000 square-foot complex with seven hangar bays capable of accommodating up to twelve airliners at a time.

Oklahoma, perhaps best known for tornados and university football teams, also has a reputation as a friendly state when it comes to attracting aviation businesses such as AAR. The state offers special tax credits to more than five hundred MROs and companies that manufacture aircraft parts. Altogether more than 120,000 aircraft workers are employed statewide. The largest maintenance facility in the state is Tinker Air Force Base, an Air Force depot maintenance center. The next-largest belongs to American Airlines. The other MROs range in size from major companies like AAR to smaller, specialized-repair shops. Centrally located from the east and west coasts, Oklahoma's a time saver for airlines bringing in planes from the four corners of the country.

Flores's first step was to visit Allegiant Air's maintenance facility at McCarran International Airport. Rather than within a spacious hangar complex, repair work on the airline's planes was done outside on a concrete ramp not far from Terminal 1. This was a clue that little complex maintenance was done there. After riding a hydraulic lift to the top of N407NV's vertical stabilizer, Flores examined the control mechanism. It was sealed behind an access panel to prevent moisture and dust from entering. He realized that if a cotter pin had worked free from a nut, the pin would likely be laying somewhere in the sealed compartment. Toro indicated that the nut and its washer were found by the airline's mechanics, but a pin wasn't. It was reasonable then to conclude that a pin had *not* been inserted in the nut at the time the rod was installed.

Initial research undertaken by Flores verified that the elevator boost cylinder on the left side of N407NV had been installed by AAR mechanics at the Oklahoma facility on May 23, 2015. A visit to that facility was next on the agenda. He kept in mind that the elevator on the left side, along with its control tab, had been removed and reinstalled by AAR less than three months before the rejected takeoff occurred.

The documentation provided to AAR mechanics for installing the cylinder required that the nut and bolt be removed from the rod in order to pull out the cylinder. The cotter pin would need to be pulled out also. Flores's investigation in Oklahoma proved that the nut had been installed without the pin. As for the MRO's paperwork trail, required to document what work had been accomplished, there wasn't much to go on. The FAA requires each maintenance and repair action on an aircraft to be accurately documented. The agency is well known for keeping a sharp eye on the presence and accuracy of such entries. Incomplete logbooks and the absence of proper recordkeeping hinder determining the causes of aircraft accidents. To Flores, the lack of complete paperwork constituted a big red flag.

To appreciate the critical role that elevators play in an MD-80, it's helpful to understand how the control system functions. Unlike Boeing and Airbus jetliners, the McDonnell Douglas series of DC-8, DC-9, and MD-80 jets don't rely on hydraulic boost systems to move their heavy elevator control surfaces. And steel cables hooked to the yokes in the cockpit don't move them either. Instead, small wing-like tabs attached to the trailing edge of each elevator cause the surfaces to pivot up or down. The pilot positions the tabs by moving his yoke forward or backward. The change in each tab's position creates an aerodynamic force that repositions the elevators in flight to raise or lower the plane's nose.

Near the top of the MD-83's vertical stabilizer sits the horizontal stabilizer, about two stories above ground level. The horizontal stabilizer pivots on bearings, enabling a pilot to precisely trim the plane's desired flight angle. The elevator surfaces are hinged to fittings at the rear edge of this stabilizer. When the pilot pushes his yoke forward, the tabs cause the elevator's trailing edge to move downward, creating an aerodynamic force to pitch the nose down. Pulling the yoke backward causes the opposite reaction and raises the nose.

During normal flight, the elevator surfaces float freely with the hydraulic cylinders damping their movements. The cylinders also serve as "gust dampers" to prevent the elevators from swinging up and down and getting damaged while the plane is parked outside in windy conditions.

What is called a "stick pusher" is built into the plane's flight control system. Should a stall condition occur, an actuating cylinder and rod (the components of N407NV missing the pin) attached to the elevator force the nose down. During flight, an AOA sensor measures the AOA of the wing and compares it to what it should be in normal flight. If the AOA is beyond limits, the stick pusher system is activated. It's designed to come into play only if a stall occurs. The system is tested before takeoff as part of a pre-takeoff check. The pilot pushes his yoke fully forward to verify that a warning light illuminates. When the warning light is lit, the system is known to be armed and operational.

A heavy maintenance check of an MD-80 and any other jet is a detailed and expensive undertaking. Its complexity requires that the plane be kept in a hangar for anywhere from two to six weeks, depending on the amount of work needed. As an MRO, AAR handled most of Allegiant Air's heavy maintenance needs.

In May 2015, N407NV was towed into one of AAR's seven hangar bays at Will Rogers World Airport in Oklahoma City for inspection and repair. The elevator controls were listed as one of the items to replace. A team of mechanics could be seen scampering around in the hangar inspecting the airframe for signs of corrosion and damage while functional checkouts of each system were performed. Two mechanics were positioned on a workstand alongside the horizontal stabilizer to remove and replace the elevator control mechanism on the left side. After wrapping up the task, they were expected to sign off on the work as completed. Before reinstalling the small access panel, however, they didn't notice that the cotter pin on the nut was missing. If they hadn't bothered to install the pin, negligence or laziness might be blamed. Flores began to think it could have resulted from a work environment at the company that didn't stress the need to pay attention to critical maintenance details.

He set out to determine if the omission constituted the negligence of one mechanic or AAR's lack of a corporate culture dedicated to safety as the first priority. Flores dove in to examine AAR's maintenance records related to the work that the MRO claimed it performed. At various times in the past, mechanics at both Allegiant Air and AAR had done work in the tail area. But as the investigation progressed, it became clear that AAR was primarily responsible for the rejected takeoff incident.

AAR and Allegiant Air had signed a five-year agreement in 2010. It called for the MRO to serve as maintenance contractor for the airline's fleet of MD-80s. According to a news release announcing the contract, AAR's group vice president said, "We're looking toward the future with an enduring commitment to providing high levels of service to help Allegiant operate its fleet safely and efficiently while maintaining their high levels of passenger service."[1] Based on Allegiant Air's well-known lack of on-time schedule performance and more negative customer reviews than positive ones, it sounded like he might be referring to another airline.

Employing thousands of technicians, AAR was ranked as the fifth-largest MRO in the world in 2012. It had also been named Aircraft Parts Supplier of the Year in an independent survey of 11,000 airline executives. Such platitudes might mean little to people outside the aviation maintenance community, but they established AAR as a major player in the worldwide MRO market. Here's what the company said on its website in 2018:

Incorporated in 1955, today we have revenues of approximately $2B with more than 5,500 employees in 20 countries. Our aftermarket expertise and award-winning market solutions, which can be integrated or leveraged separately, help customers increase efficiency and reduce costs while maintaining high levels of quality, service and safety. We are a trusted partner to airlines, militaries and OEMs delivering competitiveness so they can focus on transporting passengers, cargo and parts around the world.[2]

"Reduce costs" is the key phrase here, and it is what most appeals to chief financial officers at the airlines. Many of those executives don't know an aileron from an elevator but relish looking over corporate income statements to find any way to save money.

During September 2013, two years before the crew of N407NV rejected the takeoff, FAA inspectors found that a number of Allegiant Air's maintenance practices were deficient. In an unusual move, the agency told CEO Maurice Gallagher to stop adding new routes and buying more planes until the deficiencies were corrected. He complied, having no choice in the matter. The FAA did nothing further. In December of that year, an Allegiant Air MD-88 was ferried to AAR for a heavy maintenance check. During the plane's time in the hangar, a mechanic worked on the right-hand engine without noticing that a cotter pin was missing from a nut attached to a lever operating its fuel control. A day after the plane resumed scheduled service, it took off from Fargo, North Dakota, with a full load of passengers. As the plane climbed to cruising altitude, a cockpit warning light signaled a problem with the right engine. The pilots shut it down and executed an emergency landing. There were no injuries. But the nut had come loose. The thrust developed by the remaining engine was what kept the plane in the air.

AAR was required to report the glaring omission to the FAA. The agency told representatives from Allegiant Air and AAR to discuss responsibilities for the incident and report their findings to the FAA. The MRO promised Allegiant Air it wouldn't allow a mechanic to handle such critical work alone and sign off on its documentation. No fines were levied or enforcement actions taken by the FAA against either AAR or Allegiant Air.

In early 2015, the FAA subjected Allegiant Air's operations and maintenance facilities to increased surveillance when its pilots considered striking. This is routine action the FAA takes when it anticipates potential safety risks arising from escalating labor unrest. In April, the airline won a court order to block a pilot walkout. A month later, the FAA ended its scrutiny. It should not have done so. Forty-two jets in Allegiant Air's eighty-six-plane fleet malfunctioned in flight at least once during 2015. Engine failures resulted in fifteen of the jets needing to land immediately. Nine of the planes landed because of overheating in their tail section compartments. Six of the incidents involved burning smoke or a noxious smell in the cabin.[3]

During the latter part of 2015 and in 2016, Allegiant Air management continued to battle its employees. The airline's unionized pilots were upset over the number of cancelled flights occurring due to maintenance issues. Some of the pilots were scared enough that they wouldn't allow family members to fly on the same planes they flew. Gallagher accused the International Brotherhood of Teamsters of feeding the media unproven tales of maintenance problems.

AAR had a peripheral connection to the crash of an Alaska Airline's MD-83 fourteen miles off the California coast on January 31, 2000, killing the eighty-eight people aboard. An NTSB investigation revealed that the threaded shaft of a jackscrew that controlled the horizontal stabilizer had become worn to the point of failure. A lack of grease had stripped its threads. A large nut that moved up and down along the shaft served to change the angle of the jet's horizontal stabilizer.

High over the Pacific Ocean, the stabilizer jammed, pitching the plane into a severe nose-down attitude. The plane's dive became so severe that the pilots couldn't counteract its force by pulling their yokes completely back. The MD-83 flew upside down for a short time before impacting the ocean and breaking into pieces. Following a lengthy investigation by the NTSB, resulting in a public hearing garnering much publicity, the FAA fined Alaska Airlines $1 million for negligent maintenance.[4]

On November 3, 2004, during routine maintenance at AAR of another MD-83 for Alaska Airlines, reports submitted by three former Alaska Airline mechanics indicated their inspection of its jackscrew revealed that critical lubrication had not been performed: there was no grease visible on the jackscrew's threads. AAR was one of two MROs retained by Alaska Airlines for heavy maintenance checks. The carrier had outsourced this work to trim costs, closed down its overhaul base in Oakland, California, and terminated several hundred technicians. Alaska Airlines and AAR denied wrongdoing, and no FAA enforcement action was taken. The mechanics were branded as unhappy former employees seeking retribution against an MRO that took away their jobs.[5]

Hundreds of skilled mechanics are needed at MROs to handle an ever-expanding volume of business. More airlines are outsourcing some or all of their maintenance than ever before. Taking the family car to a neighborhood garage to fix a problem costs $75 to $120 per hour for shop labor. By comparison, AAR sold its labor to the airlines for less than $50 an hour. It's little surprise that the company found it difficult to fill vacant mechanic positions for the amount of pay being offered. However, AAR and competitive MROs couldn't afford to raise salaries appreciably because the only reason the airlines sought their services was to lower their own labor costs.

AAR was also forced to compete with U.S. government facilities when it came to recruiting employees, especially skilled mechanics. Specifically, it competed against Tinker Air Force Base, Oklahoma's largest employer of aviation personnel. The facility hired hundreds of civilian mechanics annually just to replace the workers who planned to retire.

In 2010, David Storch, CEO of AAR, told a reporter, "We have the demand for employees, but it's hard to find a skilled and trained work force."[6] Many AAR workers had migrated from Tinker, but the reverse was beginning to occur. AAR in turn trained its own workers and then lost them to the base. To counter this trend, AAR hoped to attract a new generation of young people seeking careers as aircraft technicians. AAR offered field trips to students, internships, and even scholarships.

Contrary to some opinions, it isn't true that AAR employed mostly inexperienced mechanics. Many of its technicians had decades of experience. But the seasoned mechanics would leave for better pay at other employers. The workers who remained were spread too thin to share their knowledge with less-experienced employees.

The investigation of N407NV's rejected takeoff wrapped up on August 28, 2015, and the enforcement phase began. A letter of investigation prepared by the FAA was mailed to AAR on September 9. The findings documented by Flores in his report were enlightening—"shocking" perhaps being a better word.

"Aircraft N407NV flew a total of 261 revenue flights before the nut backed off of the elevator power control boost cylinder rod end and caused the loss of pitch control," Flores wrote in his report.

> Had the nut fallen off while the aircraft was actually flying, or had the crew not rejected the takeoff, the maintenance and inspection complacent actions performed by AAR Aircraft Services personnel would have resulted in an aircraft flying without the ability to control its pitch attitude. Deliberate acts of noncompliance by company personnel resulted in improper maintenance that endangered numerous lives and properties during 261 subsequent flights.

To satisfy FAA requirements, Allegiant Air had stationed at least one technical representative on site at AAR. The technician was expected to detect maintenance errors and provide detailed oversight of any work performed. A thorough audit of AAR's maintenance documents should also have been undertaken by the airline—to make sure the entries corresponded with the work actually accomplished—before it accepted planes for passenger service and paid the MRO's invoice.

Inspector Flores was not happy. He wrote, "The action of AAR Aircraft Services, Inc. personnel borders on careless (and possibly reckless) conduct." Flores described AAR's response to his findings as "defiant and contradictory." The MRO would not admit that its employees were responsible for the maintenance errors enumerated in his report. He wrote,

If they are not in violation why are they upset that they were unable to self-disclose, additionally without mechanic signatures for the missed steps they would be unable to ascertain for certainty, who performed the missed AMM [aircraft maintenance manual] items to garner any explanations from all the mechanics involved. . . . They are clearly a repeat offender that show[s] an unwillingness to admit errors unless it will not cost the company money.

The moment that N407NV resumed scheduled flights, the nut, unsecured by a cotter pin, began moving due to normal vibrations developed by the plane and its engines. The investigation could not determine if the nut had been tightened to prevent it from loosening. Some of the evidence indicated that it had not been properly torqued. AAR's published procedures required mechanics to paint a colorful stripe of thin lacquer on a tightened nut as a visual aid to alert inspectors that the correct torque value had been applied. Once dry, the stripe stays pliable even under extreme temperature and vibration conditions. If the stripe tears, an inspector will know the nut has rotated, reducing the clamping force on the assembly it retained. The lack of both a cotter pin to secure the nut and a stripe meant that any knowledgeable and attentive inspector would immediately realize something was wrong.

AAR may have considered the cause of N407NV's rejected takeoff nothing more than an isolated act of carelessness on the part of a distracted mechanic. Flores thought of it as an egregious disregard for Allegiant Air's maintenance policies as well as a skirting of AAR's own procedures and those mandated by the Federal Air Regulations.

Executives at AAR continued to argue there wasn't enough evidence to prove that maintenance steps were missed. The evidence provided by Allegiant Air and Inspector Flores disproved that assertion. A nut had backed off the end of a rod of a hydraulic cylinder that AAR had installed. This was proof enough.

"[It's] time to stop apologizing and making excuses for the shoddy maintenance this ludicrously profitable company accepts from its cheap outsourced vendors," posted a pilot on www.airlinepilotsforum.com. "Allegiant used to have a contract with AA [American Airlines] but opted for AAR as they were cheaper. ValuJet thought SabreTech was cheaper, too.[7]

Pilots spend their careers in cockpits and worry about such things.

"My feelings in regard to this major repair organization are that the employees are underpaid, often inexperienced, mechanics and inspectors waiting for airline positions and opportunities," Flores wrote. Looking at it another way, it's not unusual for retiring FAA inspectors to be recruited by airlines and MROs to embark on new careers at the companies they may have earlier inspected on behalf of the government. Such "revolving door" appointments could cause former FAA inspectors to go easy on companies they once policed. It happens with former employees from other government agencies as well. While working for the government, they don't want to antagonize prospective future employers.

"I believe there is a culture of disregard, based on the inadequate managerial oversight identified by just the concerns identified by this one flight control installation," Flores wrote.

> Inspectors earning below the median wage and a culture of disregard is in my opinion also a detriment to safety. . . . The repair station's root cause analysis of this violation as a simple human factors concern is myopic. Deliberate decisions not to record maintenance actions (or to document incomplete work) were evident.

His report left nothing unsaid, targeting shortcomings in many areas of AAR's operations that he inspected.

> It is my opinion that there were failures at each level of personnel performing the installation of the left hand elevator, and it is only fortuitous that N407NV did not have the nut fall off while the aircraft was in flight. . . . There is a need to prevent continuing violations or potential tragedies from this repair station by imposing a hefty civil penalty to prevent other egregious complacent behavior from its maintenance and inspection department personnel.

Flores assumed that his employer would levy harsh penalties against AAR. "I recommend maximum sanction be imposed for each FAR violation identified. In addition, I recommend that a sanction be added for each of the 216 flights that were flown in violation, as AAR Aircraft Services, Inc. was causal to the flights flown in an unairworthy condition."

The inspector submitted his report in November 2015. It ended up on the desk of David Ibarra at the FAA's regional office in Van Nuys, California. Ibarra was given the responsibility for recommending the agency's next course of action. Ibarra's decision would be based on the agency's new Compliance Philosophy, introduced the same year. This philosophy encouraged the airlines and their employees to report maintenance mistakes but punished them less harshly than previously.

FAA planners created the program to encourage collaboration between airlines and the government to resolve safety concerns. It requires an airline to make voluntary disclosures of maintenance and operational errors. As far as enforcement is concerned, the emphasis shifts from penalizing companies through monetary fines to using milder, "non-enforcement" measures for remediating errors. It's more of an honor system than a punitive one. "Our evolved approach to oversight does not suggest that we are going easy on compliance," the FAA's website states about the policy. "However, FAA will not use enforcement as the first tool in the toolbox."[8]

The maintenance managers at AAR must have been pleased with the philosophy. However, not everyone who had worked at the company was happy. "Not a quality aircraft maintenance facility; upper management just wants to push aircraft out at any means," was an anonymous comment posted on a job website by a former AAR quality-control manager. There were equally biting comments from other employees.

The outcome? No fine was levied against AAR, and the FAA didn't demand changes in AAR's operations. It did write AAR a letter of correction, concurring with the steps that the MRO had already taken to prevent future mistakes. In response to the FAA's allegations, AAR responded that it would have an additional inspector sign off on maintenance of critical parts such as flight and engine controls.

No further investigation was carried out. The report was placed in a file cabinet and soon forgotten.

"Safety culture means a lot, and there isn't a good safety culture in the head shed at Allegiant," posted another pilot on the airline forum. "Hopefully, it won't take a smoking hole in the desert for the FAA to pay attention."[9]

According to the FAA, the Compliance Philosophy worked. The passengers who came close to crashing during the takeoff of Flight 436 were assured that Allegiant Air was as safe as any other airline. But was it?

The business philosophy serving as the foundation for Allegiant Air's operations had its origins in another airline: ValuJet Airlines of the 1990s. Gallagher, as the long-standing CEO of Allegiant Air, happened to be a founder of that earlier, Florida-based carrier. Five key executives from ValuJet, including three of its four founders, joined Allegiant Air when it emerged from bankruptcy. Gallagher employed a business tactic to build up Allegiant Air similar to the one he perfected at ValuJet. In simple terms, it involved buying inexpensive, well-worn planes from other airlines for cash and offering cheap fares to budget-minded travelers. The formula put into play in Las Vegas worked as well as it did at ValuJet, catapulting Allegiant Air from obscurity into its current position as one of the largest and most profitable airlines in the country.

On May 11, 1996, Flight 592, one of ValuJet's McDonnell Douglas DC-9-32s, took off from Miami for Atlanta. Within minutes, the plane ended up uncontrollable and crashed into the barren swampland of the Everglades. Upon impact, the plane was pointed nearly straight down after diving 6,400 feet in thirty-two hair-raising seconds. The plane shattered into nothing bigger than bits of aluminum and yellow fiberglass insulation, along with mutilated bodies. Amid the rock and muck, the heaviest parts dug a smoldering crater. All 110 passengers and crew were killed on impact.[10]

The twenty-seven-year-old jet had caught fire in the air, a pilot's worst nightmare. The raging flames burned through the forward cargo compartment while acrid smoke in the cabin partly blinded the pilots and choked the passengers.

Following a lengthy investigation, the cause of the accident was traced to the ignition of unexpended oxygen generators stowed in the cargo compartment. The generators were no longer usable and were being shipped to a repair facility for reconditioning. Generators like these employ an exothermic chemical reaction to produce breathable oxygen for passengers following cabin depressurization events. Unfortunately, the reaction also creates extreme heat, which can result in combustion fed by the same oxygen that the devices generate. Because pure oxygen is highly flammable, transporting such devices brings the risk they might catch fire.

Unknown to the pilots in the cockpit of Flight 592, a shipment of 144 date-expired generators had been placed in a belly compartment of the plane a few feet behind them. Several employees of SabreTech, an MRO under contract to ValuJet, had loaded the devices aboard in Miami.

Eleven minutes after the jet climbed from the runway, one or more of the devices exploded. The temperature reached 3,000 degrees. Flames burned through critical wire bundles and steel control cables as the plane's airframe began melting.

Workers at SabreTech had improperly prepared the devices for shipment. Safety caps should have been installed on each device. Doing so would have prevented an explosion. But there was another reason for not shipping them. ValuJet hadn't been authorized by the FAA to carry such hazardous cargo.

ValuJet failed to oversee its outsourced operations to prevent the hazardous material from being loaded. And the FAA's failure to keep an eye on the airline's maintenance programs, including oversight of SabreTech, contributed to the disaster.

FAA inspectors had inspected ValuJet's maintenance facilities three months before the accident. On February 14, 1996, the agency reported finding a wide range of improper practices. It then increased surveillance of the airline, including its outsourced MROs. A majority of the attention centered on the need to update obsolete manuals and repair procedures. Another problem: ValuJet had grown so fast that it couldn't hire enough experienced mechanics and inspectors to accomplish and check the work—and to watch what its MROs were doing. "ValuJet, before the big accident in the Everglades, had a number of aircraft that had to return to the field because of maintenance problems that, at the time, were the highest in the industry," said John Goglia, who chaired the NTSB public hearing for the 1996 accident.[11]

Two weeks after the accident, the FAA banned shipments of oxygen generators in the cargo compartments of *all* airliners carrying passengers. It took a fatal accident of this magnitude for the FAA to take action. The FAA then grounded all ValuJet planes for three months. Not long afterward, the airline merged with AirTran, dropped the ValuJet name, and continued doing business as though nothing had happened.

The U.S. Attorney's Office for the Southern District of Florida filed a twenty-four-count indictment against SabreTech in July 1999. Also charged were its former director of maintenance and two mechanics responsible for preparing the shipment of oxygen generators. The charges included illegal transport of hazardous materials and making false statements. A jury acquitted the employees of all charges, but not SabreTech. As a corporation, it was convicted of nine charges related to the transportation of hazardous materials and failing to properly train its employees. On appeal, a circuit court threw out all the charges except improper training.[12] SabreTech later went out of business.

Airlines have the freedom to outsource maintenance to any facility they wish, provided that it meets FAA standards. Each airline's on-site technical representatives are charged with closely monitoring the work. When heavy maintenance is subcontracted, as a majority of airlines now do, the carriers are obligated to oversee every detail of the work and make sure it is documented to guarantee the airworthiness of their planes. The airlines can't delegate responsibility for the maintenance work that MROs perform.

Allegiant Air failed to properly oversee AAR, and ValuJet made a fatal slip by not keeping an eye on SabreTech. Flight 592 became a turning point in aviation safety. It prompted a continuing public discussion about the widespread use of outsourcing at the airlines.

Allegiant Air's long-range equipment plan called for retiring its fleet of MD-80s and buying newer Airbus A319 and A320 jetliners. The rationale was based on the belief that newer jets require less costly maintenance. But "newer" is a relative term, and a newer plane can be a long way from new. The Airbus A320 first flew in scheduled service in April 1988. By comparison, the MD-80s were manufactured until 1999. As I've noted, the age of a plane is less important than careful maintenance throughout its useful service life. "An airplane that just came out of the factory can be 'old' if it's not maintained properly," said Mike Boyd, a leading aviation consultant. "Age is almost a meaningless number."[13]

As a much more complex embodiment of the electronic diagnostic systems integrated into late-model automobiles, the sophisticated level of monitoring aboard modern jets is a tremendous asset for reducing troubleshooting time.[14] It monitors the functioning of complete systems and line replaceable units (LRUs) but does not identify individual electronic or mechanical components that may have failed.[15]

When a pin, nut, or bolt falls out in flight, it's too late to save the day. Nothing other than close visual inspection by a human being can detect such faults.

Consider an incident on August 26, 1993, involving an Airbus A320 flown by Lufthansa German Airlines. A mechanic had connected some of its wiring backward. Those circuits fed signals to the plane's flight control computers from sensors activated by control sticks in the cockpit. Because the electrical connections were reversed, when the copilot pushed his stick to bank the plane to the left, the plane banked to the right. Fortunately, the copilot immediately recognized the crossed-control condition and corrected the plane's attitude. The error was easy to make because the electrical connections could be accidentally reversed. The design wasn't foolproof from a human factors standpoint. During pre-takeoff checks, the pilots didn't detect the fault nor did mechanics during an earlier post-maintenance inspection.[16]

Maintainability engineering at aircraft manufacturers is a specialty intended to prevent design flaws. Clearly, the engineers at Airbus SE in Europe missed the mark with this one.

Acknowledging the growing concern of Allegiant Air's pilots with the airline's approach to maintenance and its impact on passenger safety, the Teamsters Aviation Mechanics Coalition took a stand. Here's a description of the organization's purpose taken from its website.

The TAMC started life in September 2007 as the Teamsters Aviation Mechanics Coalition, an organization dedicated to promoting the common interests of FAA Licensed Mechanics working in the Aviation Industry as well as those unlicensed working in supporting roles. The TAMC came into existence on September 15, 2007 in Indianapolis during a meeting that included mechanics from many Teamster carriers from around the country. Those in attendance, realizing that for year's mechanics issues had largely gone unrecognized, agreed to work together to aggressively pursue an agenda to enhance aviation safety, promote work place safety and create working conditions that will attract and retain new mechanics to the industry.[17]

A report prepared by the Teamsters documented a list of unsatisfactory maintenance processes at Allegiant Air. It covered the period from September 2015 through January 2016. Within the five-month period, it found that Allegiant Air had at least ninety-eight separate and preventable maintenance failures. These included thirty-five engine problems such as failure to start and clogged filters and two instances of catastrophic failures when the rotating assemblies of the engines failed. The report cited four instances of smoke in the cabin and three instances of cabin pressurization problems. In addition, there was little or no documentation of shift turnovers. This meant that mechanics could arrive for a scheduled shift not knowing where to continue working on tasks begun on the shift just ended.

An airliner is permitted to fly with certain functions inoperative provided that a strict procedure is followed before the plane is dispatched. At Allegiant Air, the maintenance teams weren't following those procedures. Some mechanics lacked enough training and experience. Because the airline flew into secondary airports, it relied on contract mechanics and not its own employees. Some of them had little troubleshooting and mechanical experience.

The Teamsters also cited a lack of process to document equipment failures. There wasn't adequate computer equipment on site to display maintenance manuals, causing mechanics to work from instructions faxed to them from a maintenance office. The mechanics reported that the culture at the company directed them to "just move the metal," and they felt pressured to get a plane to its next station. Mechanics would ask the pilots if they would "just take the aircraft as it is."

There weren't enough spare parts, and some of them didn't work properly. Mechanics were required to cannibalize parts from grounded planes because spares weren't in stock. They reported that critical jobs, such as lubricating stabilizer jackscrews, couldn't be performed because of a lack of training and equipment. This particular accusation was stinging, given the fate of Alaska Flight 281.

"This report is just a snapshot of the problems the company is facing," wrote report author Chris Moore, chairman of the TAMC and a mechanic with thirty years airline experience.

The airline's approach to maintenance is dangerous and not up to industry standards. An emergency landing virtually every week due to maintenance issues on a fleet this size isn't normal. As one of the most profitable airlines, Allegiant should put its money back into its aircraft and stop cutting corners. Investing in maintenance and operations would mean better service to its customers and a better, safer work environment for the pilots and crew who keep Allegiant flying.[18]

Allegiant Air pilots began to warn travelers about the airline's refusal to invest in its operations and workforce. In addition to maintenance issues, they pointed to problems with employee turnover, reportedly caused by the airline's refusal to work with its pilots and their union to produce an equitable labor agreement. By the company's own admission, the resignation rate of its pilots had increased 600 percent between 2011 and 2014.

Most of Allegiant Air's pilots favored the schedules that brought them home each night (and saved the airline the cost of hotels and meals), although their compensation, benefits, and condition of the planes they flew were prime concerns. They sought a contract to earn higher salaries, enhanced health insurance coverage, added job security, and improved maintenance practices. Too many flights had been delayed or canceled due to mechanical problems.

In July 2016, after more than three years of bargaining, the pilots, represented by the International Brotherhood of Teamsters, Local 1224, ratified their first-ever contract with the airline. Considering the roadblocks they had experienced, it represented a tremendous victory. Understandably, Allegiant Air management wasn't pleased: it meant spending more money for salaries and benefits. Pilots immediately received up to a 31 percent pay increase. They originally joined the union in August 2012 following the airline's flight attendants signing on with the Transport Workers Union of America in December 2010. Mechanics, the final group of safety workers, joined the ranks of represented employees on March 6, 2018. They and the airline's flight dispatchers had voted overwhelmingly to join the International Brotherhood of Teamsters.

If it weren't for a series of other incidents involving Allegiant Air planes, the detached rod of N407NV might never have been publicized. However, the airline's problems began showing up on the front pages of newspapers, most notably those of the *Tampa Bay Times* in St. Petersburg, Florida. One of the country's most respected newspapers, the *Tampa Bay Times* has been recognized for winning twelve Pulitzer Prizes since 1964. After the paper published a series of hard-hitting articles on Allegiant Air's questionable safety record, one might think that a thirteenth Pulitzer would be forthcoming. The articles were understandable and factual.

The *Tampa Bay Times* became a huge thorn in Allegiant Air's side and a nuisance for its corporate communications people. During the summer of 2015, a prime interest of the newspaper's journalists had to do with the frequency of flight cancellations of Allegiant Air flights at the St. Petersburg-Clearwater International Airport, the paper's hometown field. Considering that the airport served as a major base for the airline, its reporters dug deep to find out what was going on. Almost all the incidents involved MD-80s, many of them having to do with their well-worn Pratt & Whitney JT8D engines. Flight 436 in Las Vegas didn't escape the paper's scrutiny either. Articles with headlines such as "One Allegiant Plane Had Four Emergency Landings within Six Weeks" may have come across as sensationalistic to some readers but were backed with facts. The newspaper pulled in plenty of inquisitive subscribers.

During the evening of April 15, 2018, millions of viewers tuned in to watch a *60 Minutes* investigative report on CBS. Correspondent Steve Kroft presented allegations and facts concerning the safety of Allegiant Air's operations—including the missing cotter pin incident of N407NV. To document the alleged wrongdoings, Kroft's staff had filed a Freedom of Information Act request with the FAA to obtain records related to the airline. The FAA took months to hand over the data. Sifting through it, Kroft's staff learned that Allegiant Air planes were three times more likely to suffer in-flight failures than flights operated by American, United, Delta, JetBlue, and Spirit. In addition to Allegiant Air, whose executives refused to be interviewed for the segment, Kroft took aim at the FAA for failing to take enforcement action, such as hefty fines, for safety infractions involving the airline.

"It has to do with a change of policy," Kroft reported during the broadcast. "Over the last three years, the FAA has switched its priorities from actively enforcing safety rules with fines, warning letters and sanctions—which become part of the public record—to working quietly with the airlines behind the scenes to fix the problems. It may well be what's allowed Allegiant to fly under the radar."[19]

The resulting publicity for Allegiant Travel Company wasn't good, its stock plummeting a day later. During the weeks following the broadcast, the company's executives repeatedly defended the airline's practices, insisting that it ran a safe operation. They stated that *60 Minutes* had aired a one-sided view and a "false narrative" about its operations and oversight by the FAA.

The *60 Minutes* segment appeared to have some short-term effect, particularly since over 10 million viewers may have tuned in Sunday evening or watched the segment online. Soon after, the Office of Inspector General for the Department of Transportation launched an investigation into the FAA's handling of maintenance-related allegations involving both Allegiant Air and American Airlines. "Our objectives now are to assess FAA's processes for investigating allegations of improper maintenance practices at Allegiant Air and American Airlines," said a memo posted online by the FAA.[20]

At the time of this writing, Allegiant Air has not suffered a major accident, as its many critics have predicted. Fewer flights are delayed now for mechanical problems. Allegiant expedited the retirement of MD-80s as promised and bought Airbus A320s and A319s, some of them new. Its stockholders and founders are more than satisfied with the airline's growth, a positive contrast to its earlier growing pains. Most of its employees are unionized and earn increased compensation.

If we dig a bit deeper, we find that some of the Airbuses, bought mainly from foreign airlines as were the MD-80s before them, are beginning to show their age. The pilots want the airline to buy new planes rather than used ones, and more of them. They have vivid memories of the schedule delays caused by mechanical failures with the MD-80s. Some second-hand Airbuses are a similar age as the McDonnell Douglas planes. This concern, along with an annoying method of scheduling their flights, brought the pilots together to vote for a strike in 2018. Allegiant Air went to court and stopped the job action as it had done in the past.

N407NV was ferried to a desert storage facility in Victorville, California, on July 2, 2018. Its working days were over. Allegiant Air flew its final scheduled flight of an MD-80 on November 26, 2018. The planes worn out, their temporary home in the desert serves as a place to remove resalable parts and melt their stripped airframes into aluminum ingots.

On February 4, 2019, *CBS News* aired the result of an eight-month-long investigation into allegations from mechanics at American Airlines and Southwest Airlines.[21] The mechanics claimed they were forced to work faster, ignore defects unrelated to their assigned tasks, and face possible termination for documenting such defects. Within a week of the broadcast, Senators Edward Markey and Richard Blumenthal sent a letter to Daniel Elwell, acting FAA administrator, demanding answers to these concerns. "In April 2018, we wrote to the FAA about reports of safety issues at Allegiant Air. The FAA's response stated that 'getting to the next level of safety requires finding and fixing hidden problems before they can cause an accident. Because everything starts with finding safety problems, compliance also requires the airline to have procedures that encourage open reporting."[22]

The senators weren't satisfied with the vague response they received. They wanted to know why the FAA had allowed the airlines to place needless pressure on mechanics to expedite maintenance work and ignore safety concerns. They asked the FAA to ensure that mechanics have the "unfettered ability to report safety concerns without fear of reprisal, including termination, from the airlines."[23]

However, Congress cannot force profitmaking air carriers to go the extra mile when it comes to maintenance—unless something catastrophic wakes everyone up. "We are constantly told we are the last line of defense. Unfortunately, we are the only line of defense," posted an Allegiant Air pilot about the decline in safety. "The lives of our passengers and crews depend on us to address the continued and needless infractions on the margins of safety. It appears no one [else] will."[24]

Note: Many of the details presented in this chapter, including dates, places, descriptions of events, conclusions, and quotes (unless otherwise attributed), were derived from Federal Aviation Administration, "Enforcement Investigation Report 2015WP390002 AAR Aircraft Services, Inc."

4

TRIPLE NICKEL

A dozen miles west of Midway Airport, tucked between the village of Clarendon Hills and the township of Hinsdale in the western suburbs of Chicago, there's a mystery yet to be solved. Buried beneath the soil in the back yard of a home, under an asphalt parking lot, or wedged under a rock could be a rusted steel bolt the diameter of a cigarette. Because that bolt hasn't been found, the world will never know for sure the cause of a tragic accident more than half a century ago. The missing bolt is thought to be responsible for what happened in the skies over Clarendon Hills during the early morning hours of September 1, 1961.

The bolt is thought to have fallen from a flight control linkage that moved the elevator control surface of a Lockheed Constellation belonging to Trans World Airlines, better known as TWA. Four minutes after taking off from Midway Airport, the plane became uncontrollable, plummeting into a cornfield and snuffing out the lives of all seventy-eight people aboard. The plane literally fell out of the sky.

From early on in the investigation of the accident, it became clear that the pilot had lost all control before the plane careened into the muddy field. After investigators from the Civil Aeronautics Board determined that the bolt was missing from the elevator linkage, a methodical ground search ensued in the hope that the bolt might turn up. The investigative team sifted the acres of charred dirt and debris where the Constellation had shed its weakened tail and dug a series of craters in the soft earth. The painstaking work consumed several days, but no bolt was found.

During the decades that followed, single-family homes built on deep lots replaced the plowed fields around Clarendon Hills Road. There's no marker at the tranquil, grassy site of this long-forgotten accident to memorialize the deaths of those seventy-eight people. In 1961, the accident ranked as the third-most-deadly aircraft accident in the nation's history. The dubious distinction of number one at the time was co-held by TWA. In 1956, one of the airline's Super Constellations crashed following a midair collision with a United Airlines DC-7 over the Grand Canyon. The death toll resulting from the crashes of those planes totaled 128 people.[1]

The early morning hours in Chicago were a blessing as the first day of September arrived. The humid heat of the summer months had begun to fade with the cooler days of autumn on the way. A mild 67 degrees registered on porch thermometers around Clarendon Hills. Although thunderstorms had moved through the area earlier, bedroom windows remained open for part of the night to admit cool air drifting in from Lake Michigan. For some residents of the largely undeveloped area, many of them farmers, a habit of retiring early and rising before dawn was a ritual tied to their chosen lifestyle. Long before midnight, they were already sound asleep. Looking forward to a long holiday weekend celebrating Labor Day on Monday, they would set aside chores, fire up a barbeque, and do nothing more than enjoy the weekend with family and friends.

Eleven miles to the east of the middle-class neighborhood, tucked inside the terminal building at Midway Airport, commotion contrasted with the tranquility of the suburbs.

From the air, Midway has been described as a square aircraft carrier stuck in the middle of a sea of homes and warehouses. Between 1932 and 1961, it attained the distinction of being the world's busiest airport. It served 10 million passengers in 1959. After nearby O'Hare International Airport opened, passenger traffic at Midway shrank by more than 60 percent. The spacious passenger facilities and longer runways of O'Hare, capable of safely accommodating fleets of new jetliners, lured the airlines away from Midway, along with their passengers. "Mile Square" Midway's runways couldn't be lengthened due to encroaching neighborhoods on each side.

The terminal's austere interior took on the appearance of a stylized bus terminal furnished with rows of plastic-covered black seats, their surfaces worn thin from years of constant use. A busy concession stand offered newspapers, cigarettes, and candy. A row of steel rental lockers graced the rear, and for $2.50 in quarters, a vending machine dispensed life insurance policies to passengers hesitant to fly. As breadwinners, husbands sought to provide continuing financial support for their wives and children should the unthinkable happen.

Waiting areas on either side of the terminal were cramped and uncomfortable. The air was humid and tinged with the smell of tobacco. Near TWA's gates, plenty of seats were available as the airline had only one passenger flight scheduled for an early morning departure. The fourteen passengers ticketed for Flight 529 paged through magazines, took smoke breaks, or strolled outside on the observation deck to watch planes take off and land. Because it was the start of a three-day weekend, some of them planned to visit families during the holiday or tuck in a short vacation. For less than one hundred dollars a ticket, they could fly coast-to-coast although the trip would not be a nonstop one.

The airline jet age was less than two years old. Only 10 percent of the nation's population, eighteen years of age or older, had flown aboard a regularly scheduled airliner. It was a big deal for first-timers.

TWA's new jets were boarding passengers at O'Hare for nonstop flights to international and domestic destinations. But the airline's piston-powered Connies, a time-honored nickname for the Constellation airliners built by the Lockheed Aircraft Corporation, continued to fly schedules out of Midway day and night. Some were filled with passengers, some loaded with freight.

With "red-eye" tourist flights, it wasn't unusual for large families to take advantage of budget fares for vacations or to visit relatives in faraway states. The airline took in much of its revenue by flying businessmen to last-minute meetings at full fare but filled the cabins with economy-minded families during the off hours. It needed to keep its planes in the air and working as many hours as possible. Flight 529 was one of those tourist flights.

As the hands of a clock on the terminal wall clicked closer to midnight, Jim Sanders could be found on the other side of the airport in TWA's flight operations room. He would serve as Flight 529's captain for its next leg to Las Vegas. Copilot Dale Tarrant and flight engineer Jim Newlin were there to greet him. Hostesses Barbara Pearson and Nanette Fidger soon joined them too. They exchanged customary introductions, sipped coffee, and shared small talk while getting to know one another. Where they stood under bright fluorescent lights, dozens of charts, airman notices, and forms were pinned to a bulletin board before them. A window overlooked an array of multicolored lights defining the airport's taxiways. The Connie they were scheduled to fly would soon come into view.

The weather at Midway wasn't a concern: scattered clouds at 10,000 feet, a high overcast on a moonless night, three miles visibility in haze and smoke, with wind blowing to the south at 9 mph.

In less than two hours, Sanders would be in the captain's seat on his way to Las Vegas, the plane's next stop. He and his crew patiently awaited the plane's arrival, scheduled to come in from Pittsburgh after originating in Boston and making a quick stop at Idlewild Airport in New York. The airliner, a model L-049 Constellation, carried a TWA fleet number of 555. The airline's crews had nicknamed the plane *Triple Nickel.*

The crewmembers lived in Southern California, and TWA domiciled them at Los Angeles International Airport. During World War II, Sanders had enlisted in the U.S. Army Air Corps and learned to fly. Piloting four-engine B-17 bombers over Germany, he and his crew survived flying a remarkable twenty-five missions. He joined TWA in August 1945 as a copilot. By the age of twenty-six he had flown Connies to Cairo, Madrid, Geneva, and Paris. He moved up from copilot to captain in June 1954, continuing to fly both international and domestic routes. By the time of Flight 529's planned departure from Midway, forty-year-old Sanders had amassed a remarkable 17,011 hours, with 12,633 of them in Connies. Sharing his love of aviation, wife Carol worked as a hostess for TWA. They lived in Manhattan Beach, a short drive from the Los Angeles airport.

Dale Tarrant joined TWA in December 1955. Born in Sturgis, South Dakota, in 1929, he attended Black Hills Teachers College and served with the U.S. Air Force from 1952 to 1955. He lived in Redondo Beach with his wife, Marian, a former Western Air Lines stewardess. Tarrant's flying time totaled 5,344 hours, with 1,975 of them logged in Constellations.

Thirty-eight-year-old Jim Newlin joined TWA in 1951, beginning his career as a flight line mechanic in Los Angeles. In 1954 he was promoted to flight engineer. Newlin was married and lived in Balboa Beach. He and his wife were raising two children from a previous marriage. He had logged 5,817 hours as a flight engineer in Connies.

Barbara Pearson, at twenty-five, had flown with TWA since August 1957. Living in Santa Monica with husband Richard, she was excited about completing this particular flight. Pearson expected to resign from the airline to devote full time to motherhood, her baby's due date being April 1962. She planned to tell her husband the good news after landing in Los Angeles.

Nanette Fidger, at the age of twenty, had been employed by TWA only since May. She began to fly scheduled routes on July 15, upon completing training. A short-timer like Pearson, Fidger intended to make only one more flight before leaving to get married.

The corporate culture at TWA in 1961 could be described as strained. For years, Howard Hughes, the company's absentee major shareholder, kept an unpredictable grip on its far-flung operations. By the end of 1960, TWA's lenders had prohibited Hughes from interfering with the management of the company. His questionable moves in arranging financing for a fleet of new jetliners resulted in the drastic action. Uncertainty, coupled with the carrier's unprofitable operations, did nothing to pacify the rank-and-file, whether they earned a living in a cockpit, a hangar, or behind a reservations desk.

On March 20, 1961, the TWA board of directors elected Charles Tillinghast Jr. as president and CEO. Pilots and mechanics considered him an unknown quantity. A career lawyer, he had no airline experience except warming a seat as a passenger.

"It was in terrible shape," Tillinghast later said of TWA operations. "By mid-1961, I thought we were looking at bankruptcy. If there was any airline that would have thrown in the towel, it was TWA."[2]

In February, the flight engineers at TWA and seven other airlines went on strike.[3] The dispute involved whether or not the new jetliners would be flown with a pilot or a flight engineer as a third crewmember. Most flight engineers had been promoted from mechanics at their airlines. They had little desire to join the pilot ranks, expecting to keep their flight engineer status and not be retrained as pilots or terminated from their chosen careers. Communication between the engineer's union and the airlines broke down completely. It became so unproductive that newly elected President John F. Kennedy appointed a fact-finding commission to investigate what drove the parties apart. Because the nation's passenger-carrying capacity was approaching a standstill with not enough crews to fly the planes, the commission's involvement ended the short-lived strike. It recommended that the jets be operated by three crewmembers, with the flight engineers trained as standby pilots in addition to performing their engineering duties. The decision signaled the end of non-pilot flight engineer careers and the emergence of pilots acting in that capacity with little practical mechanical experience.

Exposed to much negativity in the workplace, TWA employees began to wonder if their paychecks might bounce. The troubles facing the airline were distracting enough to bring worry into their lives.[4]

TWA found itself selling more tickets to tourists than to business travelers even though its route structure connected every major industrial city in the nation. Businessmen needed to arrive at destinations for sales calls or meetings as soon as possible, and not on a propeller-driven Connie at half the speed of a jet. While other airlines had ditched most of their piston-powered planes, TWA still relied on Constellations.

Tourist-class flights were flown with older L-049 Connies on an almost exclusive basis, while TWA's jetliners were assigned to international and nonstop transcontinental routes. The Connies were relegated to Sky Club Air Coach Service and refurbished with headrest covers featuring shades of beige, green, and orange. The window curtains had pastel shades, while dark blue carpeting perked up the aisles. Transforming the interiors created a warm and cheerful cabin environment.

Lockheed Aircraft Corporation manufactured many variants of the legendary Constellation for the airlines and military services. The plane's most distinctive feature was its futuristic tripletail. Unlike contemporary airliners, the Connie had three vertical stabilizers.[5] Its unique fuselage put it in a class by itself as well, having a contour shaped like the body of a dolphin. Other airliners were built with straight, tube-like fuselages.

At ninety-five feet long, the L-049 Connie was powered by four Wright Aeronautical eighteen-cylinder piston engines. Their cylinders were arranged much like the spokes of a wheel divided into two circular rows of nine cylinders each. Each engine was massive, weighing over one and one-half tons, its power output developed from 3,350 cu. in. of cylinder displacement. The power from each engine was comparable to what ten V-8 pickup truck engines could produce.[6] Originally intended for transoceanic trips, the L-049 offered a cruising speed of 313 mph.

Constellations were considered the most complicated piston-powered airliners of the time. This meant there was greater potential for mechanical failure. The plane's weight and size necessitated the use of hydraulically boosted flight controls. During an early test flight of a TWA Connie, one-half of the hydraulic system failed. A few minutes later, the other one-half did the same. Captain Hal Blackburn, one of TWA's most experienced pilots, described what it was like flying the plane with no hydraulic boost to operate the controls: "It took the combined strength of myself and two husky copilots to move that yoke."[7]

Registered as N86511 with the FAA, *Triple Nickel* happened to be the oldest Connie that TWA owned. The airline took delivery of *Triple Nickel* on December 19, 1945. Six weeks later, the plane began flying passengers from New York to France as the *Star of Paris*. A tradition at TWA and some other airlines involved painting the names of the cities they served along the sides of a plane's nose. *Triple Nickel*'s flight to Europe in February 1946 was hailed as a major milestone for TWA: the first scheduled transatlantic passenger flight from LaGuardia Field in New York to Orly Field in Paris.[8] As more advanced Super Constellations and the first generation of jet transports joined TWA's fleet, the L-049s were reconfigured to seat eighty-one passengers. The tourist class service served a burgeoning, budget-minded segment of the air traveling public. *Triple Nickel* had few creature comforts to offer its passengers and crews but got the job done, day after day. Having logged many hours in the air, the plane was well maintained and had served as a reliable workhorse for over fifteen years.

As a scheduled transcontinental flight originating in Boston, Flight 529 regularly made intermediate stops in New York and Pittsburgh followed by Chicago, Las Vegas, and Los Angeles. The flight would terminate in San Francisco. Before leaving Boston, *Triple Nickel* had several discrepancies written up by its crew. Among them was a burned-out navigation light in the tail and a leaking drain valve on a wing fuel tank. Mechanics repaired both items before the plane left Boston. Another discrepancy carried over from a previous flight was a malfunction of the system supplying cool air to the passenger cabin.[9] Not considered a "safety of flight" item, the discrepancy was again carried forward in a logbook to be repaired during a future stop.

One of the passengers boarding the plane in Pittsburgh was Harry Savage. "There were a lot of little kids running around, a lot of young people on the way to Las Vegas and Los Angeles for vacations," he recalled, noting the carefree mood of his fellow passengers.[10] A prosecutor for Allegheny County in Pennsylvania, Savage would not be continuing on to the flight's final destination as he planned to disembark in Chicago on business.

Flight 529's journey from Pittsburgh to Midway went smoothly with no hitches. The Connie pulled into a gate at 1:18 a.m. Ramp workers were told to handle its fueling quickly to keep the flight on schedule. Although there wasn't enough time for the passengers continuing on to disembark, they welcomed the few minutes available to stretch and rearrange their belongings. The captain and flight engineer arriving from Pittsburgh briefed Sanders and Newlin about the cabin cooling issue. All agreed there was no effect on airworthiness. Outside on the ramp, workers pumped enough fuel and oil into the Connie's tanks to complete the next leg. The 3,240 gallons of aviation gasoline poured into its tanks weighed in at 19,440 pounds. Newlin computed the plane's gross takeoff weight to be 94,794 pounds, well below a maximum allowable of 96,000. Checking the passenger and cargo manifests, he made sure the plane's center of gravity fell within acceptable limits. Everything checked out okay. The flying time to McCarran Airport in Las Vegas was estimated to be six hours and twenty-three minutes.

Shortly after 1:30 a.m., a TWA passenger agent announced over the public address system that Flight 529 was ready to board. It was a relief for the parents and their children already seated in the plane. They were tired and beginning to doze off. Flying after midnight was stressful but meant that families could purchase bargain tickets to stretch household budgets, making it possible to travel with several kids in tow. By contrast, business travelers opted for morning or late afternoon flights, their companies paying the much higher fares.

A gate agent opened the plane's main cabin entry door. The flight and cabin crew from Midway boarded. A TWA crew bus had shuttled them from the airline's hangar on the north ramp. Making their way into the Connie, four-teen passengers from the Chicago area followed them after trekking through the concourse. They stepped into the dimly lit cabin, soon finding their seats. Configured for tourist-class flights, the entire length of the cabin was fitted with five-abreast seating.

As departure time neared, hostesses Pearson and Fidger prepared their pas-sengers for the routine red-eye flight. Pillows and blankets were passed around. Pearson was experienced working such flights after doing so at TWA for several years. Other than the fourteen passengers boarding at Midway, the passengers already on the plane remained seated for the next leg.

Following a family visit, thirty-eight-year-old Frances Gilliam looked for-ward to joining her husband, Neil, at home in Eureka, a seaside community in Northern California. She had visited her parents in Bedford, Massachusetts. Their four children, Karen, 11; Linda Jo, 4; Denny, 14; and Tommy, 7, were buckled in for what promised to be a tiring flight involving two stops before deplaning in San Francisco.

Four women, each 20 years old, were anxious to reach Los Angeles. They were relocating there to begin adult lives working in Southern California. Carole Chase, Linda Annis, Nancy Bergstrom, and Linda Peaslee hailed from Sun-cook, New Hampshire. Close friends who had met at school, they had worked part-time jobs during the summer months to pay for the trip.

Richard Maloney, an engineer, was aboard with wife Florence and their five children. At their sides were Michael, 5; Maureen, 3; Richard Jr., 10; Mary, 8; and James, 1. Following a visit with family members in Philadelphia, they were anxious to return to suburban Canoga Park in California. While away, carpen-ters at their home had kept busy building an additional room to provide more living space for the family.

Forty-one-year-old Edward Chamberlain, an architect at Stedman & Wil-liams, hailed from Palo Alto, a suburb south of San Francisco. Along with his wife, Nancy, he was returning home following a trip to Europe. After arriving stateside, they had spent time in Connecticut visiting relatives before heading back to California. Accompanying them were their children Edward Jr., 14; Richard, 9; Grant, 4; and James, 2.

Sylvia Remnant, a 32-year-old Englishwoman, was aboard with her three children John, 10; Tym Elmer, 3; and an infant girl. She had purchased the tickets in Liverpool, England.

Of the seventy-three passengers aboard the flight, twenty were children, and fourteen were age ten or younger. Most of the passengers were continuing on from Boston or Pittsburgh. Among the people boarding at Midway were four

Chicago-area residents: a pharmacist headed to Los Angeles to visit his aging parents; a nurse traveling to San Francisco for a vacation; and two servicemen returning for duty in California following home leave.

A ramp agent rolled the loading stairs back, followed by Newlin pulling the door closed. Returning to the cockpit, he began the process of starting the four Wright R-3350 engines, each expected to develop its full 2,200 hp for takeoff. As he manipulated switches and levers at the flight engineer panel, the massive engines came to life one by one. Clouds of oily smoke poured from their exhaust stacks and swept across the ramp but quickly dissipated in the cool night air. All four engines now idling, a ramp agent guided Sanders from the gate onto a taxiway.

Tarrant picked up a microphone to contact air traffic control and read back their clearance to Las Vegas for concurrence. The Connie would be guided across the country under instrument flight rules (IFR) by following a series of airways. This involved tuning into one radio navigation station after another to hop across the country.

Sanders took the opportunity to brief Tarrant and Newlin on his planned emergency procedures should the plane suffer an engine failure or other problem during takeoff. Pilots live on the edge anticipating such events. Never predictable, the possibility of such an event causes flight crews to take these briefings seriously. During emergencies, they are aware that every second counts—and can mean the difference between life or death. Such planning helps ensure that the actions of each crewmember during an emergency are predictable and instantaneous.

Cleared by ground control, Sanders steered the Connie to a concrete run-up pad at the end of runway 22L. He twisted the steering tiller to swing the plane's nose into a gentle breeze and set the parking brake. This was the signal for Newlin to run up the engines, one on each side at a time, to check the rpm drop of their magnetos, exercise the pitch of the propellers to ensure they feathered properly, and attend to other procedural checks. Newlin gave the engines a workout, running them up to a throaty roar and watching the firing patterns of all 144 spark plugs on the scope of an electronic engine analyzer.[11]

Sitting several feet in front of Newlin, Sanders and Tarrant checked the plane's flight controls by moving the yokes and pedals for the elevator, ailerons, and rudders, taking them through their full range of movement. Sanders took care of a related task to check the elevator shift control handle next to his right leg. Should the hydraulic boost system controlling the elevator fail, something that had never happened at the airline, pulling the handle would disconnect the "power steering" and enable the pilots to operate the controls manually. It was functional.

Seat Belt and No Smoking signs lit, Pearson and Fidger returned to their seats. Cabin lights were switched off to enable the passengers to view the lights of Chicago soon after takeoff.

Final checklist items completed and ATC clearance acknowledged, Sanders received permission from the tower to roll forward, stopping just short of the runway. Cleared for takeoff, he eased the throttle levers forward, creating a loud rumble. There was enough vibration to rattle a clipboard. As the heavy machine began moving, his gaze shifted to the engine tachometer and manifold pressure gauges on the center instrument panel. Four tachometers reading 2,800 rpm and manifold pressure gauges indicating forty-six inches of mercury were good numbers. The takeoff roll continued.

Reflected in the silvery wings, orange and blue flames shot from the exhaust stacks of the engines as the Connie thundered down the 6,445-foot long concrete ribbon. In seconds, the plane would climb into a moonless sky.

Sanders moved his left hand from tiller to yoke slowly, while Tarrant called out the airspeed for him. Tarrant announced reaching V1 speed, the point of no return at which the pilot must decide whether or not to continue the takeoff. Nothing amiss, they continued. Tarrant followed with another required verbal notification by saying, "Rotate." Sanders gradually eased back on the yoke as forty-eight tons of aluminum and steel shifted from rolling on tires to being carried aloft with lift from the wings. Flight 529 took to the sky gracefully, gained altitude, and entered a right turn just past the airport.

Tarrant retracted the landing gear, soon followed by the flaps. All appeared normal. It was now one minute after 2:00 a.m., and passengers seated near a window amused themselves by watching the twinkling lights of the city pass below as the plane began a steady climb to its initial cruise altitude.

The throttles were pulled back from takeoff power. Even so, the noise made it all but impossible for the passengers to chat among themselves, but they knew it would be quieter once the plane leveled off for cruising.

One minute and thirty-four seconds after the pilots acknowledged their takeoff clearance, a controller at Midway began following Flight 529's initial progress on a radarscope. Four minutes after the plane left the runway, the image on his scope indicated that it was five miles west of the airport, proceeding on its assigned course. As another second passed, the image disappeared. Assuming it was a temporary glitch of the radar system, he had no idea that something unthinkable had just happened.

In the darkened cabin, a tremendous jolt threw anything into the air that wasn't secured. The passengers must have thought they had run into a severe air pocket, or maybe hit another plane. Rocking crazily, the Connie bounced like a speeding car ramming into a series of deep chuckholes. The force turned so violent that people were slammed down, then yanked backward; children were tossed about and battered by loose handbags and books. If not restrained with seat belts, they were rag-dolled against the ceiling. A colossal thudding noise could be heard over the familiar roar of the engines. But people seated near a window saw nothing out of the ordinary. Propellers turning, the engines were producing power. However, the front of the wings seemed to be angled up way too high, as though the plane were climbing. In reality, it was doing the opposite: losing altitude fast. The plane felt like a roller coaster dropping into a plunge. For everyone from the cockpit on back, panic set in. Engine failures and fires were not unusual occurrences with Connies. But this was unfathomable. Continuing for half a minute, the gyrations weren't showing signs of stopping. The Connie was dropping like a rock. Women screamed. Children yelled and cried. Men dug their fingers into armrests and prayed silently. The chaos would span almost a full terrifying minute.

The graceful airliner remained stuck in a nose-up attitude, trapped in a series of unforgiving aerodynamic stalls.

Faces flushed and hearts pounding, Sanders and Tarrant gripped the yokes in unison with both hands, pushing them forward, employing every bit of strength they had. They needed to lower the nose to pull out of the stalls. Consumed with a rush of adrenalin, they reacted instinctively as pilots are trained to do. They knew it would be impossible to remain in the air long enough to return to the airport for an emergency landing.

Sweating and wholly occupied in coping with the crisis, the pilots never radioed the controller at the Midway tower. Both of them were pushing on the yokes but with no result.

The Connie was not responding to the movement of the yokes, and the plane remained in the stalled condition, falling like a leaf. It appeared to recover somewhat, then entered another stall. While Tarrant continued to push against the yoke, Sanders tried pulling a knob on the thin metal handle at his side to deactivate the elevator's hydraulic muscles. Drawing on thousands of hours' experience flying Connies, he knew what to do. He suspected that the elevator boost system must have failed.

The handle was jammed. It wouldn't move an inch. Before they took off from Midway it worked fine.

Airspeed slowing with little altitude remaining and the lights of Chicago growing brighter and bigger every second, the Connie continued its vertical plunge, not unlike dropping down a shaft in an out-of-control elevator.

CHAPTER 4

Once stuck in the series of oscillations from the stalls, the plane couldn't gain any forward airspeed. The only way to exit a stall is to push the yoke forward to increase the speed, but the plane wasn't responding to the forward movement of the yokes.

The combination of an elevator jammed at an extreme angle and the pilots pushing forward on the yokes at the same time made it impossible to free the handle and disengage the boost. The crew didn't know this in the few crucial moments they had, but the handle would disengage the boost *only* if they weren't pushing forward on the yokes. Nobody had told them about this life-saving tip buried in a pilot's flight manual and largely glossed over in training sessions. Sanders pondered other options. There weren't any.

He had survived twenty-five missions during the war, enduring engine failures and enemy flak. But this was unreal. Losing their last hope for a safe recovery, the crew began experiencing the same distressing feeling being felt by their passengers. During the final seconds in the air, they could only gird themselves for the inevitable, pray perhaps, and wait for the inexorable conclusion.

A hundred feet over the darkened neighborhood of Clarendon Hills, a portion of the plane's horizontal stabilizer separated from the tail and fell to the ground.

The flickering green symbol representing Flight 529 did not reappear on the controller's radarscope. Grabbing a pair of binoculars and focusing them on the horizon over the city, a controller in the airport tower noticed a bright flash erupting west of the airport. He radioed the pilot of a Northwest Orient Airlines flight waiting to take off from the same runway that *Triple Nickel* had departed from. Clearing the plane for takeoff, he asked the captain to report what he saw in the area. Circling west of Midway, the pilot observed one-hundred-foot-high flames reflecting from the overcast sky; they illuminated the suburbs for miles around. He saw a massive cloud of smoke hovering in the same area. An American Airlines crew preparing to land also spotted the flash. They abandoned their landing approach and flew westerly to where the fire seemed to be centered. Told that a TWA flight hadn't been heard from, and looking almost straight down from altitude at an inferno engulfing the landscape, the captain reported that what he saw looked bad . . . very bad.

There was little doubt the flames and smoke represented the end of Flight 529. The plane had crashed eleven miles west of Midway Airport, one-and-one-half miles southwest of Hinsdale, a suburb of 15,000 people about twenty miles from downtown Chicago.

Shedding pieces of its airframe, the Connie had passed over Plainfield and Rogers Roads, turned north and flew along Clarendon Hills Road at almost treetop level. After enduring at least four violent stall oscillations, one of its

66

vertical fins and an attached rudder separated from the stabilizer. The assembly fell in an empty field.

The rest of the plane impacted the ground, disintegrated, and exploded in a fireball. What was once a streamlined airliner vanished in seconds, its nose auguring into the earth. It had dropped vertically more than horizontally and bounced on impact several times, the airframe shredding into pieces.

Triple Nickel ended up in a muddy corn and soybean field at 61st Street and Bentley Avenue in Clarendon Hills. The soil had become saturated by heavy rain from a thunderstorm moving through the area an hour earlier. The plane struck the ground in a slightly left-wing-low, nose-down attitude on a heading of almost true north.

To residents living under the flight path of the disabled airliner it sounded like dozens of railroads cars roaring overhead. The thunder and vibration was unlike anything they'd experienced before. The ground shaking from the tremendous explosion caused some residents to think it could be coming from Argonne National Laboratories—a sprawling Atomic Energy Commission research facility, built to develop nuclear reactors, located five miles southwest of the crash site.

The raging fire, fed by nearly three thousand gallons of high-octane aviation gasoline carried in the wing tanks, created a bewildering environment. Thick, oily smoke from the burning fuel rose thousands of feet in the placid, early morning air.

People living closest to the crash site rushed to the scene. They described the Connie's final seconds as much like an enormous scythe, chopping a swath wider and longer than a football field. Five craters had been dug, each about four feet deep, burying the sizzling-hot R-3350 engines and the heavy center section of the wing. Only shards of metal and fabric and the bodies of victims littered the field. The intense fire rendered unrecognizable most of what remained. The scene had become a blackened, lifeless landscape.

Scattered throughout the field were the possessions of people whose lives had been snuffed out: an opened book, a bathrobe, a baby bonnet, shower shoes, and crushed suitcases were among the items. A propeller blade, snapped from its hub, protruded from the ground. The outer portion of a wing had been thrown against the fence of an adjacent house. Two of the plane's husky, three-foot-diameter tires fitted to a main landing gear assembly remained unburned, resting alongside the perimeter of the fire-scorched earth.

"I woke up with sirens screaming," said Nancy Malsack, who lived six blocks from the crash site. "I quickly began to smell the unmistakable smell of burning flesh."[12]

The body of a dead woman was found clinging to an infant for a last embrace. Realizing there wasn't anything they could do to help, residents ran home to strip blankets and sheets from beds and returned to cover the bodies. Not having enough sheets to go around, they unbundled stacks of newspapers to use in their place. The sound of sirens wailed in the distance as the residents awaited teams of first responders rushing to the scene.

"I was asleep when I was awakened by a sound like a locomotive outside our window," said Charles George, a nearby resident. "I jumped up and saw a passing silhouette, and then the plane crashed in our field. A tremendous wall of flames came rolling toward our house and stopped just short, singeing crops and trees. Some of the bodies were thrown into the barn of the Broz family, just north of us."[13]

Hot engine oil spewing from fifty-gallon tanks in each wing nacelle scorched the outside walls of a home owned by Jerry and Josephine Broz. The heat melted their nylon window screens. One of the main landing gear assemblies shot through a side of the family's corrugated steel shed at the rear of the property. When first responders arrived, they found the crumpled remains of three victims there. "The plane hit the ground and bounced several times," said Josephine Broz. "We could see the wheels, the wings, everything falling apart."[14] The Broz farm is where most of the wreckage and all the victims came to rest.

"I saw the plane come into the backyard through my bedroom window," she continued. "Then the nose of the airplane landed in the cornfield." Grasping the gravity of the situation, her husband reacted instantly. "The minute she hollered, I jumped up and saw the plane in the backyard. The first thing that I said was to leave and get in the car. I called the police department, the fire department, and anyone I could get ahold of." After the explosion, all they heard was the crackling of flames. "I couldn't hear any screams or any sign of life," Broz said.[15]

It took only minutes for the firefighters and police officers to arrive, their sirens continuously yelping in the stilled air. They roared up the narrow dirt driveway leading to Broz's two-story home at 59th Street and Clarendon Hills Road. The couple lived only 450 feet from what remained of the Connie.

Before daybreak, dozens of firemen and members of suburban, county, and state police departments converged on the scene. Workers from a nearby carnival set up for the holiday weekend loaned their portable light stands to illuminate the cornfield.

"My farmyard is a cemetery without crosses," Broz said as the sun peeked over the horizon.[16] He was sickened by the sight but realized how lucky he and his wife had been to have escaped the inferno.

Tuning in a TV set in his hotel room before heading to work that morning, Henry Savage, the passenger who had gotten off the flight in Chicago, slipped into a chair in a state of shock. The macabre scene televised from the crash scene made him sick. Thinking of his experience flying into Chicago, he had heard a grinding noise when the plane took off from Pittsburgh. Awakening from a nap as the plane neared Chicago, he remembered that the plane "shook rather violently."[17] He regretted not telling anyone.

As the early morning sun peeked over the horizon, more than one hundred officials and volunteer workers began the unpleasant task of collecting the bodies. Red Cross workers crisscrossed the field all morning, driving wooden stakes with numbers pinned on them into the soil where each victim was found. From a distance, the stakes could be mistaken for crosses. The workers weren't alone. Representatives from the U.S. Post Office arrived. Their job was to retrieve whatever scorched mail had been scattered over the field. From surrounding communities, thousands of curiosity seekers trekked to the neighborhood during the first few days to view the destruction from a distance.

Several hours after daybreak, black hearses were lined up along Clarendon Hills Road. All was strangely quiet and somber as a funeral would be. The bodies were wrapped in rubber sheets and moved to the Cook County Office of the Coroner in Chicago for identification. The gruesome task would consume five days. DNA testing for accident victim identification did not exist at the time.

By mid-afternoon, Najeeb Halaby, a record-setting test pilot and second administrator of the fledgling FAA, had arrived on the scene. Accompanying him was a team of investigators to augment the work of the Civil Aeronautics Board. The public wanted answers. During evening news telecasts, Halaby assured viewers that a cause for the crash would soon be determined.

A theory about a bombing began to blossom, although there were no facts to support it. Some eyewitnesses said they heard an explosion while the plane was in the air. But seasoned accident investigators had learned to dismiss many of those accounts. The chief of the FBI's Chicago office was asked if the plane could have carried a bomb. At this early stage of the investigation he couldn't say, but a medical team that examined the corpses ruled out a bombing. The victims didn't exhibit signs typical of an explosion. Their injuries appeared more like those suffered by people involved in an automobile accident.

If it was not a bombing, the question of what caused the accident remained a mystery.

The only person who reportedly witnessed the plane's final seconds of flight happened to be an eleven-year-old boy by the name of Elmer Maves. Living three blocks south of the crash site, he didn't see any flames while the plane was in the air. But he did hear a loud popping noise, followed by a series of three less intense reports as the structure that held the vertical and horizontal stabilizers to the fuselage began to buckle and collapse.

"It was going east . . . and then it turned, and its right tail blew off," he said. "After it crashed, there was dead silence for two or three seconds. And then, all of a sudden, it exploded. Flames were like a thousand feet in the air."[18]

Although not verified, one report indicated there was a survivor. First responders hovered over the victim with lifesaving equipment. The victim was eventually covered with a sheet.

The death count was finalized in the morgue: seventy-eight men, women, children, and infants had perished. The only tribute to lives taken too soon and their next-of-kin would be a thorough investigation to determine the cause. And to make sure that a horrendous accident such as this would never take innocent lives again.

The crash of Flight 529 was traumatic for a TWA captain by the name of William Gordon. At the last minute, he had traded his assignment to fly *Triple Nickel* with Captain Sanders and moved on to another flight. He happened to be a good friend of Sanders and knew his crewmembers. Ironically, Gordon's younger brother, Robert Gordon, then a student at the University of California, Berkeley, had boarded the plane for San Francisco and died in the crash.[19]

Rodger Morphett, a ramp service agent working for TWA, helped board Flight 529's passengers while *Triple Nickel* was in New York. One of his duties involved ensuring that the airplane's landing weight wouldn't exceed limits. Three passengers needed to be pulled from the flight. Two of them were soldiers. The third happened to be a young mother traveling with her two small children. She was planning to be reunited with her husband stationed at Fort Ord in Monterey, California. Morphett convinced the reluctant woman to remain overnight in New York. After rebooking her for a flight the next day, he told her that a message would be sent to her husband to let him know about the change in plans. Then before he and a fellow worker left the airport for the night, they tried repeatedly to reach her husband without success. For many years after the accident, when Morphett and his former colleague got together, they would talk in hushed tones about whether they had really selected the woman and her kids—or if a greater power had intervened to choose her over another passenger.[20]

What no one knew at the time of the crash was that the lives of every one aboard Flight 529 were cut short because of a two-cent cotter pin that someone forgot to install.

Note: Many of the details presented in this chapter, including dates, places, descriptions of events, conclusions, and quotes (unless otherwise attributed), were derived from Civil Aeronautics Board, "Aircraft Accident Report, Trans World Airlines, Inc., Lockheed Constellation, Model 049, N86511, Midway Airport, Chicago, Illinois, September 1, 1961, SA-363."

5

DISCONNECTED

The crash of TWA Flight 529 shocked the nation. It rattled the nerves of millions of would-be air travelers enough to keep them on the ground. Finding a cause and making sure that a similar accident wouldn't happen again became the responsibility of the Civil Aeronautics Board (CAB).

Investigators from the CAB moved into position quickly. They began canvassing the burned cornfield for clues, extending the task into days. Pieces of debris were tagged, carefully segregated into piles, and trucked to a roped-off corner in one of TWA's hangars at Midway Airport. After completing the cleanup task, the investigators assumed that anything associated with the accident had been collected. Unfortunately, heartless scavengers had arrived on the scene before the first responders did. It couldn't be determined what valuables or pieces of wreckage had been carted off or whether the missing items might compromise the investigation.

"I remember chasing away someone trying to get some rings off people's hands," said Frank Trout, at the time a seventeen-year-old volunteer firefighter living nearby.[1] A mile from the site, police arrested a man. He had stolen a purse from one of the bodies. Also detained were three teenage boys who were holding a part of the fuselage when police officers stopped them. They had snatched it as a souvenir.

Other organizations joined the CAB investigation team, including representatives from TWA, the Air Line Pilots Association, the Flight Engineers International Association, the Lockheed Aircraft Corporation, the Curtiss-Wright Corporation, and the FAA. Ignoring their affiliations, they were expected to function as a team without bias. The investigation would be a coordinated effort to find the cause as soon as possible.

Members of a CAB witness group began walking door-to-door in the surrounding neighborhoods to find people who may have heard or seen the limping Connie during its final moments. More than 150 interviews would be conducted eventually.

TWA wasted no time in making a public statement. "We are cooperating with federal and local authorities in an effort to determine the cause," said Charles Tillinghast Jr., TWA's CEO. Seeking to pacify the airline's worried customers, he continued, "This was the first fatal accident involving a TWA 049 type Constellation since 1947. During this period, these airplanes have flown billions of passenger miles in complete safety."[2]

Seven investigative teams began work in earnest under the overall coordination of CAB engineers John S. Leak and Wesley Cowen. Leak was chief of the Technical Services Section, Engineering Division, in the CAB's Bureau of Safety. Cowen had joined the CAB as an investigator a year earlier.

The largest pieces of wreckage resting on the hangar floor belonged to the plane's empennage, or tail, and were portions of the plane's vertical fins and horizontal stabilizer. They were the only sizable pieces of airframe to have survived the inferno because the tail had separated seconds before the rest of the Connie hit the ground. The tail landed hundreds of feet from most of the wreckage, which gave it special significance for the investigators. The distance made it incontrovertible that a portion of the tail had broken free of the aft fuselage while the plane was still in the air. Specifically, a section of the horizontal stabilizer that supported the right vertical fin had been sheared off.[3]

There were indications that the control surface of the elevator had become stuck at the limit of its upward travel. The investigators noticed that a deformed pattern was impressed on the surface of the right rudder. It should not have been there. It was apparent that the elevator became immovable at its full-up position after the rudder slammed into it when the stabilizer broke up.

As the team sifted through the pieces of wreckage, large and small, portions of the cockpit instruments and controls were recovered. Although damaged, the shift handle used to disengage the hydraulic elevator boost system was found in its On position. It appeared that the system had been operating properly prior to the crash.

During normal flight operation, pilots of the Connie contributed only a small amount of the total force required to move the heavy elevator, a hydraulic system providing most of the muscle. The tail cone below the horizontal stabilizer enclosed the hydraulic valves and cylinders needed to actuate the rudder and elevator surfaces. Fortunate to find the components undamaged, the investigators removed them for testing in a lab. On a test bench, they functioned satisfactorily. However, a close examination revealed that a small, forged-steel arm connected to a linkage called a parallelogram wasn't connected. It could have become disconnected during the crash or at some time before the crash. Its attaching bolt was missing.[4]

From early on, a crucial question evolved: Did the impact of the crash force out the bolt that connected the arm to the linkage? Or did the bolt fall out of its hole in the arm while the plane was airborne?

The only way that the bolt could have been ejected on impact was if it had been subjected to extreme tension—that is, pulled out along its shank. Although this was unlikely, such an outcome might have resulted from severely stripped threads losing their strength or the bolt's nut breaking in half. When asked, a TWA engineer speculated that a stripped thread could be the reason for the bolt departing on impact.

All of the nuts and bolts attaching the parallelogram linkage to the elevator control system were accounted for in the piles of wreckage except one. A 5/16-inch in diameter, 2.25-inch long nickel steel bolt identified as an AN-175-21 was absent from a bushing pressed into the linkage. Appreciating the cadmium-plated bolt's critical role, the investigators scrambled to find it amid the crumpled pieces of metal, burned fabric, and coils of corroded wire lying on the hangar floor. It wasn't there. Realizing that it could be hidden under blackened dirt in the cornfield, they revisited the site to sift through the soil. Again, they returned empty-handed. Failing to locate the bolt, they thought it logical that the bolt had not been in place when the plane hit the ground. However, they knew it had to be in place during the takeoff from Midway or the plane would not have been able to lift off the runway. Four minutes after departure, therefore, the elevator had worked free of its control mechanism. But as other parties to the investigation soon came to suggest, the bolt might have exited *after* the plane hit the ground. A strong difference of opinion was emerging. Sides were being taken.

The bolt in question wasn't a garden-variety piece of hardware you might buy at Home Depot. Designated as "close tolerance," the hex-headed bolt had been machined more accurately than a general-purpose fastener.[5]

The AN-175-21 bolt also had a special feature: a hole drilled in its threaded end to accommodate a cotter pin. A steel nut, identified as an AN-320-5, held the bolted assembly together. Small slots in the nut, called castellations, enabled the cotter pin to be inserted between the castellations and through the hole in the bolt's shank. Identified as an AN-0380-2-2, the pin was a 1/16-inch in diameter and ½-inch long. It sold for two cents at any aircraft parts supply store.

Fearing that other Connies might have loose bolts, the FAA jumped into action within days. It issued an airworthiness directive mandating that all operators of model L-049 and L-749 Constellations inspect the elevator mechanisms. The action could be unusually swift because much of *Triple Nickel's* horizontal stabilizer had survived the crash and the investigators had quickly discovered the linkage with no bolt in the hole. If the tail cone had been destroyed, finding a likely solution to the mystery of what had happened would have consumed many additional weeks of detective work.

TWA responded to the FAA's directive by stating,

> TWA has completed the control system inspections on certain of its Constellations as ordered by the FAA, following the tragic accident in Chicago. The inspection of TWA 049 aircraft was completed on September 1 and 2, some days prior to the official FAA request. The FAA had ordered TWA and the other seven airlines operating these types of Constellations to inspect the aircraft to insure that "the five bolts, nuts and cotter pins in the parallelogram linkage between the elevator boost valve and boost mechanism are properly secured and safetied."[6]

It wasn't mentioned if any missing bolts, nuts, or cotter pins were discovered during the inspections. The FAA did not monitor the work in TWA's hangars.

Before World War II, flight control systems were relatively simple. Ailerons, rudders, and elevators were coupled directly to cockpit controls by steel cables, pulleys, and turnbuckles. Late in the war, the size and performance of larger planes such as the Constellation had progressed to a point where pilots needed more muscle power to help them move the cumbersome control surfaces. In response, Lockheed developed hydraulically boosted controls for its military planes in addition to the Connie. The controls brought more complexity but reduced the force needed compared to manual systems.

Yokes were provided in the cockpits of Connies to actuate the aileron and elevator control surfaces. Pedals moved the rudders. Most of the force required to move the surfaces around their hinges came from hydraulic boost similar to power steering in automobiles. Cables that controlled valves feeding high-pressure hydraulic fluid to move the pistons of boost cylinders were linked to the yokes and control surfaces. Should a hydraulic system failure occur, two handles atop the throttle pedestal in the cockpit could be pulled to disconnect the rudder and aileron cylinders, enabling the pilot to move the surfaces manually. A handle located along the left side of the pedestal disconnected the elevator boost cylinder. Pulling it shifted the elevator's control linkage to a manually operated mode. Although it would be three times more difficult for a pilot to move the elevator than with the boost operative, at least the pilot could remain in control of the plane.

At the time of the accident, the nation's major airlines outsourced a scant amount of heavy maintenance to other companies. Instead, they invested in constructing and staffing in-house repair and overhaul facilities located in key cities throughout the country. Inside gargantuan hangars, everything from minor inspections to the complete overhaul of airframes, engines, and avionics was undertaken. The facilities employed thousands of FAA-licensed mechanics, the majority of them loyal members of the machinists' union. TWA's largest overhaul and maintenance base was located at Mid-Continent International Airport in Kansas City, Missouri.[7] *Triple Nickel* checked in there during May 1959 for maintenance.

The Connie had been scheduled for replacement of components in its flight control boost system, including parts that operated the elevator. The work accomplished, inspected, and documented as completed satisfactorily, the plane returned to passenger service soon after. Further maintenance performed in November 1960 involved replacing several components dedicated to the elevator. The task included disassembling the parallelogram linkage assembly. Specifically, it involved removing and reinstalling five fasteners, including the missing AN-175-21 bolt the investigators were seeking. A final, detailed inspection of the plane's flight controls took place during a periodic check on August 7, three weeks before the accident. Nothing out of the ordinary was noted.

The CAB investigators were mystified. They couldn't understand why TWA's mechanics and inspectors didn't notice a missing cotter pin during any of those maintenance visits.

Two almost indistinguishable smudges of grease on part of the parallelogram linkage emerged as a clue.

Engineers from the CAB, working with flight control engineers assigned from Lockheed, conducted a close inspection of the linkage. They focused on the steel arm that should have been connected to it with the missing bolt. Assuming that the bolt had been installed, it would have needed to pass through a bushing pressed into the arm. A washer under the bolt head would have been seated against the outside edge of the bushing, the washer normally flush with the face of the arm. Mysteriously, two grease deposits having the consistency of modeling clay were seen on the arm. They had a thickness of 1/64 of an inch. And a pattern caused by the hex head of a bolt was visible in the residue.

During an unknown period of time, the bolt, minus a nut securing it, had moved to a point where its threaded end became lodged two-thirds of the way into the bore of the bushing. Marks cut by the threads in the outer one-third length of the bushing confirmed that the bolt had not been fully inserted. The cuts left by the threads would not have been made if the bolt had been installed properly.

In order for grease to squeeze from the bushing, a gap between the end of the bushing and either the bolt head or its washer would be required. "The heavy deposit and the splatter in the vicinity of the left bushing appeared to have come from the bushing bore, having been splattered out of the bushing by the loose, chattering bolt" stated the CAB accident report.

> In order for grease or any other material to build up on the outer surface of the left arm assembly bushing, there obviously must be a gap between the bushing and the bolt head (or washer). There are probably many ways to cause this gap but, in any case, regardless of initial cause, the nut must be loose by at least the number of threads equivalent to the maximum thickness of the grease, 1/64 inch.

Vibration of the bolt sitting in the hole had agitated the grease and packed it into the tiny gap between the bushing and bolt head. No grease was found in any other bushing in the linkage, adding credibility to the finding. It became clear that a nut had not been installed, allowing grease to migrate from the bushing as the bolt moved farther from its hole.

There was another question: Why did the grease clearly reveal the outline of a hexagonal bolt head? It seemed strange because the procedure for assembling the linkage called for using two washers, one installed under the head of the bolt and another under its nut.[8] A close inspection revealed that a washer had been installed sometime in the past, leaving its impression on the surface of the arm. Therefore, if the installation had been made in accordance with Lockheed specifications, a hexagonal pattern would *not* be seen because the washer had a larger diameter than the head of an AN-175-21 bolt.

The CAB investigators interviewed the TWA mechanic who replaced the parallelogram linkage. He said that due to tolerance variations it wasn't always possible to tighten a nut if a washer was installed under the head of the bolt.[9] He sometimes removed the washers and installed the bolt without them. This explained how the shape of a bolt head had been pressed into the grease. A washer had been installed during a previous installation of the linkage but not in November.

Sorting through the collected evidence, the investigators determined a mechanic could have failed to install the nut during the plane's maintenance in November but this wasn't probable due to the length of time elapsing from then until the day of the accident. The nut could have been over-tightened, stripping its threads. However, even a stripped nut, if a cotter pin had been inserted, would have retained the bolt. The most logical reason for the bolt's absence, although it could not be substantiated to TWA's satisfaction, was that a cotter pin had not been installed on the nut during the previous year's heavy maintenance visit.

After elevator control maintenance in November, the nut had gradually unscrewed and then fallen off, allowing the bolt to slowly drift from its bushing, splattering the thin layer of grease in the process. The bolt eventually fell out a few minutes after *Triple Nickel* took off from Chicago Midway. When the bolt exited, the boost system's valve opened to port hydraulic fluid to the up-elevator side of the cylinder,[10] causing the elevator to pivot the plane's nose to a full-up position. This resulted in the plane entering the first of several violent stalls. Sanders would have used his left hand to exert every bit of strength to push the yoke forward, while with his right hand he would have tried to pull the shift handle up to cut off the boost. The elevator remained stuck at its maximum angle, however, held by unrelenting hydraulic pressure, and it was impossible for him to pull the handle.

The predictable response to the plane's violent pitch up, and the series of stalls, was to continue pushing forward on the yoke. That's how pilots are trained to recover from a stall. Unfortunately, doing this in *Triple Nickel* prevented shutting off the boost. Pushing on the yokes meant that a much higher force was needed to pull the shift handle up, causing the crew to never regain control.[11]

No record existed of previous problems with the elevator boost systems of Constellations operated by the airlines. However, the military services did suffer a fatal accident and a non-injury incident while flying military versions of the airliners. The cause was attributed to the inability of the pilots to shift the boost to manual operation. The CAB investigators uncovered a shocking similarity to what had happened to *Triple Nickel*. Following an incident involving a U.S. Air Force C-121, a transport version of the Connie, the Air Force ordered that a research study be conducted to determine possible failure modes of the boost system.[12] The finding: when the shift system was tested on a mock-up supplied with simulated air loads, moving the handle couldn't be accomplished when a force of one hundred pounds or more was pushing the yokes forward.

Surmounting this potentially deadly handicap in flight, the pilots of the C-121 had landed safely after a harrowing ride from high altitude. The crew of a U.S. Navy R7V, another militarized variant of the Connie, was not as fortunate. Several people witnessed the plane's fatal plunge into the ground at Taft, California, on May 14, 1958. The R7V had made several 360-degree turns with its nose positioned at a steep angle. Never regaining the altitude it lost in the turns, the plane remained stuck in orbit and coming dangerously close to the barren fields below. Suddenly, a severe pitch-up movement occurred and the plane was whipped into a steep bank. Flying at an altitude too low to recover, the R7V slammed into the ground, killing everyone aboard.

A Navy investigation discovered that a bolt connecting the parallelogram linkage to the spool of a hydraulic valve controlling the boost cylinder had backed out. It wasn't the same bolt missing from *Triple Nickel*, but the outcome was just as deadly. Uncontrolled movement of the spool caused the cylinder's piston to push the elevator, causing the nose to rise sharply. The R7V descended in this fashion all the way from 12,300 feet to where it crashed, the pilots struggling continuously in a futile effort to pull out from the series of stalls.

Like that of the *Triple Nickel*, the shift handle of the R7V was found in the On position. The handle had not been pulled out, likely because the pilots couldn't muster enough strength between them to do so.

The falling R7V had endured five successive accelerated stalls. Most of its airframe absorbed the intense shaking caused by the extreme air loads, but the metal skin, stringers, and bulkheads in the aft section of the fuselage failed. Similar to what happened to *Triple Nickel*, the R7V's horizontal stabilizer structure cracked, turning the plane into a falling brick.

Lockheed scheduled a series of tests for the Navy similar to what the Air Force had conducted. The tests revealed that with extreme elevator deflections, moving the handle couldn't be accomplished if forward pressure was being applied to the yoke. The report, authored by Lockheed flight control specialists, stated in part,

> A study of the curves reveals the marked effect of [control] column forces on shift force, but also that there is a reasonable amount of column force allowable. The conditions permitting a shift to manual have considerable latitude, depending upon surface moment, restraining column force, and surface angle. Within these limits, many opportunities would be present, permitting a shift to manual position.

Combining these findings with what was learned about *Triple Nickel*'s final moments, the CAB investigators felt that the opinion of the Lockheed engineers represented a hit-and-miss approach to designing an emergency system for an aircraft. Assuming that the controls could jam, as they did in Chicago, the investigators disputed the test report by responding, "Particularly in an unmanageable regime, and if a corrective mechanism is available, a pilot should be offered a positive correction, not opportunities-within-limits." For Lockheed to admit that the ergonomic design of its boost system might not be failsafe appeared to be asking too much from the time-honored manufacturer.

It would seem that recovering from a steep, nose-up attitude would be a simple, straightforward procedure for a pilot. But this boost system had a dangerous peculiarity. In the shift from boost to manual, a change of the system's mechanical advantage lengthened the connection between the yokes and the arm that moved the elevator. The shift moved the yokes back in concert with the elevator. When the boost system hydraulic valves operated properly, the elevator was free to move downward because it was assisted by air pressure pushing against the control surface. If the yokes weren't being pressed forward, the controls would complete the shift successfully. It's assumed that *Triple Nickel*'s pilots applied forward pressure in an attempt to exit the stall and *then* tried to make the shift. Because the elevator had already moved up more than 16 degrees at that point and remained stuck there, the lifesaving action came too late.

There was no possibility that Sanders, or any other pilot, could have brought *Triple Nickel* under control and landed it safely. The seventy-eight people aboard had taken off in an airliner with a loose bolt resulting from a missing cotter pin. If the pin had been installed, everyone would have arrived at his or her destination safely. Instead, they died in a cornfield. It had nothing to do with pilot error, bad weather, engine failure, or sabotage. It was pure negligence on the part of one or more employees contributed to by a design flaw that existed in the emergency flight control system of all Constellations.

To present its findings, the CAB convened a hearing at Midway Hotel in Chicago on September 27, 1961. At times, the testimony turned into a showstopper.

A TWA mechanic, not identified by name in the CAB investigation report, testified that he installed the parallelogram linkage in November 1960. "I am sure all bolts were installed, properly torqued, and safetied," he replied when asked about the task. Then, thinking about what he had just said, he added, "I do not remember specifically working on plane 555." He either truly couldn't remember or made the comment to avoid perjuring himself. Either way, the statement seemed to contradict his testimony of a minute earlier. However, the mechanic wasn't solely responsible. The inspector checking his work and his supervisor would be equally guilty.

During the 1960s, accident investigation methodologies centered on the failure of mechanical parts more than what led up to their failure: the human factor. Mechanics and inspectors working on the Connie's elevator mechanism testified that the job had been completed correctly. Defending them, the managers at TWA didn't concur with the CAB investigators who stated that the bolt was lost during flight.

"The airline would not admit culpability where there wasn't a 100 percent certainty," said David Kent, who as a child lived in the area where the plane had crashed. "Every TWA mechanic, and likely the pilots for the airline, would tell you that the airline was at fault."

Bill Aitken was the head mechanic for TWA at Midway Airport. Kent talked with him. "I could not get Bill to tell me that much," he said. "But I suspect it had something to do with his position as main liaison between the feds and TWA."[13]

Assuming that the cause of the accident had nothing to do with a missing cotter pin, the airline could offer no explanation as to why the Connie became uncontrollable in the air and crashed. If the pin wasn't the cause, what was it?

Each participant testifying at the hearing denied culpability. If the bolt had been found, a metallurgical analysis in a laboratory could have disclosed the length of time it had been lodged in the bushing and roughly when it fell out.

Because the elevator linkages of TWA's other Constellations had been installed correctly, it became obvious that an individual rather than systemic failure of the airline's maintenance policies had resulted in the accident. A mechanic could have become distracted for any one of a dozen reasons.

The CAB's conclusion in its final report made no reference to a maintenance error: "The probable cause of this accident was the loss of an AN-175-21 nickel steel bolt from the parallelogram linkage of the elevator boost system, resulting in loss of control of the aircraft." The key word here is "probable." It's included in all causes cited by the CAB and years later by the NTSB in its own reports. Without an admission of guilt from any of the parties involved, and with no bolt to admit into evidence, the investigative findings were taken more as conjecture than fact by many observers.

Following the hearing, TWA management remained resolute in its position regarding the bolt. In the October 16, 1961, edition of *Skyliner*, the airline's employee newspaper, it reported in blunt terms: "CAB investigators were of the conclusion the bolt may have come off in flight. TWA officials contended the bolt came off on impact."[14]

As far as the CAB was concerned, the case was closed. Its teams had gathered evidence, unearthed clues, and produced what was thought to be the cause. The accident may have resulted from a distracted, overworked mechanic who, in haste, had forgotten to insert the pin. And his work should have been checked.

The work life of an aircraft mechanic can be sweaty, tiring, and occasionally dangerous. Much of the heavy maintenance, including work performed by TWA at its maintenance facility in Kansas City, was conducted in the middle of the night. Surveys reveal that workers on "graveyard shifts" are significantly less efficient than those on daytime shifts. If a mechanic works a rotating shift, moving between three different time periods, fatigue reaches an all-time high. It takes three or four days for a body's circadian clock to adjust to such changes, and without those three or four days, sleep deprivation is the result. And a sleepy mechanic can easily make mistakes.

In addition, airline maintenance facilities of the 1960s didn't require drug testing of their employees. Alcoholism ran unchecked in most of society, a problem affecting the aviation industry as well. And much as today, the onset of behavioral problems, including the effects of ADHD, depression, and anxiety, further exacerbated poor employee performance. In addition to substance abuse, mental health concerns were not discussed openly or always treated during the middle of the last century. If a mechanic began his shift impaired due to mental distraction or substance abuse, it could result in driving a rivet wrong or forgetting to install a cotter pin.

Exactly when the bolt fell from *Triple Nickel* continued to be a matter of conjecture, with no shortage of opinions. TWA representatives reiterated that the bolt sheared apart on impact, pieces of it falling free. The company offered no further comment, particularly from CEO Charles Tillinghast Jr. The corporate communications staff remained mum as well. In 2011, I asked Jerry Cosley, TWA's retired vice president of public affairs, about the accident. Although quite verbal about other issues affecting the airline during his lengthy career, when it came to *Triple Nickel* he offered, "No comment." Cosley had been at the scene of the accident in Clarendon Hills and had watched the CAB investigation unfold.

Winding up its investigative work on November 22, 1961, the CAB leadership recommended to the FAA that the mechanism used to shift the elevator boost to manual control be modified. Their rationale was based on the belief that the instinctive actions of a pilot should be sequential in nature rather than simultaneous. The recommendation called for a redesigned mechanism to relieve hydraulic pressure *before* a pilot would be allowed to move the shift handle to gain manual control, regardless of how much force was being applied to the yokes.

A position paper prepared by Georg Kohne, a senior captain for Lufthansa German Airlines and an experienced Constellation pilot, offered a clarification of the plane's safety problems. Kohne, along with several other pilots, had been involved in a recent project to restore and fly a Connie in scheduled service. He wrote,

> The Lockheed Constellation series may well be the most attractive and interesting design of all airliners. However, its safety record does not at all qualify for any positive ranking. Many, way too many, Connies were lost in operation . . .

frequently caused by poor ergonomic design or a demanding, complicated or misleading system layout being at least a contribution, if not the root cause.[15]

On March 8, 1962, the FAA responded to the CAB's recommendation for a design change via letter. It stated that the pilot's flight manual for the plane had been revised by Lockheed to include "procedures for turning off the elevator boost with an uncontrollable elevator." The letter went on to say, "In view of the excellent service history achieved by this aircraft since certification in 1946, we believe there is insufficient justification to require design changes to accomplish your total objective."

The FAA took into consideration the overall safety record of the Connie, beginning when it first entered commercial service; a "probable" and not conclusive cause of the accident; and the likely cost to the airlines to modify the shift mechanism. These were the reasons why it vetoed the CAB recommendation. The FAA ignored the frantic environment that must have existed in the cockpit during *Triple Nickel*'s final minute and why this kind of accident could happen again. The FAA was more attuned to studying parts failing than the people or processes that caused them to fail. It would take time for the agency to appreciate how a small error made by a mechanic could bring down an airliner. It was obvious that it hadn't taken into account the boost issues affecting the military C-121 and R7V.

Those few words in the FAA letter were not what the hard-working CAB investigators wanted to hear—or the family members and friends of passengers who had perished.

L-049 Connies continued to fly for TWA up to an FAA deadline in 1962, when they were retired from passenger service. The agency had mandated that weather radar systems be installed in airline transports, including Connies. The modifications would be costly, requiring expensive rewiring and installing radar nose cones. In response, TWA decided to sell its entire L-049 fleet.[16]

Because a bolt was never found, investigators could not *positively* ascertain what happened. It boiled down to whether lapses of maintenance and inspection practices at TWA were responsible for the accident. Whether they were or not, the airline was rumored to have made an unknown number of out-of-court settlements to families of the victims.

TWA struggled through dour financial conditions in 1961, exacerbated by the layoff of seasoned employees and the fielding of a fleet of new jets that brought with it extreme debt. A sharp division of opinion continued to worsen the relationship between management and the rank-and-file. Under CEO Tillinghast's leadership, the board of directors voted to diversify the businesses that

TWA owned by acquiring properties such as Hilton International and Century 21 Real Estate.

Following the Airline Deregulation Act of 1978, TWA was spun off from the holding company that owned the non-aviation enterprises. Renegade financier Carl Icahn soon acquired control of the airline via a leveraged buyout. The airline's financial death appeared on the horizon. Drained of many valuable assets, TWA slipped heavily into debt, which forced the sale of its moneymaking international routes. TWA ended up in Chapter 11 bankruptcy in 1992 and again in 1995. A year later, the airline almost shut down following the disastrous explosion of Flight 800 off the New York coast, killing the 230 people on board.[17] In 2001, a weakened TWA filed for bankruptcy a third and final time, the carrier's assets having been acquired by American Airlines in January of that year. TWA flew its last scheduled flight on December 1, 2001.

Compounding the sorrow following the Flight 529 tragedy, the unthinkable took place two weeks later about twenty miles from Clarendon Hills. At 8:57 a.m., on September 17, Northwest Orient Airlines Flight 706, a one-year-old Lockheed L-188C Electra, crashed shortly after departing O'Hare International Airport. All thirty-two passengers and a crew of five aboard the four-engine turboprop airliner were killed instantly. As with *Triple Nickel*, the plane became uncontrollable at a low altitude, impacted the ground, and was instantly consumed by fire.[18]

Electra N137US had flown from Miami, Florida, to Milwaukee, Wisconsin, the day before the accident. The next morning the plane flew into O'Hare. It underwent routine servicing and a change of crews before taking off to continue on to several destinations in Florida.

The pilots acknowledged their takeoff clearance while taxiing and were cleared to make a running takeoff from runway 14R. Upon passing the runway's 8,000-foot marker, the plane rose about 100 feet—slightly lower than an Electra would usually be on departure. The plane then began a right turn, still climbing, but it still wasn't more than 300 feet in the air.

The bank to the right increased dramatically. When the bank reached 45 degrees, the pilot made a short, garbled radio call to O'Hare tower, alerting the controller of an emergency. The roll continued to a frightening 60 degrees, the plane's wings now tilted almost vertically, and the heavy plane began to lose what little altitude it had gained. Uncontrollable, it was about to slam into the ground. It's possible the pilot tried to reach the runway to land. But there wasn't enough altitude remaining.

The right wing brushed high-tension power lines paralleling the tracks of the Chicago Northwestern Railroad. The lines severed instantly, a bright bluish flash erupting. The disabled Electra maintained its forward momentum, banking 85 degrees from the vertical and reaching a nose-down attitude of 10 degrees. Its wing struck the railroad embankment, the plane cartwheeling and its nose digging into the ground 380 feet from first contact. Settling right side up, it then slid 820 feet, shredding pieces of its airframe along the way, the debris strewn across an area 200 feet wide by 1,200 feet long. Orange and red flames marked the spot where the burning hulk came to rest. A billowing mushroom cloud of black smoke spewed into the air.

Bystanders at the airport had observed the plane's banking increase steadily, with an aileron that appeared to be stuck in a right-wing-down position. The CAB investigators began to suspect that the aileron's control system could have jammed. Normal pilot recovery techniques, such as moving the rudder, modifying engine power, or adjusting aileron trim tabs may have proved successful in overcoming a steep bank if sufficient altitude had been available. But the pilots were flying not much above rooftop level.

When investigators had dismantled what remained of the plane's components, the evidence pointed to a loss of control resulting from a disconnected steel cable in the aileron control system. This caused the aileron on the right side to throw the plane into a steep roll that made returning to level flight impossible.

Cables attaching the yokes to the aileron hydraulic boost system had been disassembled for maintenance two months before the accident. A thin piece of safety wire that secured a cable connector had *not* been replaced after the cables were reinstalled. Without the safety wire in place, the connector gradually unscrewed until it separated completely during takeoff. The cable disconnected, it wasn't possible for the pilots to apply enough opposing aileron force to level the wings and regain control of the plane.

Eight discrepancies involving the aileron control system of N137US had been reported by different pilots from June 27 to July 11. The latter date was also when the boost assembly was replaced. The plane went on to fly a total of twenty-nine scheduled passenger flights with a defective part. Little effort had been made by the airline to determine the cause of the problems or to correct it. The CAB investigation report noted that the lack of attention reflected a "casual attitude" in dealing with what turned deadly.

Further investigation disclosed that the training of mechanics at the airline had been sporadic. No specialized training existed for mechanics working on the Electra's complex flight control system. The mechanic who installed the replacement boost assembly had not received any formal training. Although an informal, on-the-job training program existed, with instructors available to mechanics for consultation, the program wasn't in full swing at the time. It was the *first time* that any Northwest mechanic had worked on the flight control rigging of an Electra.

The CAB team members concluded that the probable cause of the accident was a mechanical failure of the aileron control system due to improper replacement of its boost assembly, resulting in a loss of control at too low an altitude to recover. The investigators determined from testimony presented at a public hearing that the airline's maintenance and inspection personnel showed an "ignorance or disregard of published directives and instructions."[19]

The accident paralleled what had brought down TWA Flight 529 only seventeen days earlier: negligence in maintaining a critical part of the flight control system. In the case of the Electra, it wasn't about inserting a cotter pin. It involved a mechanic who forgot to attach a two-inch-long piece of safety wire to secure a cable that controlled an aileron.

Flight 706 became the fifth major accident involving an Electra since the big turboprop's introduction two years earlier. After several fatal accidents of the newly introduced Electra, the press had begun to scornfully refer to the plane as a "flying coffin." Such publicity created a firestorm of mistrust with the traveling public. As a result, the Electra was deemed unsafe and many people felt it should be grounded.[20] The FAA in turn was alleged to have ignored the plane's structural shortcomings while allowing it to continue flying. Through a herculean engineering effort and major financial investment by Lockheed, the structural weaknesses plaguing the plane were fixed at no cost to the airlines. After Lockheed modified each Electra, the planes went on to serve as reliable passenger airliners and freighters for decades.

The CAB's investigation completed, the FAA disciplined Northwest Orient Airlines. However, the laissez-faire culture existing in its hangars took years to eradicate. Following major organizational changes, the long-established airline continued onward for almost fifty years, serving air travelers throughout the world. In 2008, now renamed Northwest Airlines, it merged with Delta Air Lines.

It is natural to consider *Triple Nickel* the "granddaddy" of fatal accidents caused by simple maintenance errors. Over the decades following the crash, efforts to prevent similar accidents have fallen short of expectations. After each accident or incident, detailed investigations followed, and recommendations to not repeat mistakes were made, but missing bolts and screws continue to plague the world of aviation to this day.

Twenty miles from O'Hare airport in Clarendon Hills, the corn stalks and barns are long gone. Homes set on deep lots, interspersed with groves of trees as tall as eighty feet, have replaced them. Much of the surrounding land is covered with dense foliage and grassy areas where children go to play. Jerry Broz, the farmer who owned the land where the Connie crashed, never plowed the 200 by 1,100-foot former debris field. It remained undisturbed. Decades later, scars left in the earth by the crash of *Triple Nickel* have disappeared. On Labor Day weekends, a number of senior citizens in Chicago, and people who follow aviation history, make it a point to remember what took place in that muddy cornfield two hours after midnight so many years ago.

"Today, the area is a stand of trees that began to grow in the corn and soybean field after the crash," said Kent. "Many of the old-time residents of the area attended a public hearing years back to subdivide the land for homes. One resident, Bob Del Sardo, said, 'Leave it alone . . . that area is hallowed ground.' The developer went home."[21]

Note: Many of the details presented in this chapter, including dates, places, descriptions of events, conclusions, and quotes (unless otherwise attributed), were derived from Civil Aeronautics Board, "Aircraft Accident Report, Trans World Airlines, Inc., Lockheed Constellation, Model 049, N86511, Midway Airport, Chicago, Illinois, September 1, 1961, SA-363."

6

BOXES AND PEOPLE

The weather in California's Sacramento Valley isn't always what the chamber of commerce likes to promote. During the winter and spring months, it's not unusual to find highways and airports socked-in under thick Tule fog. In summer and fall, long days of bone-dry heat set in, bringing eye-watering smog. On Wednesday, February 16, 2000, there was no fog and no heat wave. The daytime temperature hovered around 60 degrees with puffy white clouds dotting a blue sky. In aviation terms, it was close to CAVU (ceiling and visibility unlimited).

Sacramento bustled with people attending school, working in state office buildings, or visiting an automotive auction yard in Rancho Cordova, a city one dozen miles east of the state capital in Sacramento County. The king-size yard, owned by Insurance Auto Auctions, occupied a flat expanse of land at 11499 Douglas Road. The company is a leading auctioneer of used sedans, coupes, SUVs, and pickups.

People looking to buy an inexpensive car were there to examine recent additions to the inventory. Among the hundreds of vehicles parked in long rows one might find an older Chevy, a late model SUV, or a perhaps a sporty BMW.

Insurance Auto Auction's business office sat in a corner of the forty-two-acre yard, with plenty of separation from nearby homes and strip malls. The yard was surrounded by barren fields in 2000 because the region's real estate developers hadn't yet grabbed the land to erect cookie-cutter tract houses. The auction company's owners chose the location to be certain they would have sufficient acreage to expand car storage in the future. The only major industrial facility in the area was Mather Airport, one mile away.

During the afternoon of February 16, more than three hundred prospective customers dropped by the yard, many of them bidding on cars. Mild weather brought out a fair-size crowd with the yard remaining open for business until five o'clock. Adding to the excitement, big jets occasionally taking off from Mather served as a treat for anyone having even a passing interest in aviation.

Mather Airport, owned and operated by Sacramento County, is situated on level land about twelve miles east of downtown Sacramento, on the south side of US Route 50. It's the site of the former Mather Air Force Base, closed in 1993 by the Base Realignment and Closure Act, better known as BRAC. As a government commission, BRAC had orchestrated the closure of many military installations around the nation following the winding down of the Cold War.[1] Due to the BRAC decision, the military airport was transformed into one serving commercial and private aviation. United Parcel Service moved its operations there from Sacramento International Airport to take advantage of the airport's spacious ramp for loading and unloading jet freighters and to make use of its uncrowded 11,301-foot runway.

During the 1990s, an airline by the name of Emery Worldwide joined UPS at Mather to ship freight to its main hub in Dayton, Ohio. In common with UPS, Emery operated a fleet of four-engine McDonnell Douglas DC-8 jetliners converted to freighters. Emery had come into existence flying only two planes, but within ten years its fleet numbered more than ninety jet freighters serving 185 cities throughout the world.

After World War II, Emery Air Freight became the first freight forwarder to be awarded a license as a common carrier by the CAB. Over the next three decades, Emery's shipments were carried aboard planes operated by scheduled airlines. To boost capacity in 1976, Emery began chartering the planes of other carriers. By 1979 it had grown into a nationwide freight delivery service with sorting hubs operating in Dayton, Ohio, and Smyrna, Tennessee. Building on this success, the company adopted a new name: Emery Worldwide Airlines. In 1984, undergoing further expansion, the airline acquired the first of forty-three DC-8 jets. Each was modified with two oversize loading doors and strengthened floors to transport unusually heavy loads of cargo.

Emery ranked third in size behind UPS and FedEx, the latter boosting its revenues by acquiring the Flying Tiger Line. In 1993, Emery won a ten-year contract from the U.S. Postal Service, the win helping the airline post its first profit since 1986.

Choosing Dayton for a hub wasn't a quick decision made by Emery executives. They discovered that 78 percent of the cities in the United States where the airline had customers were located within a ninety-minute flight of Dayton

International Airport. Eager to create jobs and expand the city's tax base, Dayton leased millions of square feet of ramp space to Emery for loading and unloading its dozens of planes simultaneously. An expanding economy caused the company to grow so fast that it built a sixteen-story control tower to direct its ground traffic at the airport.

Deep in the bowels of the Dayton sorting facility, operations at night never stopped. Pallets loaded on forklifts moved swiftly through a building and onto the ramp. It took a large cadre of workers to push more than 3 million pounds of freight through the hub every night. To streamline the process, barcode readers identified and tracked each item, which was then placed in a container designed to fit the cabin of Emery's jets. Mechanical lifts, known as "K-loaders," kept busy loading and unloading containers or pallets on dozens of planes. Operations at the hub were carefully orchestrated, taking on the appearance of a military mission.

Emery transported mostly heavy business-to-business shipments. Although it delivered more than eighty thousand small packages a day, its specialty was shipping oversize products and industrial equipment. Thinking that it might be profitable to deliver a greater volume of high-priority envelopes and small packages on an overnight basis, Emery acquired Purolator Courier in 1987 to boost its revenues, a move that later turned into a financial nightmare.

In April 1989, Consolidated Freightways bought rival Emery Worldwide. "Emery was not going to make it on its own," George Robertson, an air cargo analyst, told the *Los Angeles Times*. "That's why it was sold."[2] All cargo-carrying airlines were facing challenges in remaining profitable even though the volume of shipments had climbed. Increased competition from freight forwarders became the problem because they worked with the major passenger airlines. The mainstream airlines had cut shipping rates below what Emery was charging because they weren't dependent on the cargo business to make money. Selling tickets to passengers continued to be the major source of their revenue.

In return for $230 million, Consolidated acquired Emery's extensive network of air routes, a valuable list of customers, and the immense sorting facility in Dayton. The marriage of the two firms created the largest heavy cargo shipper in the nation.

There were, however, skeptics questioning the viability of the merger. "The merger won't reduce a significant amount of capacity or increase the amount of pounds shipped," said Theodore Scherck, president of the Colography Group, a major transportation consulting organization. "There is still too much capacity for too little freight."[3]

Following the merger, Emery's revenues began a steady climb. All looked well partly because it had won another contract from the U.S. Postal Service in 1997. The $1.7-billion windfall required it to operate the government's Priority Mail network along the east coast. Unfortunately, a lengthy strike at UPS the same year threw Emery into a tailspin. Emery was suddenly shipping three times more cargo than before the strike. The demand necessitated the hiring of additional employees in Dayton and nine more flights. Taking into account the costs involved in ramping up its operations, Emery didn't profit from the extra business.

A trim, thirty-five-year-old resident by the name of George Land called Placerville, California, home. In common with his neighbors, Land had gravitated to the Sierra Nevada foothills to enjoy its unhurried outdoor life rather than live amid the hustle of a sprawling metropolis. Land's job enabled him to live almost anywhere: he was a pilot and had been working for Emery Worldwide Airlines since September 1996. Conveniently, some of his flights landed at and departed from Mather Airport, a quick thirty-three-mile drive from his home in the Gold Country. A seasoned pilot, Land had logged 4,511 total hours, 2,080 of them flying DC-8s as a copilot. On February 16, he would join two other pilots for an early evening flight from Mather to Emery's hub in Ohio.

For Land and the two pilots joining him, Emery Flight 17 would be a routine trip. The captain assigned to the flight, forty-three-year-old Kevin Stables, hailed from New York. In addition to Stables and Land, rounding out the crew was thirty-eight-year-old flight engineer Russell Hicks. He and wife Connie were residents of Sparks, a fast-growing suburb east of Reno, Nevada. They had been married for only five weeks. Hicks had accumulated almost 9,800 hours in the air, mostly as a pilot with United Airlines, including 675 hours as a DC-8 flight engineer.

To prepare for a long day flying across the country, Stables actually started out on the afternoon of February 15. He traveled from Albany to Dayton as a passenger on an Emery flight. Airline pilots refer to such positioning flights as "commuting." Arriving in Dayton, he transferred to Emery Flight 18. It was scheduled to fly a load of cargo directly to Mather and then on to the Reno/Tahoe International Airport, followed by a return hop to Dayton. Due to a minor mechanical issue, the flight sequence was reversed to a landing initially at Reno and then at Mather. It had already been a long day for Stables by the time he reached Reno. He hadn't been at the controls from Albany to Reno but sat behind the pilots and read a book. At Reno, the schedule called for a change of crews. Stables took over from the captain who had flown into Reno, while Hicks joined Stables as flight engineer. Designated Flight 17, the crew went on to Mather and landed there about 6:15 p.m. Land joined them at the airport.

Born in Schenectady, Stables had earned a private pilot's license at the age of sixteen. Following graduation from high school and community college, he went on to attend Embry-Riddle Aeronautical University in Daytona Beach. Before joining Emery on October 19, 1994, he had flown for several commuter airlines, eventually logging more than 13,000 hours. He and his wife, Kathleen, lived in Berlin, a picturesque, sparsely populated town in upstate New York.

When the DC-8 the crew would take to Dayton was new, it came from the California plant of McDonnell Douglas on March 21, 1968. Manufactured as a DC-8-61, it was powered by four noisy Pratt & Whitney JT3D-3B engines, each producing 18,000 pounds of thrust. In June 1983, the engines were replaced with CFM International CFM56-2-C1 fanjets, each engine now producing 22,000 pounds of thrust. The CFM56 was to become a sought-after engine for retrofitting older airline transports. A big selling point was its compliance with the FAA's latest noise and emission regulations. And it burned far less fuel than the obsolete, fuel-hungry Pratt & Whitney engines.[4] The plane was re-designated a DC-8-71. It was then converted to a freighter in April 1993, resulting in the *F* added to its designation. Emery bought the plane on March 27, 1994.

The DC-8-71F that Stables was flying carried FAA registration number N8079U. Previously operated by several other airlines, it had flown around the world for a quarter century before Emery acquired it. The airframe had amassed 84,447 hours by February 2000, the plane having made 33,395 takeoffs and landings. The plane had peeling paint and scuffed surfaces, but appearances don't matter when it comes to hauling freight. "Passengers complain but boxes don't" is a favorite saying of cargo pilots who have previously flown passengers.

Within minutes after the DC-8's arrival at Mather, a team of handlers had arrived at its side, erecting portable light stands, pushing ramps into place, and hooking up ground support equipment. The workers would unload, refuel, and reload the jet for its nightlong trip to Dayton. The first task was to unload the cargo with K-loaders moved into place near the open doors. Packed containers and stacked pallets were pulled from both main and belly cargo compartments and rolled to an adjacent storage area. The incoming cargo removed, the evening's outgoing load consisted of barrels of automotive transmission fluid, containers full of clothing, and boxes of fuses used to activate automobile air safety bags. None of the items was considered hazardous.

In Emery's operations room, Stables exchanged pleasantries with Land and began reviewing the evening's flight plan. The two pilots accompanying Hicks examined the departure documents, consisting of a load sheet, fuel load, dispatch papers, and weather data. All appeared satisfactory, with no extreme weather events expected along the 1,792-mile route. At Mather, the winds were calm with a visibility of ten miles, a ceiling of 7,000 feet, and an air temperature of 46 degrees. Flying conditions could not have been better.

Each of the pilots knew that Emery and the other cargo-carrying airlines had experienced problems with inadequately secured cargo. Emery planes were especially vulnerable because they transported heavy loads that other carriers wouldn't handle.

In 1997 there had been a fatal crash at Miami when the latches holding a pallet in place hadn't been secured properly. It was Flight 101, a DC-8-71F operated by a Miami-based freight carrier named Fine Air. The cargo slid aft, rendering the jet uncontrollable on takeoff. Five people were killed, including the driver of a car struck by the plane.[5]

Emery had a long history of improperly secured cargo. Straps and locks holding pallets in place would fail, causing the cargo to shift. "Emery knew they were having trouble with cargo shifts," said Steven Weinstein, a former pilot at the airline. "I, personally, was on over a dozen flights where the FAA came out, inspected airplanes, and made us replace the cargo straps because they were unsafe."[6]

In addition to Emery's cargo loading problems, McDonnell Douglas jets were sensitive to foreign objects jamming their controls. On September 8, 1970, a DC-8-63F freighter operated by Trans International Airlines crashed shortly after taking off from JFK International Airport in New York. The plane rotated to an extreme nose-high attitude of at least 60 degrees, stalled, and smashed into the ground from an altitude of 500 feet. The NTSB ruled the probable cause of the accident to be "a loss of pitch control caused by entrapment of a pointed, asphalt-covered object between the leading edge of the right elevator and the right horizontal spar web access door in the aft part of the stabilizer."[7]

On the Mather ramp, flight engineer Hicks conducted a preflight inspection of N8079U's exterior while keeping an eye on the cargo loading operations. At the same time, mechanics from Emery and a contract maintenance company helped check the plane's engine oil levels, tires, and brakes and handled the refueling chores. Hicks and the mechanics didn't spot any discrepancies. Now, long after sunset, it was dark in the southwest corner of the airport. The mechanics had set up portable light stands along the left side of the plane to illuminate the open cargo doors for loading and unloading. But there wasn't any lighting set up along the right side. Hicks used a flashlight to find his way around the plane.

The containers and pallets were moved into the interior and secured to the floor at multiple locking points. The heaviest cargo was stowed over the wing near the plane's center of gravity. Lighter loads were positioned fore and aft.

A Southwest Airlines Boeing 737 MAX 8 departs the airport in Boise, Idaho. The carrier currently has in its fleet and ordered more MAX airliners than any other airline. *Gerald Howard. Reproduced with permission.*

An American Airlines McDonnell Douglas DC-10-10 departs Los Angeles International Airport in November 1995. One of the airline's DC-10s crashed on departure from Chicago on May 25, 1979, killing 273 people. *Duncan Stewart. Reproduced with permission.*

N407NV, an Allegiant Air McDonnell Douglas MD-83 that nearly crashed on takeoff from Las Vegas, Nevada, on August 15, 2015, climbs out from the same airport during an earlier flight. *Sebastian Sowa. Reproduced with permission.*

N86511, a TWA Lockheed L-049 Constellation, is seen taxiing for takeoff months before crashing near Chicago, Illinois, on September 1, 1961. All seventy-eight people aboard Flight 529 died in that crash. *American Aviation Historical Society. Reproduced with permission.*

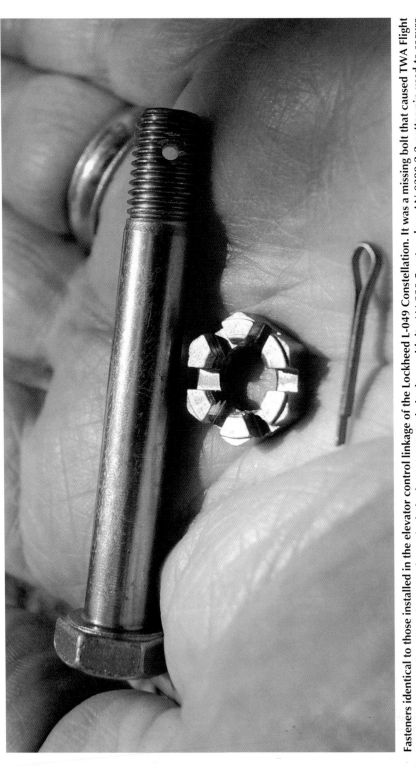

Fasteners identical to those installed in the elevator control linkage of the Lockheed L-049 Constellation. It was a missing bolt that caused TWA Flight 529 to lose control and crash. Parts shown include the AN-175-21 bolt along with its AN-320-5 nut and an AN-0380-2-2 cotter pin used to secure the nut. A mechanic had failed to install the pin. *Author photo.*

A Northwest Orient Airlines Lockheed L-188 Electra prepares to depart Midway Airport in Chicago. At nearby O'Hare International Airport on September 17, 1961, an identical Electra crashed on takeoff, killing all thirty-seven people aboard. *American Aviation Historical Society. Reproduced with permission.*

An Emery Worldwide Airlines McDonnell Douglas DC-8-71F pauses along a taxiway. On February 16, 2000, an identical plane crashed in a deserted car auction yard in Rancho Cordova, California. Its crew of three was killed; the jet and hundreds of cars were incinerated. *Detlev Borstel, Germany. Reproduced with permission.*

N66534, a Resort Airlines Curtiss C-46, awaits its next flight. N66534 crashed at the Louisville, Kentucky, airport on September 28, 1953, killing twenty-eight of the forty-four passengers and crewmembers aboard. *American Aviation Historical Society. Reproduced with permission.*

N8405H, a Western Air Lines Convair 240, is ready to board its passengers. On February 13, 1958, N8405H crash-landed in the Southern California desert near Palm Springs. It was destroyed by fire but the twenty-one passengers and crewmembers survived. *American Aviation Historical Society. Reproduced with permission.*

On September 11, 1991, a team of mechanics at Continental Express failed to install forty-seven screws securing the left leading edge to the horizontal stabilizer of an Embraer Brasilia. Flight 2674 crashed because of the oversight, killing the fourteen people aboard. Pictured is a handful of those screws. *Author photo.*

A lightweight, single-engine personal jet, the Cirrus SF50 (also known as the Vision Jet), was introduced in 2016. In April 2019, the FAA grounded all Vision Jets until their defective angle-of-attack sensors were replaced. *Alex Zothique. Reproduced with permission.*

Should a load shift too far from the plane's center of gravity, regaining control of the jet could be impossible.

Emery's loading supervisor was the last person to visit the cockpit crew that night, handing the crew a final accounting of the evening's load. After Hicks reviewed it, he used the supervisor's tabulations to calculate N8079U's center of gravity. The supervisor exited with a signed copy of the loading document and a completed weight and balance form. The data indicated that the load would be lighter than the more usual 75,000 pounds.[8]

Inside the cabin at 7:33 p.m., Hicks double-checked the load to make sure the fourteen containers and four pallets were tightly secured. The cargo doors were closed and latched. Returning to the cockpit, he settled into the flight engineer's seat directly behind Land to work his way through a lengthy checklist prior to starting the engines.

Because Stables had taken off from Reno and landed at Mather, Land would make this takeoff. Stables would taxi the plane using a tiller at his side and handle radio communications.

They began the routine ritual for starting the engines. The first CFM56 awakened and settled into an incessant whine. Hicks repeated the procedure to start the other three. He notified a ground handler via intercom that all four engines were idling satisfactorily. Umbilical cords connected to a ground power unit and an air cart were unhooked and moved a safe distance from the plane.

Releasing the parking brake and nudging the thrust levers forward, Stables guided the DC-8 from the cargo ramp. Taxiing slowly, Land gave his takeoff briefing. There is a mandatory requirement that the pilot in command advise all crewmembers of what action he will take should an emergency happen on departure.

At 7:41 p.m., Stables radioed they were taxiing from the ramp to runway 22L. Because there was no air traffic control tower at Mather, they and other pilots in the vicinity would broadcast their intention to take off or land and their current position on a common radio frequency called Unicom. Stables set the flaps at 15 degrees while Land conducted a check to determine if full freedom of movement existed for all the flight controls. The yokes were rotated left and right, then forward and backward, hitting their mechanical stops each time. Rudder pedals were each pressed all the way to the floor. No obstruction or binding was noticed with any of the controls.

Taxiing to the runway, they spotted a helicopter off in the distance.

Land commented, "I've never really been in a helicopter, you know."

Hicks chuckled in response, "[It's] really weird going that slow in the air though. I don't like it,"

Land said, "Hey, you're hanging by that bolt, you know."

Again chuckling, Hicks said, "Yeah . . . 'Jesus nut,'" referring, as many pilots do, to the part of a helicopter that such aircraft depend on to stay in the air.

This short bit of levity between the men, preserved on the cockpit voice recorder, would serve as a haunting memory of the horror they were about to experience.

At 7:47 p.m., Stables radioed terminal radar approach control (TRACON) in Sacramento to advise the controller that Emery Flight 17 was number one for takeoff from Mather. No other planes were in line waiting. He also requested that their IFR flight plan for Dayton be opened. The TRACON controller responded: "Emery 17 . . . you're released for departure, report airborne."

Stables acknowledged, "We'll call you in the air."

As Land pushed the thrust levers forward with his left hand, a reassuring, throaty roar emanated from the fanjets spooling up. The 140-ton plane began gathering speed. A distance marker along the runway's side identified the first mile they passed.

Serving as nonflying pilot, one of the duties handled by Stables involved monitoring the takeoff speed. Watching the airspeed indicator he called out "Eighty knots," with Land responding, "Eighty knots . . . elevator checks." This involved a quick check of the elevators by moving the yoke and making sure they weren't stuck. They were not. Reaching 145 mph, Stables announced, "V1," seconds later followed by "Rotate." Passing 168 mph, Land applied slight rearward pressure to his yoke, causing the plane to leave the pavement.

But something didn't seem right.

Upon passing rotation speed, the nose angled up more than usual. Land had not moved the yoke back much at all. He instantly released the backpressure and pushed the yoke forward slightly. Three seconds later Stables called out, "V2" followed by "Positive rate," the plane starting to climb with the runway passing well below them.

But the DC-8 seemed to fly where it wanted to go, not where Land wanted. The pilots were dumbfounded because neither of them had moved the controls. There were no gusts or air turbulence in the area to cause the erratic flight path. The situation worsened, with the upward pitching showing no sign of decreasing. N8079U slipped into a left turn, steepening to about 35 degrees, all within ten seconds.

Pushing the yokes forward didn't help. To counteract the force, Stables set the horizontal stabilizer trim to a fully pitch-down position. It didn't do anything.

"We're going back . . . c.g.'s waay [sic] out of limits," Land exclaimed, referring to the position of the jet's center of gravity. He was going to try turning around to land on the runway they had taken off from a half-minute earlier. Shifting cargo probably caused the problem— or so they guessed.

Six seconds after the decision to circle back to the runway, Hicks asked Land, "Do you want to pull the power back?" Two seconds later, the hum of the engines' rpm decreasing was followed by the clatter of the plane's stick shaker. The jet was about to stall. Shrill, incessant sounds of warning horns and bells clamored for the crew's attention.

Land blurted out, "Oh, shit," with Stables responding, "Push forward." Stables radioed the TRACON controller that they were in the midst of an emergency.

As the plane climbed to 1,000 feet, the left bank instantly decreased from more than 30 degrees to 13, then zoomed up to 25, followed by decreasing to 12. They were all over the sky, and dangerously close to the ground. N8079U was acting much like a paper kite wavering in a breeze.

Land said, "You steer . . . I'm pushing." Stables would try to arrest the erratic wing rocking, while Land continued the attempt to get the nose down.

Feeling helpless sitting at the flight engineer's station behind his fellow pilots, Hicks blurted out, "We're sinking. . . . We're going down, guys."

Two seconds later, the ground proximity warning system's "Whoop, Whoop, Pull Up" horn sounded. Land yelled over the noise, "Power!" They were descending through 679 feet in a steepening left bank. The descent didn't stop until the plane reached 601 feet, then the plane began climbing again. As it did, the left bank angle increased, reaching a steep 45 degrees, then decreasing. It was like sitting on a roller coaster.

Seconds later, Hicks said, "There you go," followed by Stables yelling, "Roll out!" both in strained voices.

Stables radioed the TRACON controller, "Emery [17 has an] extreme c.g. problem." The DC-8 continued its crazy climbing and diving episodes coupled with erratic banking. Even though the plane had been loaded properly, the pilots must have been haunted by memories of fellow pilots who died because cargo shifted in flight.

Hicks yelled over the racket, "Anything I can do, guys!" Stables said to Land, "Roll out to the right." Land responded by uttering, "Okay . . . push." They didn't know what to do next. Nobody would. Nothing yet had helped them regain control of the floundering jet. These were white-knuckle, gut-wrenching moments.

The bank angle of the right wing decreasing again, the ground proximity warning system alert continued its distinctive sound. Land uttered, "We're gonna have to land fast." After a right bank came a left one and so on. "What I'm trying to do is make the airplane's pitch match the elevator," he said. "That's why I'm putting it in a bank."

N8079U stayed in a left turn headed toward the runway they had taken off from. Stables told Land, "Bring it around."

Their actions were useless. While the pilots maintained nose-down pressure on the yokes, they also banked, trying a different approach to hopefully control both the pitch and roll. Hicks adjusted the engine thrust slightly. The plane rolled and pitched, climbed and descended again, as the crew tried different combinations of control inputs and engine power settings. The plane's movements were unpredictable, and the pilots fought the erratic movements in total futility because the elevator control surface needed to level the nose was broken and beyond their control to fix.

At 7:51 p.m., the plane was little more than 200 feet above the ground. Making matters worse, it was stuck in a steep left turn. Stables may have recalled that the wingspan of a DC-8 was about 142 feet, leaving only a few dozen feet between the tip of the left wing and unforgiving terra firma. The plane was close to a near-vertical bank.

The DC-8 was bound to crash. Perhaps for a second or two, the crew may have become stunned by the realization that they were nearing the end of their lives.

Land yelled, "Power!" then exhaled loudly.

A second later, the cockpit voice recording preserved the loud noise of the crash.

N8079U slammed into the deserted automobile auction yard in a left wing low, slightly nose-up attitude. The yard was one mile east of where they departed. The wing initially contacted the overhang of a roof on a two-story building along the southeast edge of the yard. The jet then pancaked onto the tops of the parked vehicles. Fragments from its airframe were jettisoned hundreds of feet, most of the fiery wreckage cascading in all directions across the field, followed by a river of thousands of gallons of blazing jet fuel.

"I saw the pilot try to pull up four times," eyewitness Lee Elrod told a reporter from the *Los Angeles Times*. "He'd get to about 2,000–3,000 feet and drop again. Finally it made a left bank and just dropped to the ground and exploded."[9]

A large portion of Insurance Auto Auction's forty-two-acre yard burst into flames. The gasoline sitting in the tanks of stored cars fueled an immense fireball, seen for miles in the moonless sky. Automotive gasoline is more volatile than kerosene-based jet fuel, and an estimated two hundred cars would be destroyed. The destruction cut a swath about 250 yards wide by a quarter-mile long.

Stables, Land, and Hicks were killed on impact. The only person injured on the ground was a security guard. His injuries were minor. If the crash had occurred a few hours earlier, dozens of customers milling around the yard would have died.

Throughout the night, families living in the residential areas of Rancho Cordova were subjected to repetitive explosions caused by gasoline igniting in the tanks of the cars. The firefighters had their hands full in trying to contain the fuel-fed fire. They prevented the flames from spreading to adjacent properties, waiting for the inferno to burn out from fuel exhaustion.

By dawn, the smoke and embers billowing over the Sacramento Valley resembled the aftermath of a bombing. Parts thrown into the air by the explosions, coming from both the plane and the cars, ended up comingled in a smoldering expanse of metal scattered over the melted asphalt.

There was little in the wreckage to readily identify parts of the jetliner. With the exception of the fanjet engines, portions of the wings, and the empennage, much of the melted and blackened pieces of metal were unrecognizable.

During the excruciating three minutes the crew struggled to regain control of the DC-8 after takeoff, their thoughts likely turned to cargo shifting as a cause of the control issues. A later investigation would prove them wrong. Similar to Allegiant Air Flight 436, an unsecured nut had fallen out and one of the plane's elevator control surfaces became jammed. Unlike the fortunate passengers and crew aboard Flight 436, however, the Emery pilots were already in the air with no possibility of getting the plane back on the ground safely.

Note: Many of the details presented in this chapter, including dates, places, descriptions of events, conclusions, and quotes (unless otherwise attributed), were derived from National Transportation Safety Board, "Aircraft Accident Report, Loss of Pitch Control on Takeoff, Emery Worldwide Airlines, Flight 17, McDonnell Douglas DC-8-71F, N8079U, Rancho Cordova, California, February 16, 2000, NTSB Identification AAR-03/02."

7

UNDER THE RADAR

Sleepy viewers tuning into eleven p.m. newscasts on February 16, 2000, opened their eyes wide. A towering mass of flames was seen rising from the remains of the Emery DC-8 in Rancho Cordova as cars continued to explode in the auction lot, one after another. Within hours, the news segments were beamed into homes stretching from San Francisco to San Diego and, by dawn, the entire nation.

The FAA office in Sacramento immediately notified the NTSB headquarters in Washington, DC, of the accident. It was the correct protocol to follow. However, it wasn't necessary because the newscasts in Los Angeles had led off with the story. An investigator from an NTSB regional office had already left for the crash site.

Within hours, the NTSB had assembled a "go-team" led by an investigator-in-charge. Not long after dawn on February 17, the team departed the nation's capitol. Flying to Sacramento, the investigators drove to the accident site during the late morning hours. It was a busy month for the agency: three weeks earlier an Alaska Airlines jetliner had crashed into the Pacific Ocean.[1]

A go-team typically includes a leader from the NTSB, an air traffic control specialist, a meteorologist, a human-performance expert, an expert trained in witness interrogation, an engine specialist, and consultants in hydraulics, electrical systems, and maintenance records. Remaining in Washington, other specialists await the arrival of cockpit voice recorders (CVRs) and flight data recorders (FDRs) for analysis.

The NTSB is forced to conduct its investigative work under intense scrutiny from both the media and the public. Because air travel constitutes a daily routine for millions of passengers, fatal accidents are instantly publicized, causing anxious travelers to immediately demand the reason for the accident. It's disappointing for the public to learn that it can take a year or more for the agency to pin down a probable cause.

Relying on teamwork, the NTSB requests assistance from manufacturers, airlines, and, by law, the FAA. This expanded group enables the agency to leverage its limited resources by culling the technical talent of companies, entities (such as a pilot's union), and individuals who may have peripheral involvement with an accident. Members of the media, lawyers, and representatives of insurance companies aren't allowed to participate in any phase of an investigation. Their interest is understandable, however. Millions of dollars in liability judgments and the reputations of corporations are tied to the probable cause that emerges.

The first two days of an investigation are critical because the evidence at a crash site is fragile and still undisturbed. Once visitors traipse through a debris field, the clues begin to disappear. Until the go-team arrives, law enforcement personnel secure the area to protect it from curiosity seekers. When examining the site, team members don't touch the wreckage; instead, they take photos from various angles, measure distances, and prepare detailed notes for future reference. While the investigators undertake the sweaty fieldwork, the NTSB Materials Laboratory in Washington prepares to extract the voice recordings from the plane's CVR and decipher aircraft performance data from its FDR.

When electronic flight recorders became required equipment aboard the nation's airliners in 1967, the job of an accident investigator was helped immeasurably. Although the devices are often referred to as "black boxes," they are actually painted a bright orange color to help investigators locate them in the wreckage of a crashed plane. Most importantly, they are designed to survive both severe impact and fire. Recorders retrieved from twisted wrecks are often dented and burned but their contents remain uncompromised. When TWA Flight 529 crashed in 1961, recorders were still in the future. But for well over fifty years now, CVRs and FDRs have been standard equipment aboard all airliners. They are required by international regulation, overseen by the International Civil Aviation Organization.

The CVR preserves conversations between the pilots along with radio calls to and from air traffic controllers. It even records any noise in the cockpit, including such subtle actions as the click of a switch. The FDR has a different role than a CVR. It stores details of the plane's performance, recording dozens (and often hundreds) of parameters collected from sensors that monitor the airframe and engines. The performance samplings are stored in memory on a second-by-second basis.

When a plane carrying a load of passengers has an accident, it's front-page news. But when planes that transport cargo crash, unless people on the ground are killed, the accidents seldom garner headlines. The loss of Emery Flight 17 happened to be different. The repetitive explosions and acres-long firestorm were witnessed by thousands of people for miles around. Because the disaster occurred adjacent to a heavily populated area, there were immediate outcries demanding a reason for the crash.

From early on in the Emery investigation, it seemed logical that cargo breaking free of its restraints and moving the plane's center of gravity back would be the cause of the plane becoming uncontrollable. TV stations and newspapers publicized this shifting cargo theory without delay. They pointed to past accidents caused by improperly secured loads. Meanwhile, the investigators followed a slow, methodical approach and didn't entertain such conclusions.

As the investigators combed the charred wreckage in the auction yard, they came across an important clue. It had nothing to do with shifting cargo. Examining what remained of N8079U's empennage, they noticed that a bolt was missing from a pushrod designed to move a control tab for the elevator on the right side. The bolt's castellated nut and cotter pin were also missing. If the bolt had been secured with a nut and pin, the investigators knew there was no way it could have fallen from its hole.

In common with the MD-80s that Allegiant Air and other airlines flew, the elevator flight control system of a DC-8 is tab-driven. That is, the yokes aren't mechanically linked to the elevators. They connect to small, airfoil-shaped tabs hinged at the rear of control surfaces that serve as elevators. During flight, movement of the tabs results in the angle of the elevators changing, the plane's nose then moving up or down.

Pulling back on the yoke sends the tab down. The resulting aerodynamic force moves the trailing edge of the elevator up, pushing the nose up. Pushing the yoke forward moves the tab up, forcing the elevator trailing edge down, thereby dropping the nose.

The operation of the tab depends on the installation of a single bolt that connects the pushrod to a crank fitting affixed to the tab. What disconnected in N8079U's empennage was the bolt that connected the fitting to a bearing in the pushrod, resulting in the tab disengaging. The now-uncontrolled elevator forced the plane into an extreme nose-up attitude. Despite the pilots applying forward pressure on the yokes, the aerodynamic force resulting from the tab's incorrect position could not be overcome.

Examining the bolt, investigators didn't find that its threads were stripped or its shank was sheared. Breakage of the bolt's nut or cotter pin seemed unlikely. The bolt had separated from the crank fitting because it was not properly secured. Either the nut was never installed or it had been installed *without a cotter pin.*

Investigators speculated that the bolt had loosened and worked its way partly out of the hole during the plane's takeoff from Reno. During takeoff from Mather, vibration resulting from rumbling down the long runway then could have freed it. Or perhaps the bolt fell out after a bumpy touchdown in Rancho Cordova or during the routine flight control check that Land performed during takeoff.

The investigators also surmised that the plane's most recent inspection or its subsequent maintenance might offer clues as to what happened. They set out to determine where and when the negligent assembly work had taken place.

Maintenance departments at the scheduled airlines make use of procedures extracted from an aircraft maintenance manual (AMM, or a similar acronym). The AMM is used for generating "task cards." Offering detailed procedural instructions, the cards ensure that mechanics follow proper procedures and document the tasks they complete.

At most air carriers, the inspections of planes range from daily walk-around checks by flight crews to service checks conducted by line mechanics at terminal gates to major checks performed at an airline's maintenance base or an outsourced maintenance facility. A letter of the alphabet designates each of these checks. The three most common checks are A-checks, C-checks, and D-checks.

An A-check involves a general inspection of the plane's interior and exterior. It's typically performed on a biweekly to monthly basis, depending on how much the plane flies. The schedule for a C-check depends on the airline, type of plane, and how many hours or cycles have been flown since the last check. The frequency of a D-check, categorized as heavy maintenance, again depends on the type of plane and how it's operated. A D-check can consume several weeks. In a worst-case scenario, this can extend to months. Disassembling the entire plane and putting it back together again may be the best way to describe a D-check.

In addition to N8079U missing a cotter pin, the Emery accident had something else in common with the Allegiant Air incident. Emery's heavy maintenance had been outsourced to a large MRO. And much like Allegiant Air, the MRO wasn't in Central America or Asia but in the United States. Its name was Tennessee Technical Services (TTS). The Emery plane underwent a D-check there in November 1999, three months before the accident.

Based in Smyrna, Tennessee, TTS began operating as an MRO in May 1998, less than two years before the accident. The FAA-approved facility specialized in undertaking repair work for DC-8s and other jet transports. In October 1998, after passing a safety audit conducted by Emery, TTS was placed on the airline's list of approved MROs. It went on to offer Emery a variety of services, including heavy maintenance and many less complex tasks.[2]

The MRO in Smyrna operated from a hangar capable of accommodating four DC-8s at a time. An adjacent building served as a repair and overhaul facility for aircraft components. From its beginning to March 2001, TTS had completed maintenance work for 173 planes, including Emery's jets. At the time of Flight 17's accident, the MRO employed ninety-one licensed mechanics and twenty inspectors.

TTS had been awarded the FAA's Diamond Certificate of Excellence Award every year from 1998 to 2001 for its participation in the FAA Aviation Technician Training Program. In an attempt to improve the competence of mechanics and their employers, the FAA had organized the program. According to TTS managers, the company had designed its own training curriculum based on the federal program. The MRO and the FAA had cemented a solid working relationship. Time would tell if it was too cordial.

When Emery added TTS to its list of approved MROs, the airline sent quality-control representatives to Smyrna to train the TTS inspectors in Emery's procedures. The employees trained by Emery were the only inspectors permitted to work on its planes.

The mechanics chosen to perform checks of Emery's planes weren't newcomers. The lead mechanics and inspectors working on N8079U each had between twenty and forty years of experience. They were especially skilled in maintaining DC-8s. All work at TTS was accomplished under the watchful eye of at least one technical representative stationed on site by Emery. However, the MRO faced the same kind of labor problems AAR encountered in handling Allegiant Air's business. Hiring a sufficient number of qualified mechanics and inspectors to fill empty positions became a never-ending headache. Increased salaries brought in more-experienced technicians, but the associated increase in labor costs put the company at a competitive disadvantage when bidding against other MROs for contracts. TTS needed to remain competitive, but its profit margins were already razor-thin. Not only did it compete with other MROs, it competed with the maintenance departments of its airline customers as well. Whatever organization could do the work cheapest got the business.

The Rancho Cordova investigation erupted into a blame game played back and forth. Each party set out to protect its corporate turf. Determining the responsibility for the accident boiled down to finding a key piece of missing information: the last person who worked on the elevator flight controls of N8079U.

Pilots at Emery had become frustrated with the airline well before the accident. Their union leaders had begun gathering complaints as early as the spring of 1999. There were allegations of too many maintenance deferrals, a "mom and pop" mentality resulting in "broken aircraft, unseasoned mechanics, exhausted crews, and constant delays" according to a report forwarded to the FAA in September 1999.[3] It further stated,

> EWA [Emery] is out of the regulator's eye. . . . Why are the authorities continuing to turn a blind eye? If we have an accident in the near future, the subsequent investigation will show sainthood on the part of ValuJet when compared to Emery. . . . Emery crews are living on borrowed time.[4]

A stinging communiqué came from Thomas Rachford, chairman of the Air Line Pilots Association Council 110. A DC-8 captain at Emery, Rachford told the FAA of "crews pushed to fly exhausted, cargo doors opening, engines flaming out, engines burning up. . . . I can't say it any clearer: This airline is going to put a hole in the ground and kill someone. Please do not let this fall upon deaf ears."[5] The letter was mailed to the FAA in September 1998.

Sixteen months later, the crash in the auction yard validated his prediction.

Five months after the accident, Emery pilots authorized a strike. Contract talks between the union and airline stretched twenty-seven months with no tangible progress. The Air Line Pilots Association reported that 96 percent of the airline's 483 pilots had approved striking. They asked for job protection, better pay, and a limit on what flight time was logged by nonemployee pilots, which caused the flight hours of the unionized pilots to be reduced along with their pay.[6]

Fourteen months after the accident, an Emery DC-8 crash-landed in Nashville, Tennessee. An incorrect part had been installed during assembly of the plane's left main landing gear. Fortunately, no one was injured.

The FAA threatened to revoke Emery's license after finding one hundred safety violations during an inspection conducted in January 2000—one month before the accident. The license was *not* revoked. Despite six FAA inspections within two years, plus a stream of safety violations and complaints voiced by pilots dating from 1996, the FAA did nothing until August 11, 2001, when it again threatened to pull Emery's license. This was eleven days before the NTSB planned to conduct a public hearing regarding Flight 17. The FAA's inadequate monitoring of the airline would then be aired for all to hear.

On August 13, Emery's Palo Alto–based parent company, CNF, grounded its entire thirty-seven-plane fleet until the FAA was satisfied that the violations were remedied. The hearing was cancelled temporarily. The ruckus caused by the grounding of the Emery fleet and the airline being shut down was the reason. In December of that year, Emery and a CNF subsidiary, Menlo Logistics, merged to form Menlo Worldwide, a firm that no longer transported cargo. Menlo Worldwide abandoned the airline business and left the FAA holding the bag. The company's planes were sold or repossessed, while Emery's employees went to work somewhere else.

After concluding the on-site and laboratory investigative phases, the NTSB categorized its findings in publicly accessible files with input welcomed from any organization having involvement. A flurry of new information was submitted to the NTSB, most of the participants placing blame for the accident on other organizations.

TTS mechanics were aware that the drilled-shank bolt, castellated nut, and cotter pin were mandatory items to ensure an airworthy installation. Emery mechanics insisted that TTS mechanics didn't properly secure the bolt during the D-check. However, it became apparent that Emery mechanics could have worked in the area of the plane where the missing bolt would have been installed after TTS completed the check. Shifting blame back and forth, each side offered a different version of what they believed happened.

Emery offered the first theory:

> Loss of elevator control that resulted from the loss of the bolt connecting the right-hand elevator pushrod to the elevator control tab crank fitting. The loss of the bolt was due to the failure of the TTS mechanics conducting the D-check to install the cotter pin, or the nut and cotter pin, to safety the bolt properly. Contributing to the accident was the failure of the TTS inspector to identify the missing hardware at the time that the work on the elevator control tab installation was completed during the D-check installation.

In stark contrast with this statement, TTS offered its own opinion. It indicated that several maintenance actions had been performed by Emery mechanics *after* TTS completed the D-check. This could have resulted in the bolt falling out that connected the pushrod to the crank fitting. Offering evidence, TTS cited Emery's troubleshooting efforts with an elevator damper on the DC-8. The work had been performed because of repeated pilot write-ups. TTS noted,

> The likely cause was a failure at the control tab clevis fitting due to either a failure of or improper securing of the nut, bolt, and/or cotter pin. This resulted in the pilot's inability to control the aircraft. Improper and inadequate maintenance performed by (Emery) likely caused the bolt/nut assembly to come loose or fail during the fatal takeoff.

The next opinion came from the Air Line Pilots Association.

> Evidence and analysis indicates that the bolt which attaches the pushrod to the tab crank fitting for the right-hand . . . elevator control tab was jammed in the airplane nose up (ANU) position. . . . Although the root cause for the loss of the bolt is unknown, the most likely scenario is that the bolt's locking hardware was either never or improperly installed after maintenance activity by Emery. . . . Given the . . . vague and/or ambiguous work card and maintenance guidance, the sparse aircraft logbook write-ups . . . regarding both the damper reversal and the B-checks, it seems highly likely that the elevator system linkage was parted by (Emery) during one of those maintenance actions, and that locking hardware was either never or improperly reinstalled.

Seeking to distance itself from multimillion-dollar lawsuits, Boeing, having acquired McDonnell Douglas Corporation in 1997, took a middle road in the dispute by responding,

> Boeing believes that the probable cause of this accident was improper maintenance practices that led to the separation of the control tab pushrod from the control tab crank (fitting), a subsequent restriction of the control tab in an extreme trailing edge down position, and the subsequent loss of control of the airplane. . . . The right elevator control-rod-to-control-tab-crank joint was improperly installed either during the . . . "D" check at TTS, or during troubleshooting at Emery, for the flight crew reported difficulty with flaring the aircraft.

There had been egregious shortcomings in maintenance and maintenance oversight. The FAA's deputy operations inspector assigned to Emery, Mark McConaughy, felt that what he learned about the accident didn't make for complacency. He told NTSB investigators, "I suggested to my superiors the possibility that a criminal investigation needs to be opened."[7]

Completing the task of assembling the voluminous amount of documentation and acknowledging countless comments, investigators prepared for the public hearing to present what facts were known at that point. Expert witnesses would be called to testify under oath and assist board members in formulating a probable cause. Excluded were media, family members, lawyers, and insurance personnel.

On May 9, 2002, the hearing was convened after being cancelled in August the year before. The NTSB board members and investigators examined a vast array of damning evidence about sloppy maintenance. The hearing was recessed after two long days and before the FAA officials in attendance had been questioned. There wasn't a need. The FAA's public image could be likened to that of a tough cop keeping the airlines in line. Based on data assembled by the NTSB, combined with interviews of Emery employees, the opposite became apparent. The FAA had not taken enforcement action against the airline, in spite of so many violations affecting flight safety.

Bruce Robbins, former director of engineering at Emery, testified during the hearing that he considered the maintenance deficiencies "warts" common to any airline. NTSB board member John Goglia responded, "I think we've found cancer."[8]

The NTSB's last step in the process involved publishing a final report citing a probable cause for the accident. Safety recommendations to prevent future accidents were also forwarded to the FAA. If the NTSB didn't offer recommendations, there would be no impetus for the FAA to improve safety. Over the years, close to 80 percent of the recommendations the NTSB has made to the FAA have been acted upon favorably. But any recommendation for Emery to improve its operations would be moot at this point. The airline had shut its doors forever.

One of the NTSB's recommendations was to retrofit all DC-8s with a redundant flight control system. This would also affect DC-9s and MD-80s. The recommendation stated, "Require Boeing to redesign DC-8 elevator control tab installations and require all DC-8 operators to then retrofit these installations, such that pilots are able to safely operate the airplane if the control tab becomes disconnected from the pushrod."[9]

The recommendation was ignored.

As is frequently the case, the NTSB's final report was sobering in its conclusions but it did not assign specific blame for what happened, didn't identify a responsible party, and didn't address the work culture existing at TTS or Emery as contributing causes.

> The National Transportation Safety Board determines that the probable cause of the accident was a loss of pitch control resulting from the disconnection of the right elevator control tab. The disconnection was caused by the failure to properly secure and inspect the attachment bolt.

N8079U's accident suggests what *could* have happened to Allegiant Air Flight 436 departing Las Vegas. Both events occurred during takeoff after failures of the elevator control system and, more specifically, failures brought on by missing cotter pins. The design of the MD-83's system was patterned after that of the earlier DC-8.

"Nobody cares," said Captain Rachford about the number of cargo planes crashing. "Until we wind up wiping out a schoolyard, then all of a   den everyone will be on board. Then everyone will say, 'We told you so, we told you so.' Until we kill 250 or 300 people because a plane crashes somewhere, people won't do anything."[10]

Donald Land, father of Emery pilot George Land, was upset that the FAA allowed non-airworthy jets and unqualified people and companies to operate. He said, "It is time to stop the killing."[11]

The once-mighty cargo airline called Emery Worldwide is no more, an obscure footnote in commercial aviation history. Tennessee Technical Services is also gone. Emery's former flight crews and mechanics are retired or work elsewhere in the aviation industry. At the end of 2018, the Emery sorting center in Dayton, once occupied by hundreds of workers, remained abandoned as well as the impressive sixteen-story control tower. The ghostly concrete ramp that once played host to dozens of DC-8s each night is cracked and sprouting weeds.

Note: Many of the details presented in this chapter, including dates, places, descriptions of events, conclusions, and quotes (unless otherwise attributed), were derived from National Transportation Safety Board, "Aircraft Accident Report, Loss of Pitch Control on Takeoff Emery Worldwide Airlines, Flight 17, McDonnell Douglas DC-8-71F, N8079U, Rancho Cordova, California, February 16, 2000, NTSB Identification AAR-03/02."

8

THEN AS NOW

It is easy to conclude that propeller-driven Constellations are one-half-century-old relics that offer nowhere near the safety offered by today's jetliners. And there's the mistaken belief that the jets coming off the assembly lines at Boeing and Airbus are somehow immune to the missing hardware issues that caused earlier accidents. They are not.

China Airlines Flight 120 made a smooth touchdown at Okinawa's airport on August 20, 2007. Its pilots didn't know that a bolt had fallen from a slat mechanism in the wing of their Boeing 737NG, putting a gaping hole in a fuel tank. As the plane taxied to the terminal, a ramp worker noticed an enormous plume of fuel pouring from the wing. The pilots shut down the engines immediately, but the fuel ignited a few seconds later, flames quickly engulfing the fuselage. Miraculously, the 165 passengers and crewmembers evacuated without serious injury. The fire destroyed a near-new jetliner all because a worker on an assembly line at Boeing forgot to install a washer on a bolt.[1]

Today's jetliners are equipped with avionic systems only dreamed of fifty years ago. Color weather radar, collision avoidance warning, GPS navigation, LCD instrument displays, and automatic flight control with a capability to land in near 0-0 weather conditions, top the list. What hasn't changed in most planes are the mechanical linkages, cables, and push-pull rods that move control surfaces on the wings and tail. A 1930s-era Douglas DC-3 shares the same kinds of hardware with today's Boeing 737. Bolts, nuts, and cotter pins connect the parts of both old and new airframes, and missing hardware still causes accidents. The computerized diagnostic and fault isolation systems aboard newer jets still can't detect a missing nut, washer, or pin. It remains the job of a human being to visually detect those discrepancies.[2]

Missing hardware presents a problem not only for the airlines. FAA records document that general aviation aircraft, ranging from single-engine private planes to helicopters, suffer many accidents attributed to hardware problems. Because they depend on rotors rather than fixed wings to remain aloft, helicopters are the most vulnerable.[3]

Revisiting an era of aviation before *Triple Nickel*'s accident in 1961, it's worthwhile to consider whether maintenance errors, especially those involving missing hardware, were a recurring cause of accidents. Research shows they were.

One airplane seemed to suffer an inordinate number of accidents traceable to this cause: the twin-engine, propeller-driven C-46 built by Curtiss-Wright in the 1940s. Pilot error topped the list for many of its accidents, but mechanical failure, often triggered by missing hardware, was also dominant. It wasn't because C-46s were poorly designed. They often crashed as a result of maintenance carelessness.

If you were to stand next to a C-46 on a ramp, it would seem monstrous. The nose extended twenty-one feet above the ground, while the bulging fuselage offered more than 2,300 cu. ft. of space to transport eight tons of cargo and passengers. The span of its wing, at 106.5 feet, was about the same as that of a Boeing 727. The wing area alone totaled 1,360 sq. ft., about the same square footage as the floor plan of a small house.

On September 28, 1953, a fully loaded C-46 registered as N66534 to Resort Airlines crashed as it attempted to land at the Louisville, Kentucky airport. Twenty-five passengers and its crew of three were killed. Sixteen surviving passengers suffered serious injuries. Ironically, Resort Airlines had been named winner of the National Safety Council's aviation safety award a year earlier. The council recognized the carrier for flying 7,749,000 passenger miles from March 1950 through December 1952 without suffering a passenger or crew fatality.[4]

N66534 departed North Philadelphia Airport for Louisville at 1:03 p.m. Thirty-three-year-old Wharton Moller served as captain, assisted by copilot John Pickel, two years older. Stewardess Dorothy Bush handled duties in the cabin. Moller had 7,500 hours aloft, an impressive 4,634 of them at the controls of C-46s. Pickel was also well qualified: 6,850 total hours with 2,300 of them logged in this type of plane.

Under contract to the U.S. Army, Resort Airlines transported soldiers from Camp Kilmer in New Jersey to Fort Knox, Kentucky. Moller's plane was one of five C-46s chartered from the airline. Kilmer had once served as the nation's largest processing center for troops heading overseas or returning home. On

September 28, a group of soldiers from Puerto Rico were eager to undergo processing for reassignment. All of them were infantrymen—most of them recently fighting North Korean troops. The men had been flown to Kilmer from their homes in Puerto Rico after brief leaves with family members. They were then bused from Kilmer to Philadelphia.

The afternoon flight from Philadelphia was routine, the weather cooperating along the planned route. Approaching Standiford Airport in Louisville, Moller requested landing clearance from the control tower. He was cleared to land on runway 24.

As Moller executed a straight-in approach and arrived over the runway's threshold, a controller in the tower noticed that the approach appeared normal—that is, until Moller began pulling the nose up to land. After gaining altitude, the heavy C-46 dropped, hitting the runway with an earthshaking thud and ballooning back into the air. In response, Moller shoved the throttles forward, the engines developing full horsepower. But the plane began pitching up even more. It entered an unusually steep climb, the nose yawing to the left as the AOA of the wings steadily increased.

Picking up a pair of binoculars, the controller focused them on the plane's tail, seeing that a part of the elevator on the left side was hanging free in the wind. He radioed Moller to warn him but received no response.

The C-46 continued climbing steeply then entered a turn to the left about 300 feet over the runway. The plane stalled, dropped instantly, and hit the ground, crumpling its nose and left wing. The fuselage cracked into two large sections, the forward portion immediately engulfed in flames fed by gasoline pouring from damaged wing tanks.

Moller and Pickel died on impact. Twenty-four-year-old stewardess Bush was critically injured, and a day later, she died. Sixteen passengers of the forty-one aboard were in critical condition. The remainder died alongside the runway of burns, blunt trauma, or smoke inhalation.

Most of the survivors were seated in or near the tail section. The injured were discovered screaming and muttering invocations to "Maria," the Virgin Mary in Puerto Rico's Spanish language. When the fuselage split open, some of the soldiers had been thrown clear of the wreckage and roughed up. The less fortunate were incinerated in what remained of the fuselage. Ambulances rushed the injured to hospitals with severe burns, broken bones, concussions, and internal injuries. Along the runway, scorched duffle bags were scattered about. A few bodies were tossed as far away as a hundred feet, some decapitated.

"The plane was afire when we arrived," said Marion Hopper, an American Airlines employee who worked at the airport. "At least fifteen or twenty persons were either lying dead or moaning pitifully." Ed Schmitt, a captain with the city fire department echoed those observations: "It was just one mess of screams and moans. Nobody could talk coherently."[5]

Corroborating the observations of the controller, several other witnesses had focused their eyes on the dangling elevator. The approach appeared normal to them until the tires were about to touch the runway. Each agreed that the plane then began a steep climb culminating in the unrecoverable stall.

N66534 had struck the pavement at a 50-degree nose-down angle, the left wing banked down 30 degrees. Most of the wreckage ended up strewn along the left side of runway 24, the forward section of the fuselage shoved back into the left wing's center section. The remainder of the wing was severed at its juncture with the fuselage. Inside the cabin, the violent crash caused every passenger seat to be ripped from the cabin floor and tossed about.

Investigators from the CAB focused on the tail as an area of interest due to the eyewitness reports. Remarkably, the horizontal stabilizer and elevator on the right side, together with the vertical stabilizer and rudder, had survived the ordeal undamaged. The left horizontal stabilizer had buckled upward in two areas but remained attached to the fuselage. The inboard two-thirds of its elevator stayed fastened to the stabilizer by hinges. The outboard one-third was found resting on the runway.

The mystery of what happened to N66534 would be solved unusually fast. It became clear that a bolt had exited a hinge bracket that retained the left elevator. This caused the outboard one-third of the control surface to loosen and flap in the wind stream. The C-46 then became uncontrollable.

Unlike the *Triple Nickel* investigation eight years in the future, the missing bolt was found inside the aluminum elevator. But its nut and cotter pin were *not* found even after a sweeping search of the runway's surface. Because the bolt hadn't fractured, it was obvious that its nut must have come loose and allowed the bolt to fall away.

The bolt discovered in the rubble, designated an AN5-13, was not the correct bolt specified by the C-46's manufacturer. It should have been an NAS55-14. The bolts may have looked similar, but the correct bolt's tolerances were tighter. The bolt in the wreckage was severely worn around its shank, especially in the area where it rested on a steel bushing pressed into the hinge bracket. A close examination disclosed that the wear pattern on the inside of the bushing and the outside of the bolt's shank closely matched. The pattern indicated that the bolt had been fitted in the bracket before eventually exiting.

An examination of the bushing revealed that its surfaces didn't meet the required specifications for hardness. As proof, its interior passage had been

beaten out of round. Because the bushing was made of softer metal than specified, it's likely the bushing's worn surface resulted from vibration caused by the
undersized bolt. The incorrect bolt's shank was also shorter by one-eighth of
an inch compared to the bolt specified for the installation. Due to this shorter
length, the bolt had a weaker grip and several of its threads rested directly
against the wall of the bushing. If the correct bolt had been installed, it would
have fit snugly in the bushing with no threads abrading the wall.

Microscopic examination of a slot designed to retain a cotter pin in the
castellated nut for the bolt revealed the existence of a slightly deformed area at
one end. This meant that a pin had been installed in the slot at some point. A
flake of brass fell from the slot, but no other pieces of non-ferrous metal were
found. The presence of the debris could have resulted from the use of a brass
cotter pin.

During examination of the remainder of the tail area, a brass cotter pin *was*
found. It secured a nut holding another part. The other cotter pins installed
in the airframe were made of steel. Mechanics from Slick Airways (functioning
as an MRO and conducting heavy maintenance checks for Resort's planes) reported that they didn't use brass pins. The mechanics at Resort said the same.

The CAB's attention shifted to Slick Airways. The government had certificated Slick as a scheduled air carrier in 1949. It began flight operations by
purchasing surplus military Curtiss C-46s from the Reconstruction Finance
Corporation. But it wasn't the best of times to start a cargo airline. There were
other non-scheduled cargo airlines competing with the major airlines and forcing the upstart carriers out of business by slashing shipping rates. Slick somehow survived. Despite losing six C-46s in accidents during its first five years in
business, it became the dominant scheduled airfreight carrier in the country at
the time. Because the airline had acquired expertise in repairing its own planes,
it took on maintenance work for C-46s belonging to other carriers. Resort Airlines was one of them.

From July 8 to July 11, 1953, the mechanics in Slick's hangar at the San
Antonio airport conducted a heavy maintenance check for N66534. The tasks
included a complete inspection of its airframe and engines. Although removal
of the right and left elevators was required for overhaul, the CAB investigators
discovered that only a single work order and parts replacement sheet had been
prepared to document the task. The only paperwork in existence pertained to
the *right* elevator. Queried about the omission, the mechanics and inspectors
didn't recall doing any work on the left elevator. This was not correct.

An inspection of what remained of N66534's left elevator revealed a number
of safety violations: unapproved bearings, wrong bolts, and the remains of a

brass cotter pin. Slick had sole responsibility for the discrepancies as no work had been done on the elevator after the plane left Slick's hangar.

A number of possible scenarios were considered. First, the bolt had not been installed during the elevator's overhaul in San Antonio. Or it was installed but later removed for an unexplained reason. Or, finally, the bolt was correctly installed but its nut or cotter pin was omitted or subsequently lost. The last scenario seemed most probable.

The bolt, nut, and pin would have been subjected to heavy vibration for an unknown period of time. Constant vibration from the plane's 2,000-hp Pratt & Whitney R-2800 engines might have gradually worn away part of the pin and freed it. The bolt would then have begun slipping out as its nut unscrewed because the cotter pin wasn't in place to stop it.

The bolt worked free during the final approach into Louisville. Moller's angling the nose up for landing resulted in the first moderately large elevator deflection after the bolt was lost. When Moller pulled the yoke back for the flare, the downward force on the left elevator caused it to fail, and the pilots couldn't apply enough forward pressure on the yokes to counteract the plane's nose-up pitch. Applying engine power only made things worse as it produced an even steeper climb that ended in the crash.

Shoddy paper records at Slick became a clue that the company's maintenance practices were a hit-and-miss proposition. The records were so incomplete that it couldn't be determined who had worked on the left elevator. When queried about the lack of documentation, no one would take responsibility for the work.

The investigative team also conducted a survey of all commercially operated C-46s. Several planes, including another one owned by Resort, didn't have the correct NAS-55 hinge bolts installed.

To document its findings, the CAB scheduled a public hearing in Louisville on November 23, 1953. The board's final report was damning.

> The Board determines that the probable cause of this accident was structural failure of the left elevator in flight, causing loss of control. The left outboard hinge bolt backing out of the assembly brought about this structural failure. The underlying cause was improper maintenance which resulted in the installation of hinge bolts and bearings not meeting specifications, and inadequate inspection which failed to detect this condition.

The blame landed squarely on the mechanics and inspectors at Slick Airways, although poor oversight of their work by employees of Resort Airlines compounded the errors. If a qualified inspector from Resort had been assigned to the Slick facility and had kept a close eye on the work, the accident would not have happened.

Western Airlines' long-standing slogan was *The Only Way to Fly*. The long-established carrier offered scheduled flights to Hawaii, Alaska, Canada, and Mexico City—and as far eastward as Minneapolis. Although Western Airlines faced stiff competition from major airlines on many of its routes, its schedules and friendly service were popular with business and leisure travelers alike.[6]

One of Western's flights was scheduled to fly from Los Angeles to Las Vegas, then on to San Diego, with an intermediate stop in Palm Springs. At Los Angeles International Airport during the early morning hours of February 13, 1958, a twin-engine, propeller-driven Convair 240 was readied to fly to McCarran Field in Las Vegas. FAA-registered as N8405H, the plane had just received a clean bill of health following a maintenance check in the airline's overhaul facilities at Los Angeles International. The mechanics there were equipped to handle all levels of maintenance for the airline's fleet of piston-powered Convair 240s and Douglas DC-6Bs.[7]

Manufactured in December 1948, N8405H had accrued a total of 22,516 hours in the air. At ten years old, it was still in the prime of its service life, maintained by Western's cadre of mechanics. Maintenance was seldom outsourced to MROs in the 1950s and most of the larger airlines operated their own large-scale overhaul facilities.

An hour before its first flight of the day, the Convair was moved from the maintenance area to a gate at the passenger terminal on Avion Drive. Its pilots then arrived and conducted their preflight inspection. This was especially important because flight-critical parts of the airframe had been disassembled and reinstalled less than a day earlier. Aware of the work, the pilots didn't notice anything out of the ordinary.

Dick Schumacher served as captain assisted by copilot Jim LeBel. In the cabin, stewardess Barbara Grimes would handle passenger service. Forty-year-old Schumacher had joined Western in February 1945, destined to remain a pilot at the airline for his entire career. He had accumulated a total of 9,845 hours, including 3,547 at the controls of the carrier's Convair 240s. LeBel, age thirty-one, had been hired in September 1954, racking up a total of 5,240 hours, 785 of them in the Convair. Twenty-four-year-old Grimes joined Western in July 1957.

The plane departed Los Angeles International on schedule to begin its flight across the southwestern desert to McCarran Field. The crew appreciated the absence of fog or rain along the way. Approaching Nevada, they anticipated

60-degree temperatures unlike the scorching heat typifying the region during the summer months. Within an hour, they were taxiing off the runway at McCarran.

After the plane had pulled up to a gate, those passengers whose flight ended at the gambling resort disembarked. The plane was then refueled with 330 gallons of gasoline. Schumacher took a walk around the Convair to stretch his legs and check for anything abnormal such as a significant engine oil leak, a tire needing air, or a dent in the fuselage caused by an errant baggage cart. All looked okay. After a short stay at the gate, the pilots regrouped in the cockpit just long enough to sip a cup of coffee. In the cabin, eighteen passengers ticketed for Palm Springs, the next stop, or the flight's final destination in San Diego were seated by Grimes.

Baggage loaded and N8405H ready to go, Schumacher and LeBel breezed through the routine checklists and cranked the eighteen-cylinder, 2,000-hp Pratt & Whitney R-2800 engines. The engines brought to life and idling, Schumacher requested a taxi clearance from McCarran ground control. Receiving one promptly, they proceeded to their assigned runway.

Following an engine run-up to check magneto firing and propeller feathering, Western Flight 19 was cleared for takeoff at 12:30 p.m., fifteen minutes behind schedule. With LeBel occupying the captain's seat, they began the 250-mile hop to Palm Springs. Schumacher sat in the right seat to supervise LeBel and assume the customary duties of a copilot. Before the advent of flight simulators, it was normal practice to give copilots as much flying time as possible before they moved up to captain.

Upon reaching a planned cruising altitude of 10,000 feet, both the crew and their passengers gazed at the vivid colors of the Mojave Desert passing below. Not unexpectedly, they encountered mild turbulence due to thermals rising from the warmer ground. To smooth the ride, Schumacher received clearance to climb to 12,000 feet. In the calmer air, the remainder of the trip to Palm Springs was relaxing, and N8405H touched down there at 1:30 p.m.

The stopover was brief, its purpose to disembark and board passengers. The pilots remained in the cockpit. Taking into account a change in the number of passengers aboard and the amount of fuel burned, the pilots calculated the plane's weight to be 35,655 pounds, 4,742 pounds less than the maximum allowable for takeoff. The load was properly distributed within center of gravity limits. Everything appeared shipshape. After the plane had been at the gate for six minutes, its engines were restarted for the short hop to San Diego. Remaining in the left seat, LeBel taxied the plane to the far end of the runway for takeoff. Checks of the engines and a myriad of instruments monitoring the plane's systems showed normal indications. Schumacher alerted Grimes over the intercom they were ready to depart. She took her seat after making certain that the belts for her passengers were snug.

At 1:42 p.m., roaring down runway 31, N8405H lifted off gently. All went according to plan as the plane passed over the departure end of the runway and began a slow climb over the desert. On reaching 30 feet, Schumacher pulled up the landing gear and later retracted the flaps. As the plane climbed to 550 feet, LeBel called for him to reduce engine power for the climb. Schumacher moved the throttle levers back. They were now moving along at 178 mph. LeBel made a slight bank to the right to maintain adequate distance from another aircraft in the vicinity and rolled out on course.

Then the serenity of the afternoon was suddenly shattered for the crew and passengers. They tensed up after hearing and feeling a loud grinding noise and jerking motion. It sounded much like metal splitting. Schumacher heard it and thought that a structural part of the fuselage could be failing. At the same time, the plane's nose dropped sharply. LeBel pulled back on his yoke in an attempt to bring it up. The yoke moved backward just fine, but the elevator didn't respond.

On the ground, several witnesses had noticed that at least two pieces of silvery metal fell from the plane soon after takeoff. Most of them thought the pieces may have come from the wing on the right side.

Inside the cabin, a passenger seated along the right side by a first-row window watched outside in horror. A section of the wing had broken loose. It flopped up and down for three or four seconds before departing in the wind stream. Its loss exposed innards of the wing containing wiring and plumbing lines. A fellow passenger saw the same part flash by his window.

Unable to see the inboard section of the right wing from the cockpit windows, LeBel and Schumacher were not aware that the wing had been damaged. The plane was exceedingly difficult to control; it continued to shake violently.

The buffeting made it impossible for the passengers to pull their seat belts tighter and hold on. Cups stored in the galley spilled onto the floor. Grimes was pushed against a bulkhead, her cap thrown from her head. There wasn't a pattern to the shaking. It continued in both up-and-down and side-to-side jerky motions.

Descending at a steep angle had now brought them dangerously close to the ground—low enough to spot sagebrush dotting the rock-strewn terrain. LeBel continued to pull his yoke back to try leveling the plane. But the rapid descent couldn't be arrested. Schumacher moved the trim wheel for the elevator to its full nose-up position. The pitch attitude stayed the same.

Confused, both pilots pulled back on the yokes in unison but still couldn't raise the nose; the plane remained stuck in a mild dive. The elevator was ineffective.

Schumacher wasn't interested in troubleshooting the problem. He only wanted to get the sick Convair back on the ground, hopefully in one piece. At this point, a crash landing would be fine. The pilots agreed that an emergency landing was inevitable. But first they had to find a way to get the nose raised. They had only seconds to do so before hitting the ground.

Whatever the problem was, the pilots knew they needed to build up additional airspeed to increase the lift developed by the elevator. This would help raise the nose, their only hope of regaining pitch control and making a safe landing.

LeBel pushed the yoke forward to *steepen* the dive, which reached nearly a 45-degree angle, while advancing the throttles to develop almost 4,000 hp. The maneuver was risky, but they'd run out of options. The airspeed increasing to 276 mph, and the added lift developed by the elevator resulted in the needed pitch control.[8]

Maintaining full takeoff power and a scary 300 feet from the ground, LeBel successfully pulled the nose up. At 50 feet, the plane about to scrape the tops of the sagebrush, Schumacher lowered the landing gear. Enough control now existed to get the plane back on the ground.

LeBel was able to raise the nose to almost a horizontal landing attitude. It wasn't a normal landing attitude but close enough. They braced themselves as the plane hit the ground, its main landing gear striking the rock-strewn surface with tremendous force. Roaring across uneven, brush-covered sand, the plane bounced up and down several feet at a time. Schumacher shut down both engines; there was now no propeller reversing to slow the plane down.

The eighteen-ton airliner continued working its way over the rocks and flora, flattening everything in its path before finally striking a series of boulders. It slid to a halt after slamming into the largest of them.

Thirty seconds earlier, they had been in the air. Now the plane was stopped in a mostly intact, upright condition. The fuselage, the left wing with its engine, and the empennage had held together. In the cabin, the noise level had gone from deafening to total silence. But the peaceful interlude would be short-lived.

A wall of flames erupted like a blowtorch, fed by hundreds of gallons of high-octane gasoline pouring from a ruptured tank in the left wing. Spreading along the left side of the fuselage, the flames licked around the cabin windows. Evacuation was Schumacher's immediate order upon smelling the fumes. Any delay could prove fatal. Fortunately, the flames hadn't yet spread to the right side of the plane. Grimes herded her passengers through the emergency exits while Schumacher forced open the passenger entry door along the right side to provide further egress. One of the passengers broke a leg after becoming entangled in a seat belt while trying to step through a narrow window exit.

It took less than a minute for everyone to escape the cabin and run for their lives.

Dumbfounded that they had survived such a horrific accident, they then turned and watched an explosion finish off what remained of the Convair. It was remarkable that no one was killed, but five of the eighteen passengers sustained serious injuries. The crew was fortunate to have suffered only scratches. Landing the plane in one piece and escaping the fire was nothing less than a miracle.

N8405H had smashed into the ground about four miles northwest of the departure end of runway 31. Debris from the fuselage and wings defined the ground path of the rampaging plane. The crash site consisted of mounds of drifting sand strewn with hundreds of half-buried rocks. Tracks carved in the sand by the landing gear stretched for over six hundred feet. One hundred feet from where the plane had stopped after its left main landing gear struck the immovable boulder lay the heavy gear assembly, sheared off by the impact and tossed past the boulder.

Upon ground impact, the propellers of both engines had snapped off from their shafts. Much of the right wing was gone, the extreme force of the crash having hurled it almost 1,200 feet from where the plane first hit the ground. Sitting a few feet away from the wing, its engine and main landing gear had dug into the sandy soil.

A piece of aluminum that formed the leading edge of the right wing landed about one-half mile from the end of runway 31—three and one-half miles from where the Convair crash landed. The aluminum leading edge had been screwed to the front of the wing structure between the fuselage and right engine. The curved piece, measuring fifty-two inches long by twenty-five inches wide, was fitted with piano hinges along its top to allow pivoting upward for inspections. When the leading edge was closed, a row of twenty-seven screws along its bottom fastened into a row of self-locking nuts mounted along the lower edge of the wing spar.

Because several passengers had witnessed pieces of the right wing failing, CAB investigators began by examining what remained of that portion of the airframe, most of it incinerated. They took a close look at the nuts affixed to the wing spar that served to retain the screws. A magnifying glass came in handy for determining whether the threads in the nuts were stripped. But the holes showed no evidence of elongation or tearing. The presence of the screws, or pieces of them remaining in the holes, would confirm they had been installed and secured by the nuts at the time of the accident. But there were no screws, or any pieces of them, remaining in any of the nuts, and a search of the ground surrounding the accident site failed to turn up the screws. As for the leading edge, it had survived its five-hundred-foot fall largely intact.

Following the maintenance check in Los Angeles, the Convair had flown a total of only two hours and nine minutes. To learn more, the CAB investigators queried the employees at Los Angeles International who were responsible for the plane's operational airworthiness.

N8405H had been pulled from passenger service and towed into the Western Airlines hangar at 4:00 p.m. on Tuesday, February 12, the day before the accident. A lead mechanic on the evening shift told his crew to remove all inspection panels from the airframe, including the screws retaining the leading edges of both wings. Once the leading edges were opened up, an inspector documented several minor discrepancies needing repair. Two of them were in the right wing. The discrepancies, or "squawks," were signed off as corrected at 12:30 a.m. on Wednesday when the midnight shift came on duty.

At 3:30 a.m., the mechanics were told to close the inspection panels and leading edges. A lead mechanic told the workers under his supervision to perform most of the tasks. To help, a mechanic borrowed from an engine crew got involved. He was told to reinstall the right-wing leading edge and secure any open access panels.

The work involved checking the metal strip that retained the twenty-seven nuts. He then unhooked the leading edge from its raised position and lowered it into place.

He finished up the tasks at approximately 4:00 a.m.

The CAB investigators convened a public hearing in Los Angeles on March 28, 1958. The mechanic assigned from the engine crew testified about the actions he took that night. He said that after lowering the leading edge into a closed position, he inserted a few screws in holes along its lower edge for alignment purposes, tightening them only partially. He used screws from his toolbox because he couldn't find the screws that another mechanic had removed earlier that evening. The "missing screws" statement was disputed by two other mechanics. They testified that the screws were wrapped in a rag hanging from the edge of the right wing.

Because the evidence revealed that *no* screws had been installed, the mechanic was queried about whether he might have forgotten to install them. In response, and as documented in the investigation report, he said, "It just doesn't seem like they were in it." After further questioning, he mentioned a litany of personal issues causing extreme stress in his life. It became apparent to the investigators that mental distraction likely resulted in his forgetting to install the screws.

The lead mechanic had been responsible for making sure all leading edges and inspection panels were closed and secured using the correct hardware. When asked about the details of his work, he said that each panel hadn't been checked "screw by screw." Instead, his personal philosophy was to conduct a cursory inspection of the exterior surfaces of the entire plane. Not knowing if each screw retaining the leading edges had been installed, he assumed that a visual check would reveal if the head of a screw protruded above the surface, indicating it was loose. Each screw needed to be flush with the airframe skin. He also expected that the mechanic he borrowed from the engine crew would do everything correctly, saying, "I shouldn't have to check everything."

When the shift for the engine mechanic ended, the man told the lead mechanic to advise the day shift that each inspection panel had been closed properly. He didn't mention the leading edges.

Another lead mechanic testified that he always completed such work by checking the panels for proper placement, looseness, and missing screws. He was emphatic in stating that it was the only correct way to do the job.

Western Airlines didn't rely on employees designated as inspectors to handle all its inspection tasks. Ensuring that the leading edges were secured was *not* an inspector's responsibility. The inspection function was delegated to a lead mechanic on a given shift. In fact, the company's maintenance manual required it: "The lead mechanic will make a walkaround inspection of the aircraft to ascertain that all access doors, plates, openings and cargo pit lining is [*sic*] in place and secured and sign off the applicable line of the master card."

It became apparent that the cause of the accident rested on the carelessness of a mechanic and his immediate boss rather than a systemic failure of Western's safety culture.

The final verdict offered by the CAB surprised no one. "The Board determines that the probable cause of this accident was the failure of a mechanic to secure properly the right wing leading edge section as a result of which the unit separated in flight. This improper installation was undetected because of inadequate inspection."

Engineers found it incredible that the leading edge section had remained attached to the wing for the entire distance from Los Angeles to Palm Springs. Only a handful of screws had retained it. If this section of the wing had separated at a higher speed, the resulting forces could have caused the plane to break apart in midair.

Captain Schumacher was fortunate to have escaped injury and possible death during the crash landing. But his luck didn't last. On March 31, 1971, a Western Airlines four-engine Boeing 720 crashed at Ontario International

Airport in California. It happened during a training flight with no passengers aboard. Schumacher and four other crewmembers aboard were killed. A bracket supporting a hydraulic actuator that moved the rudder had failed, causing a complete loss of directional control. Both accidents, separated by thirteen years, were the result of mechanical failure—or more accurately, carelessness.

Note: Many of the details presented in this chapter, including dates, places, descriptions of events, conclusions, and quotes (unless otherwise attributed), were derived from Civil Aeronautics Board, "Aircraft Investigation Report, Resort Airlines, Inc., Louisville, Kentucky, September 28, 1953, SA-285"; and Civil Aeronautics Board, "Accident Investigation Report, Western Airlines, Inc., Convair 240, N 8405H, Near Palm Springs, California, February 13, 1958, SA-329."

9

UNSCREWED

The passengers aboard Western Airlines Flight 19 were fortunate to have survived their crash landing in the Southern California desert. Thirty-three-years later, the passengers aboard Continental Express Flight 2574 in Texas weren't as lucky, all of them dying in a horrific, preventable accident. Determining what happened to Flight 19 wasn't much of a mystery. But nailing down the underlying reasons for Flight 2574's demise would tax the intellect and stamina of its investigators to the fullest.

In August 1953, a Houston-based airline named Trans-Texas Airways (TTA) began operating scheduled flights to thirty-six airports stretching from El Paso to Memphis. It never earned a stellar reputation for reliability or luxury but did provide essential air transportation for millions of people. TTA's oil-splattered DC-3s and Convairs had seen better days. Making primarily short hops to smaller cities and crisscrossing over forests, the airline was labeled "Tree Top Airlines" by its detractors. The carrier's brand desperately needed upgrading to project a fresh image to the public, and so in April 1969, Trans-Texas Airways became Texas International Airlines after the CAB approved scheduled flights to several cities in Mexico.

For an airline unprofitable since 1966, the bold transition incurred massive debt and generated little income. Losing millions of dollars each year, Texas International was acquired in 1972 by a holding company called Jet Capital Corporation and headed by thirty-two-year-old financial impresario Frank Lorenzo. Born in New York, Lorenzo had attended Columbia University and followed that by earning an MBA from the Harvard Business School. Growing up a mile from LaGuardia Airport in Queens, Lorenzo not surprisingly began his career as a financial analyst at an airline.

The bank account at Texas International was nearly depleted when Lorenzo took over. He capped its outflow of cash, slashing employee wages and benefits. No sooner had the ink dried on the agreement to buy the airline than he began firing employees. To cut benefits further, he ordered ticket agents to do some of their work on a part-time basis. In response, their union struck. Retaliating, Lorenzo hired replacements willing to work for less money. Members of Texas International's other unions walked off their jobs in sympathy with the agents. Unrelenting, Lorenzo shut the airline down for four months to "restructure" its operations—and further economize.

In the wake of this unprecedented labor unrest, Lorenzo cut some airfares in half to attract budget-minded customers. Because the low fares meant cutting the payroll even further, the action exacerbated his already sour relationship with the unions.

Bargain fares were popular with people accustomed to riding crowded Greyhound buses. But for seasoned travelers desiring higher standards, competitive airlines grabbed much of Texas International's business. Poor employee morale, erratic service, and dirty planes also caused them to fly on other airlines.

Gaining wind of Lorenzo's future intentions, the unions planned a lengthy strike. He had already threatened to follow through with large-scale layoffs and deep cuts in benefits for employees who had survived his earlier actions.

In 1980, Lorenzo formed Texas Air Corporation, a holding company for Texas International Airlines. He then went on to acquire Continental Airlines in 1982 and merged the two airlines, Continental becoming the surviving brand. The labor problems didn't subside. They got worse. During nineteen months of negotiations, Continental Airlines and the union representing its mechanics couldn't reach an agreement. The mechanics went on strike in August 1983. Continental continued its flight operations by hiring whatever non-union mechanics it could find. A few weeks later, the airline filed for Chapter 11 bankruptcy. After the filing, the pilot's union struck to protest wage cuts. To Lorenzo, pilots were no different than racecar drivers—being paid for enjoying a hobby. And airline mechanics were nothing more than glorified grease monkeys.

During the bankruptcy proceedings, Continental's lawyers insisted that the airline's labor costs were still too high, leading to the possibility that the airline might go out of business. The unions claimed that bankruptcy was nothing more than a ploy to eliminate the labor contracts. They were right. The workers' appeal went nowhere, however, when the court handed down a ruling that permitted the airline to void *all* its union contracts. In retaliation against disgruntled employees, Lorenzo fired a third of them, tore up the labor contracts in public, and dropped most of the airline's routes.

In September 1986, Continental Airlines emerged from bankruptcy a far leaner company. After slashing costs to the bone, it began to turn a profit. That same year Continental Express came into existence as a subsidiary of the airline. Beginning with deregulation of the nation's airlines in 1978, major air carriers had begun scheduling flights to less-traveled destinations using planes operated by smaller regional carriers. Lorenzo formed Continental Express after rationalizing that a single regional airline, wholly owned by Continental Airlines, would be cheaper to operate than paying independent commuter airlines to provide the service. Once again, it was a matter of cutting costs and exercising control for the dictatorial Lorenzo.

Continental Express emerged from the complicated merger of four small airlines controlled by Texas Air Corporation. They were Provincetown-Boston Airlines, Bar Harbor Airlines, Rocky Mountain Airways, and Britt Airways. In 1991, Rocky Mountain's operations were folded into Britt Airways. The fast-moving changes were hard to follow on Wall Street and impossible to decipher for even seasoned air travelers. Although branded Continental Express, the airline would operate under Britt's FAA air carrier certificate until November 2011.

Lorenzo pursued airline ownership as a game, moving companies around like pieces on a chessboard. The shuffling of executives in each of his companies was confusing, leading to morale problems throughout the ranks of Texas Air Corporation employees. On the front lines, pilots and mechanics suffered the most.

When regional carriers began operating turboprop-powered Embraer EMB-120 Brasilia airliners in 1985, the compact planes showed promise of revolutionizing short-haul air travel. Manufactured by Embraer (Embresa-Brasileira de Aeronautica S.A., headquartered in Sao Paulo, Brazil), the Brasilia evolved by incorporating hundreds of suggestions from airline executives, pilots, and mechanics. For the first time in commercial aviation history, regional airlines connecting rural communities would operate a plane specifically designed for them. Powered by two robust Pratt & Whitney PW118 turboprop engines, each of them producing 1,800 shaft horsepower, the Brasilia proved to be the fastest and most economical small airliner of its day.[1]

Following overnight maintenance at Houston Intercontinental Airport (now George Bush Intercontinental Airport), a Continental Express Brasilia taxied from the hangar area to a gate at the passenger terminal. It was shortly before dawn on September 11, 1991. The plane was about to endure a full day in the air making "milk runs" to a handful of cities in the southwest. FAA-registered as

N33701, the plane had been purchased by Continental Express from Embraer on April 15, 1988.[2]

In the cockpit of the plane sat its captain, twenty-nine-year-old Brad Patridge, studying the departure documents for Flight 2574. Clint Rodosovich, forty-three, would assist him as copilot. Awaiting the passengers was thirty-three-year-old Nancy Reed, the flight attendant. Both of the pilots were captains, each highly experienced flying the Brasilia. Patridge, hired on October 10, 1987, had accumulated 4,243 total hours. About 2,468 of them were at the controls of a Brasilia. Rodosovich was even more experienced with 11,543 hours, 1,066 of them acquired in the plane. Hired by Continental Express on March 12, 1990, at least 10,300 of Rodosovich's hours had been logged flying airplanes and helicopters at other companies. A decorated military veteran, Rodosovich had served in Vietnam flying attack helicopters during the war. Although he wasn't the captain of Flight 2574, the chief pilot permitted him to maintain his status as a captain. They were lacking copilots at the time and he was needed to fill the position.

It would be a tiring day for the three-person crew, necessitating that they rise well before dawn and not expect to leave for home until late in the day. The flight legs would require a rapid succession of takeoffs and landings.

Following a 7:00 a.m. departure, the Brasilia's first stop would be Laredo International Airport. Patridge assumed that everything in the plane was airworthy. But neither pilot was aware that a dozen mechanics and inspectors had crawled over its airframe a few hours earlier to replace a de-icing boot on the plane's horizontal stabilizer.[3]

Patridge and Rodosovich paged through each item on their checklists methodically, started the engines, and taxied to Houston's active runway. Departing on schedule, the flight was uneventful—at least for the pilots. A passenger deplaning in Laredo later recalled being awakened by an unusual vibration that rattled a soda can on a tray in front of him. He asked flight attendant Reed if he could move to another seat. He did so but neglected to tell her or one of the pilots about the vibration.

Eleven passengers boarded N33701 in Laredo. There was plenty of room because the cabin could seat as many as thirty people. Two of the passengers planned to disembark in Houston; the rest of them were scheduled to board connecting flights. One of them was fifty-one-year-old Maria Guillermina Valdes Villalva, the director of a college in Mexico and a prominent social activist. She was on her way to attend the graduation of her daughter. The others included six people from Monterrey, Mexico.

Before departing Laredo, the pilots calculated the plane's takeoff weight to be 22,272 pounds, including 1,815 pounds of passengers, 259 pounds of cargo, and 3,100 pounds of fuel. This was 3,081 pounds below the maximum allowable of 25,350 pounds. The load was positioned well within center of gravity limits. As for the weather, there were no significant advisories in effect. They were good to go.

N33701 departed the Laredo runway at 9:09 a.m. for the ninety-minute flight back to Houston. Following a normal takeoff, the plane reached a cruise altitude of 25,000 feet. Rodosovich was handling radio communications with air traffic control, and the controller soon instructed the flight to descend one thousand feet. It wasn't necessary to remain at a higher altitude because Houston wasn't far away. They would soon descend and prepare for an approach to the airport.

Rodosovich made radio contact with the radar controller in Houston at 9:49 a.m. Five minutes later, the controller told the flight to "cross five miles southwest of Intercontinental at and maintain niner thousand." Rodosovich radioed back, "Okay, fifty-five miles southwest of Intercontinental at niner thousand, we're out of flight level two four zero." The controller instructed him to make a heading change. Rodosovich confirmed the request as Patridge adjusted a knob on the autopilot panel to align the plane with the requested heading.

The CVR captured sparse conversation between the men during the flight. Neither pilot voiced any problem on the recording. A call from Rodosovich at 9:54 a.m. confirming further instructions from air traffic control was the crew's last radio transmission.

At 10:03 a.m., the CVR picked up the sound of loose objects and papers tossed around the cockpit. A heavy grunt from one of the pilots could be heard. No words were spoken, no yelling or profanity. More-familiar sounds included audible alerts produced by the plane's warning systems. The intensity of noise increased: loud cracking and rumbling—followed by a mysterious, gentle swish of wind.

Then the recording stopped.

Inside the Brasilia, an abrupt force had tossed people and objects about. The plane's nose pitched down sharply. Two seconds later, all hell broke loose. The pressurization failed, windows cracked—and the fuselage structure began twisting. Unbelted passengers were hurled against the cabin walls and ceiling. A furious flow of cold air entered the cabin, hitting the passengers like a tornado. Sections of the fuselage breaking apart, the passengers gasped their last breaths in a state of panic. The plane's oscillating downward plunge accelerating, it is likely they lost consciousness.

Data from the plane's FDR revealed that N33701 began descending at the moment the abrupt pitch change occurred. The change caused a massive, negative, vertical acceleration. The descent was followed by erratic changes in roll, yaw, and heading. There was no way Patridge or Rodosovich could have arrested the deadly descent.

Before the loss of radio communication, two radar controllers coordinating the flight in Houston were relieved by another person from the next shift. During a briefing, they noticed that the symbol representing N33701, transmitted from the plane's ATC transponder, had disappeared from the screen. At 10:05 p.m., the controller taking over tried contacting the pilots. There was no response.

There was no response from the crew because part of the plane's tail section had snapped off in midair. This was followed by much of the left wing separating and bending under the fuselage; a broken fuel line then started a fire. The $8 million Brasilia plummeted like a rock for more than two miles. Smashing into the ground, it belly-flopped, ending up fairly upright, its fiery fuselage embedded in the plowed soil of a cornfield. Pieces of wreckage were strewn over a four-mile stretch of southeast Texas farmland, the tranquil area known as a winter home for huge flocks of geese and other migrating waterfowl.

"I was in the field about two miles from where it landed," said seventy-six-year-old Charlie Labay, a rice farmer living nearby. "It was just spinning and just coming straight down."[4]

Another farmer who witnessed the plane break apart in the air called Guadalupe Villarreal, the police chief in nearby Eagle Lake. It was 10:10 a.m.

"I thought at first it was a crop duster," Villarreal said. "Once I got there, I contacted the fire departments and told them they didn't have to come. It had nearly burned itself out."[5]

The fire chief and the town's volunteer firefighters had already been dispatched, driving the first of two 350-gallon, four-wheel-drive fire trucks. Arriving at the scene in ten minutes, they could see that the fire had destroyed much of the airframe. They poured enough water over the wreckage to extinguish whatever hot spots remained. Several ambulances also rushed to the scene. There was no need. It was obvious that everyone aboard the plane had died.

The plane came down about fifty-five miles west of Houston and seven miles southwest of the town of Eagle Lake, population 3,900. The area was planted in corn, and some of it was pastureland. Before the fuselage of N33701 hit the ground, small pieces of its airframe fell like confetti, scattering over the fields. The Colorado River flowed north to south a mile or two west of the site. A private pilot flying along the course of the fast-moving river reported seeing a piece of floating wreckage. It would never be found.

The first responders saw several charred bodies in the crushed fuselage. Because they were bunched up, at first it was difficult to tell how many there were. "I could tell there were no survivors when I got there," said Jose Ugarte, an Eagle Lake physician and regional medical examiner for the FAA.[6]

The bodies of two passengers had been ejected by the impact, landing about twenty feet from the wreckage. The bodies of both pilots remained in the cockpit, strapped in their seats. The structure surrounding the cockpit had partly collapsed but had escaped much of the fire damage. The victims pinned in the cabin were burned beyond recognition.

There was nothing the first responders could do except pull tarps over the remains. Wooden stakes were driven into the soil to mark where the two bodies were thrown. The largest pieces of wreckage lay in a twisted heap of metal. Bits of yellow fiberglass insulation littered the field.

An NTSB go-team was dispatched from Washington, DC without delay. By late afternoon of September 11, 1991, the investigators arrived on the scene. They didn't know it then, but the accident would rank as one of the most perplexing cases of their careers.

The group of investigators traveled a bumpy, single-lane road outside Eagle Lake to reach the cornfield, joining local officials and the FAA's own people. A coroner arrived to conduct the delicate task of removing the remains to perform autopsies. The debris field was almost the size of a football stadium, and pieces of the airframe could be seen everywhere. The NTSB team began the tedious process of photographing hundreds of pieces of wreckage, large and small. Each part was tagged for later reference, with a map drawn and keyed to where each piece was discovered. The debris field was so huge that a helicopter needed to be chartered to search for wreckage outside the immediate area.

Hundreds of parts of the Brasilia, including all eight of its propeller blades, were located within about a one-mile radius of the crumpled fuselage. Most of the fuselage came to rest in one place. The lower portion of the forward airframe was heavily crushed. As expected, the landing gear assemblies were found in a retracted position. The left engine and propeller assembly, minus its four blades, hit the earth 370 feet south-southwest of the fuselage. There was no indication of an anomaly occurring in either the engines or propellers prior to the in-flight breakup. Damage resulting from the inflight gyrations is what overstressed the airframe and engines, twisting and tucking the left wing under the fuselage. A wing tip landed one-fifth of a mile west of the fuselage. The aft fuselage section, including the upper two-thirds of the vertical stabilizer, suffered severe damage. Some of its structure and metal skin remained attached to the tail cone. Smaller pieces were discovered in a horse corral a mile west of the fuselage. It was as though the plane had exploded while high in the sky.

Autopsies of the three crewmembers and eleven passengers conducted by the Harris County Coroner's Office revealed they had suffered traumatic injuries caused by the impact. Although two people were ejected on impact and thrown into the cornfield, the other victims were crushed inside the cabin. There was no indication the fatalities had resulted from burns or physical trauma before impact.

Fanning out from the site, the investigators discovered what would become their most important clue. The horizontal stabilizer had landed more than six hundred feet west-southwest of where the fuselage did. Clearly it had broken free of the fuselage *before* the plane hit the ground. More mystifying, the entire leading edge formerly attached to the stabilizer's left side wasn't found.

The CVR and FDR were recovered from the aft fuselage. There was minor damage to their orange-painted cases but they hadn't been subjected to fire. The recorders were flown to the agency's computer analysis laboratory in Washington, DC. Arriving at the lab, the mass of electronic data would be downloaded to recreate the events that culminated in the crash. An initial analysis revealed that a clear CVR recording existed with no loss of tonal quality. The FDR readout was also acceptable and expected to yield helpful aircraft performance data.

To recreate the sequence of events leading up to the crash, the NTSB relied on evidence gathered at the crash site, statements from witnesses, and data from the recorders. Aircraft performance data and engineering calculations provided by Embraer were used to study the plane's erratic motions during its last minute aloft. Flight parameters existing at the time of the plane's sudden pitch down, including airspeed, altitude, acceleration, and attitude had been recorded by the FDR. The weather during the flight was calm. Therefore, clear air turbulence or gust loads weren't thought to be a factor causing the plane to disintegrate.

Data downloaded from the FDR indicated that N33701 had descended through 11,500 feet at a speed of 299 mph after it abruptly pitched downward and entered the steep dive. The data indicated that a force of at least three negative Gs was attained one second after the upset.

During the first six seconds of the upset, the right wing rolled down between 10 and 15 degrees. At the same time, a lateral push of as much as one-half G was felt. Immediately following this short slice of time, the plane continued a roll to the right—moving 160 degrees in one second—the maneuver comparable to half of a pronounced snap roll. During that second, the pitch attitude reached 86 degrees, the nose beginning to point almost straight down. The left wing and engine broke free from the fuselage at that point. Seconds later, monstrous air loads resulted in the horizontal stabilizer separating and falling free from the remainder of the airframe.

The investigators remained focused on wondering why the leading edge had separated *before* the stabilizer itself did.

A damaged horizontal stabilizer would compromise the aerodynamic lift that pushes down the tail, a force required to sustain level flight.[7] The stabilizer separation caused an extreme change in pitch, and the wing stalled. Each of the two leading-edge sections forming the stabilizer's airfoil was held in place by forty-seven machine screws spaced along the edge's upper side. An equal number of screws retained it along the bottom. To fly into icing conditions safely, rubber boots were glued to each of the leading edges to shed any ice that might adhere.[8]

None of the screws intended to secure the upper side of the left leading edge were found in the debris field. And there was no indication of undue stress in the nuts that would have anchored those screws. More telling, it appeared that *no screws had been installed*. It was strange that the screws along the lower side were found screwed into the stabilizer. Its glass fiber leading edge appeared as though it had been torn from the stabilizer, causing a portion of it to be pushed into the turbulent wind stream. Not capable of enduring air loads resulting from 300 mph speeds, it separated from the stabilizer. The wind stream hadn't appreciably distorted the stiff, composite-reinforced part during the flight into Laredo. But during the return journey to Houston, the leading edge loosened to a point where the plane's speed and vibrations tore it apart.

It wasn't the best of times for Continental Express or the nation's airlines in general. The accident raised grave doubts in the minds of the traveling public about the safety of flying. On April 5, 1991, four months before the Continental Express accident, Flight 2311, an Atlantic Southeast Airline's Brasilia carrying twenty-three passengers and crewmembers, crashed near Brunswick, Georgia, the result of the malfunction of a mechanical governor, the propeller of the plane's left engine slipping into reverse pitch as the plane was nearing an airport for landing. This created tremendous drag that destroyed much of the lift produced by the left wing, and the plane rolled and pitched uncontrollably before crashing. Everyone aboard died, including former Senator John Tower, his daughter, and astronaut Manley "Sonny" Carter Jr.[9] The passenger list made for front-page news.

By 1989, Continental Airlines was serving 133 airports around the world and carrying about 9 percent of the nation's airline traffic. It offered more than 1,250 daily departures. Satisfied with what he had achieved and looking forward to profiting from other business endeavors, Frank Lorenzo sold his stake in the bankrupt airline in 1990. Continental Airlines merged into Continental

United Holdings in 2010 and lost its longtime identity as an airline. Today it's a part of United Airlines Holdings. Following the merger of Continental with United, Continental Express was renamed "United Express."

Note: Many of the details presented in this chapter, including dates, places, descriptions of events, conclusions, and quotes (unless otherwise attributed), were derived from National Transportation Safety Board, "Aircraft Accident Report, Britt Airways, Inc., d/b/a Continental Express Flight 2574, In-Flight Structural Breakup EMB-120RT, N33701 Eagle Lake, Texas, September 11, 1991, NTSB Identification AAR-92/04."

❿

BLAME GAME

A major airline accident upsets everyone, especially people who work for the airline. When fellow employees die, a somber mood fills the offices and hangars for weeks. Aside from the human drama, the most immediate task for the CEO is damage control: convincing the public that the accident was not an indication of anything wrong with the airline's operations.

When the NTSB investigators first visited the headquarters of Continental Express adjacent to the Houston airport, they weren't welcomed with open arms. Its managers projected a sullen, remote persona. The perceived lack of cooperation wasn't understandable, considering that three of the airline's employees had been killed. The managers displayed anxiousness yet didn't appear to be in a rush to assist with the investigation. Ignoring these observations, the investigators organized the tasks ahead of them and began visiting departments in the company that may have had a connection to the tragedy.

They researched the maintenance history of the Brasilia that had crashed, especially any repair work on the horizontal stabilizer. This involved reviewing records and work procedures together with interviewing employees responsible for the plane's maintenance during the hours before the accident. The investigators discovered that the group of employees assigned to aircraft N33701, consisting of mechanics, inspectors, and supervisors, represented about 23 percent of all workers on the evening shift and 21 percent of those working the midnight shift. Together, they represented approximately 15 percent of the *entire* maintenance workforce at Continental Express.

N33701 had received an inordinate amount of attention from the mechanics and inspectors that night—or so it appeared. It confused the investigators that so many workers had been involved in the plane's maintenance. FAA regulations required that a lead mechanic be assigned to each of the airline's shifts. The position had not been filled. Instead, a supervisor who oversaw the mechanics assumed that role. This signaled that something hadn't been right. However, the airline had complied with all FAA airworthiness directives affecting the Brasilia.

At Continental Express, the FAA-approved procedures that dictated how Continental should maintain its fleet of planes were contained in a company bible called the General Maintenance Manual (GMM). The manual included a section on a Required Inspection Item (RII) program that mandated special inspections of components considered critical to flight safety. These included flight controls.

One section of the GMM stated that "personnel performing maintenance will follow and be familiar with the instructions as outlined herein. . . . Instructions and information, contained herein, bring Continental Express into compliance with the appropriate Federal Aviation Regulations. For this reason, it is essential that the contents be followed." This constituted a stern warning that was not to be ignored.

The GMM stressed the importance of completing all required maintenance and inspection forms to assure that nothing would be overlooked. It included information on how to write up shift turnover forms so that supervisors overseeing a later shift of employees would be aware that work accomplished by a previous crew had been completed—*or* only partly completed. Incomplete work was to be noted on the reverse side of a task card, detailing the specific maintenance step at which the work stopped. In addition to the cards, several other methods were offered in the GMM for handing work over to mechanics during shift changes.

An examination of maintenance records revealed that on August 26, 1991, a fleet-wide campaign had been initiated to inspect the rubber de-icing boots on all the airline's Brasilia airplanes. When it came to N33701, an inspector noted that the boots on its horizontal stabilizer had "dry rotted pin holes entire length." The inspector documented the condition on a task card as an item "to watch." Taking action the day before the accident, the maintenance control office in Houston told a supervisor on the midnight shift to have his mechanics replace both the right- and left-hand boots on the stabilizer.

The task was expected to require assistance from employees assigned to the midnight shift only. However, seven mechanics, four supervisors, and three quality-control inspectors would eventually get involved in the work during an eight-hour span of time.

Changing either one of the boots meant that a fiber-reinforced leading edge would need to be removed from the stabilizer by first removing a set of screws that attached the leading edge to the stabilizer. After a new boot had been glued to the leading edge, the leading edge would be reinstalled on the stabilizer using the set of screws removed earlier.

Pulling off a worn de-icing boot, removing the screws holding the curved leading edge to the stabilizer, replacing the worn boot, and reinstalling everything might be handled during a single work shift. At Continental Express, the task ended up spanning two shifts consisting of a plethora of mechanics, inspectors, and supervisors. But even then the job ended up only half-completed. The saying "Storm it with manpower" didn't apply that night.

At 8:00 p.m., a supervisor assigned to the evening shift and transferred from duty at the passenger terminal arrived at the hangar to oversee the boot replacement work. It was decided to have the evening crew handle the work although maintenance control had initially assigned it to the midnight mechanics. After discussing the task with another supervisor, he towed the plane into a hangar. By 9:30 p.m. it was parked under bright lights in a hangar capable of accommodating two of the turboprop airliners at a time. The supervisor had earlier told two of the mechanics assigned to him to remove the boots from both sides of the horizontal stabilizer. They got busy.

The mechanics, assisted by an inspector who volunteered to help, reached the T-tail of N33701 by standing on a hydraulic lift and began the disassembly portion of the work. Twenty feet over the floor of the hangar, the workers peeled away most of the boot stuck to the leading edge on the right side. The next task involved removing the screws on the lower side that held the leading edge to the stabilizer.

At 10:00 p.m. the supervisor walked into the hangar, glanced upward, and saw his mechanics kneeling on top of the stabilizer's right side working on the boot and leading edge. It appeared to him that everything was progressing satisfactorily. He didn't notice if any work had begun on the left side.

After removing the screws on the top of the right leading edge, the twenty-eight-year-old inspector who had volunteered his assistance to the evening supervisor walked across the top of the twenty-three-foot wide stabilizer to its left side. He then pulled out *all* the screws holding the top of the left-hand leading edge to the stabilizer. He didn't touch the screws on its bottom. Working on the other side of the stabilizer, the other mechanics ignored him.

At 10:05 p.m., an inspector assigned to the midnight shift arrived at work earlier than usual and noticed that most of the boot on the right side had been peeled off. He glanced at the task card assigned to the inspector who had helped remove the screws. He was surprised to see that no entry was penned in. At 10:30 p.m. the inspector who performed the work made a notation. It consisted of one sentence: "Helped the mechanic remove the de-ice boots." He did not mention removing the screws on the top of the left-hand leading edge. That inspector then clocked out and went home. But before leaving, he placed the screws he had removed in a small plastic bag and hung it on a work stand next to the tail.

The supervisor who had arrived for the midnight shift asked his evening counterpart if work had begun on the left side. The man looked toward the tail of N33701 and said, "No." The midnight supervisor told him that work on the right side could be finished that night but the left-hand boot would need to be replaced on another day. There wasn't enough time to replace both boots during his shift because the plane was scheduled for an early morning departure.

One of the two mechanics on the evening shift who had helped remove the boot on the right side of the stabilizer was told to stop further work on N33701. He was needed to finish a task begun earlier on another plane. After this he left for home. The second mechanic who had helped remove the boot on the right side of the stabilizer told the supervisor he was nearing the end of his shift too so he would "turn over" the remaining work on the right-side boot to a mechanic on the midnight shift. Verbally notifying a midnight shift mechanic to finish the work, he locked up his toolbox, clocked out, and headed out the door.

The midnight shift began at 10:30 p.m. What happened during the next few hours set the stage for the eventual fate of N33701.

The latest mechanic assigned to the task never worked on the boot. Instead, he verbally turned the task over to another mechanic on his shift. A game of musical chairs had begun. The latter mechanic testified at a later NTSB hearing that he couldn't remember receiving the turnover request and never saw the bag of screws the evening inspector said he had placed on the work stand.

Another mechanic on the midnight shift was instead assigned to finish the task. He asked the outgoing evening supervisor how much work had been done on N33701. The supervisor pointed to the plane's tail before speaking. He said that a few stripped screws had caused his mechanics to lose time removing the leading edge. The work was not completed. The mechanic asked if the work on a boot had begun on the left side. The supervisor said that he didn't think there was enough time to replace it. The inference: he was unsure if any work had begun on the left side. At 11:00 p.m., that supervisor went home. He didn't talk with the supervisor who would be his counterpart on the midnight shift—the man who would now be responsible for managing the job's completion. By 11:30 p.m., the two mechanics who had worked on the right-hand boot and leading edge that evening had also gone home. Because little had been documented on task cards, the history of what work had been completed turned into guesswork.

Two mechanics on the midnight shift were told to wrap up the work on the right side of the stabilizer. The stuck screws on the leading edge were drilled out and the part was pulled off the stabilizer. A new boot was bonded to it on a workbench in the hangar. Meanwhile, N33701 was towed from the hangar to make room for another plane. The plane relocated to a darkened area of the ramp, there wasn't much illumination to guide the mechanics while they reinstalled the assembled boot and leading edge. Flashlights had to suffice.

The supervisor and the two mechanics didn't know that the screws on the top of the left-hand leading edge had been removed. No entry had been made on a task card to document that action. The supervisor on the evening shift had elected to begin work on the boots to ease the midnight shift's workload but he didn't issue cards to the mechanics on his own shift. They were part of a package assigned to the later shift. As a result, no entries were made on the cards to advise the later supervisor and his mechanics how much work had been done. Throughout the night, they assumed that the mechanics on the evening shift had worked on the right side only.

Finishing up the work, an inspector climbed atop the stabilizer to both install and then inspect tubing that supplied compressed air to operate the pneumatic de-icing boot on the right side. The inspector had no way of knowing that the screws on top of the other leading edge weren't installed. It was difficult to spot small details ten feet away in a poorly lit area. Although the man had been trained as an inspector, he had no reason to look for the dozens of empty holes where screws had been inserted a few hours earlier.

The entire evening shift was now at home. The midnight shift assumed that all was well with N33701 once the new boot had been glued in place, the leading edge reinstalled, and the work had passed inspection.

As dawn neared, the plane was moved from the maintenance area to the passenger terminal for its first flight of the day.

The GMM governing the importance of detailed inspections stated, "Continental Express has established a list of items that requires a concentrated inspection (RII) on any work performed on those items. This list includes items that could result in a failure or malfunction that could endanger the safe operation of the aircraft."

In an attempt to deflect some of the airline's liability, the airline's management was of the opinion that removing and replacing de-icing boots *did not constitute RIIs*. If they did, the boots would need to be examined by a senior quality assurance inspector, costing the airline additional time, labor, and money. The inspector on the midnight shift who approved the plane for flight was under the impression that the boot wasn't an RII. His cursory look at the horizontal stabilizer, without undertaking an inspection of the leading edges on both sides, satisfied him that all was well.

Engineers at Embraer, the manufacturer of the Brasilia, argued that the FAA considered the boots and leading edges RIIs because they were considered parts of the horizontal stabilizer assembly.

Disagreeing, Continental Express officials stuck to insisting that the boots and leading edges were *separate* components and not an integral part of the stabilizer. The airline was unusually blunt in stating that if the manufacturer or the FAA had wanted the components to be treated as a single RII, they should have made it clear.

An examination of the plane's logbook revealed that nothing had been entered to document the work performed a few hours earlier. The pilots were not told about it even though the work affected flight safety. Because the work was classified by the airline as routine scheduled maintenance, there was no airline policy requiring the crew to be notified. As for the FAA, there wasn't a regulation requiring that flight crews be made aware of *routine* maintenance.

Even so, if the pilots had been informed of the work and had inspected the plane at the gate, they could not have discovered the missing screws. The top of the horizontal stabilizer towers two stories above the ground, and they would not have been able to see the screw holes from ground level during their preflight inspection. There was no possibility at that point of benefitting from two sets of eyes to detect the deadly oversight.

The individual errors and an apparent failed maintenance culture at Continental Express were difficult to unravel. NTSB investigators concentrated on uncovering systemic reasons for the accident as well as errors made by inadequately trained supervisors, mechanics, and inspectors.

The GMM required that specific procedures be used when initiating shift turnovers. These steps included briefings by mechanics to supervisors, briefings by outgoing supervisors to incoming supervisors, completion of maintenance and inspection shift turnover forms, and the documentation of incomplete work on task cards. If these or *any* of the correct procedures had been followed, N33701 would not have crashed.

The inspector on the evening shift who assisted the two mechanics remove the screws failed to fill out a shift turnover form. If he had provided one to his replacement and reported the work as being started on *both* leading edges, the accident would not have happened. As an inspector, he was thought to possess a "second set of eyes"—considered necessary in overseeing work performed by mechanics. By assuming the temporary role of mechanic, he no longer functioned as an inspector. He had been hired as a mechanic in July 1989. In October 1990, he was promoted to inspector. He received a warning from his supervisor in August 1991 for having "missed a crack" while checking a section of an airframe. A second warning came his way a month later because "he did not finish all paperwork required . . . missed 15 task cards." Continental Express management placed him on probation. The actions the inspector took during the night of September 11 continued this pattern of marginal performance. According to the airline's written policy, "there is no precise formula for applying discipline." No action was taken after a specific number of warnings. The vague policy had proven ineffective.[1]

Everyone, the mechanics, inspectors, and supervisors, was responsible for the accident, some of them making use of practices that violated FAA regulations. Senior managers at Continental Express had not ensured that the correct procedures would be followed and enforced, resulting in the plane being dispatched in an unsafe condition.

And insufficient surveillance by FAA safety inspectors gave the airline carte blanche to do whatever it wanted.

The dispute of whether the boots should be RIIs or classified under a less-critical standard dragged on. Assuming an unflinching defense, Continental Express management insisted that the boots were typically replaced separately from leading edges on a calendar basis and could not be considered an integral part of the horizontal stabilizer. The airline again pointed out that if these "non-structural" leading edges made of reinforced glass fiber were thought to be so critical to flight safety, Embraer should have identified them as RIIs.

Embraer reiterated its position by stating that the boots and leading edges were parts of the horizontal stabilizer assembly, meaning they were flight-critical.

The conclusion on the part of the NTSB was that Continental Express erred in not designating the removal and replacement of the boots as RIIs. By themselves, the boots were separate parts and didn't constitute RIIs. However, because the leading edges needed to be pulled to remove and replace the boots, and the leading edges were flight critical, the boots and the leading edges together constituted RIIs. The extra inspection required by an RII should have revealed the existence of the missing screws. It might have prevented the accident.

Under pressure, Continental Express finally relented and dismissed its argument.

The remaining concern was whether so many missteps constituted isolated instances of mechanic negligence or systemic neglect within the corporation.

The influence of executives and senior managers is more difficult to identify than the actions of employees doing the work, but the effects of failed management decisions are pervasive, affecting an airline's operations at all levels. The investigators were faced with determining what level of the company's organization, from shop supervisors up to the CEO, was responsible for a dangerous work culture that had become institutionalized.

The investigators didn't believe that the mistakes were related solely to the actions of the employees working on N33701. There were no indications of drug abuse, criminal activity, or abnormal psychological behavior among them. But none of the workers had followed prescribed turnover methods in the GMM and they had disregarded other established procedures. The inspectors were among the worst offenders. Their reckless attitude suggested that management had not established an effective safety program to ensure that the work would be performed and documented properly. In reality, it meant that no one was keeping an eye on the store.

The investigation shifted to assessing the FAA's effectiveness in monitoring airline maintenance practices. The NTSB came to the conclusion that the FAA wasn't much of a watchdog, especially at Continental Express.

A former maintenance inspector at the FAA reported that he coped with a "tremendous" workload while monitoring Continental Express. This limited his effectiveness in determining if proper safety practices were being followed. During his assignment to the airline, from February 1989 to June 1991, the fleet underwent dramatic expansion. The inspector worked by himself for about a year at the Houston base. During that time, his manager assigned him a number of unrelated, time-consuming duties. When the airline slipped into bankruptcy, its maintenance operation required more surveillance, but no one was assigned to help him. This limited amount of time affected the depth of his on-site inspections. Although he kept up with the FAA's mandated minimum number, they were incomplete. He characterized the workload as "extremely full," requiring him to work both evenings and weekends.

Technicians at Continental Express queried by the investigators said they noticed FAA inspectors in the hangar infrequently, providing estimates of "perhaps a couple times per month at maximum," "once every two months," "every two or three months," and "once every three months, and the last visit might have been six or seven months before." A supervisor on the evening shift said that FAA visits were always announced with one day's advance notice. It gave the workers enough time to straighten up the hangar and try to bring the maintenance files up to date.

The FAA inspector's limited visits to the hangar floor meant that all deviations from procedures in the GMM were impossible to detect. And he was forced to rely on incomplete records that didn't reflect the actual work accomplished.

Shortly after the accident, a National Aviation Safety Inspection Program (NASIP) team from the FAA conducted an inspection of the entire maintenance program at Continental Express. A letter dated November 18, 1991, sent to the airline's management from then FAA Administrator James B. Busey, stated, "During our inspection, the team favorably noted that Britt Airways (doing business as Continental Express) has implemented an internal evaluation program. The inspection revealed very few safety deficiencies, a fact we attribute, in part, to the success of your internal evaluation system."

An NTSB concern centered on the limited scope of an NASIP inspection that failed to uncover problems the NTSB thought contributed to N33701's accident. The FAA survey didn't find *any* employees who didn't adhere to the shift turnover procedures. After the accident, the airline took little action to comply with those procedures. The NTSB felt that a thorough review of previous shift turnover records would have revealed serious deficiencies. The program's scope needed to be expanded.

The NTSB recommended that the FAA observe actual maintenance and repair work in the hangar and how it was documented to make sure the work complied with the GMM and Federal Air Regulations. It recommended that the NASIP emphasize hands-on inspection of equipment and procedures as well as make unannounced spot inspections.

The FAA agreed with the suggestions and said it would implement them but didn't announce a timeframe for doing so.

The NTSB's probable cause statement concerning the crash of N33701 was unusually lengthy:

> The National Transportation Safety Board determines that the probable cause of this accident was the failure of Continental Express maintenance and inspection personnel to adhere to proper maintenance and quality assurance procedures for the airplane's horizontal stabilizer deice boots that led to the sudden in-flight loss of the partially secured left horizontal stabilizer leading edge and the immediate severe nose-down pitch over and breakup of the airplane. Contributing to the cause of the accident was the failure of the Continental Express management to ensure compliance with the approved maintenance procedures, and the failure of FAA surveillance to detect and verify compliance with approved procedures.

Examining the official accident report, the executives at Continental Express were upset because the probable cause pointed to management incompetency.

Said a new release issued by the airline,

> While Continental Express does not fundamentally disagree with the N.T.S.B.'s
> probable cause finding (failure of personnel to adhere to prescribed procedures),
> the airline strongly disagrees with the board's conclusion that management fail-
> ures and inadequate F.A.A. surveillance contributed to the accident.[2]

The NTSB board voted 3–1 to accept the report's probable cause statement.
Member John Lauber dissented, refusing to accept a report that blamed the
workers in the hangar but cited the airline's management as only a "contributing
cause." He felt that top management's lack of a commitment to safety had set the
stage for this accident. That flawed corporate culture had permeated *all* levels
of employees, finding its way down to the mechanics and inspectors who then
adopted a lackadaisical attitude.

On July 21, 1992, Lauber wrote,

> I am perplexed by the majority decision that the actions of Continental Express
> senior management were not causal in this accident. . . . The multitude of lapses
> and failures committed by many employees of Continental Express discovered
> in this investigation is not consistent with the notion that the accident resulted
> from isolated, as opposed to systemic, factors. The series of failures, which led
> directly to the accident were not the result of an aberration, but rather resulted
> from the normal, accepted way of doing business at Continental Express. . . . Se-
> nior management created a work environment in which a string of failures, such
> as occurred the night before the accident, became probable.

Lauber felt that the probable cause stated in the report should be revised.
Specifically, he wanted it to say that the accident was caused by "the failure of
Continental Express management to establish a corporate culture which encouraged and enforced adherence to approved maintenance and quality assurance procedures." He didn't forget the FAA. "Contributing to the accident was
the inadequate surveillance by the FAA of the Continental Express maintenance
and quality assurance programs."

The loss of N33701 sparked widespread public concern about airline safety.
The airworthiness of the Brasilia itself wasn't questioned. The concern had to
do with the questionable management culture at this and other airlines. The
legacy of Lorenzo's outlandish leadership repeatedly came to mind. His cost-
cutting tactics and constant abuse of employees were well known and, in some
fashion, likely contributed to the end of N33701.

Air travelers found it incomprehensible that items appearing as insignificant as a handful of screws could bring down an $8 million airliner. Lessons learned from this accident were expected to ensure that another like it would not happen again. Unexpectedly, the *same* mistake was repeated.

Senior management at Continental Express didn't learn much from the crash of N33701. Fourteen months later, on December 9, 1992, another Brasilia operated by the airline experienced an incident caused by a set of screws that someone forgot to install. This time the screws were located on the wing rather than the tail. Shortly after takeoff, the copilot of the plane felt a heavy vibration in the airframe and a slight chattering of his yoke. The crew decided to return to the airport they'd just departed from. An investigation revealed that fourteen screws were missing from the aileron on the left wing. A mechanic had not reinstalled them when the aileron was replaced. Compounding the error, an inspector failed to notice that the screws weren't there. The NTSB's finding:

> The National Transportation Safety Board determines the probable cause(s) of this incident to be: The assigned mechanic's failure to reinstall the attachment screws and the quality inspector's inadequate inspection of the completed work. A factor was the complacency of the maintenance personnel.[3]

The safety culture at Continental Express had not improved.

Halfway around the world, the same kind of mistake that brought down N33701 reappeared. It involved the same model plane, same leading edge, same set of missing screws, and a similar group of distracted mechanics. A span of almost seven years separated the two events, this one taking place in France rather than over a cornfield in Texas.

During the early evening hours of September 29, 1998, a Brasilia took off from runway 26 at Clermont-Ferrand Auvergne Airport in France. Registered as F-GTSH, the plane was operated by Regional Airlines, a major regional carrier in France. It began a flight to Pau, on the northern edge of the Pyrenees, with twenty-six passengers aboard.

Making a left turn at 14,000 feet, the pilot felt a jolt followed by strong vibrations. The crew decided to land immediately. The vibrations intensified when the plane slowed for its final approach to the runway. Fortunately, they were able to land without further incident.

After landing, the crew noticed that the left-hand leading edge and the outer portion of the horizontal stabilizer were missing. Following maintenance on its tail on September 10, the plane had flown 114 hours in passenger service. During this time in the air, the Brasilia had flown with that near-fatal flaw in its stabilizer. Unlike the crew and passengers aboard Continental Express Flight 2574, the crew and passengers of F-GTSH had luckily escaped death.

On July 27, 1998, managers at Regional Airlines had ordered the replacement of the de-icing boots on eight Brasilia airplanes to comply with a fleet refurbishment program. F-GTSH was the fifth plane scheduled for repair, the work to be accomplished over several days. A new boot, glued to the existing left-hand leading edge, was installed on September 2.

It wasn't possible for investigators to learn anything about how the missing leading edge failed. The part was never found. However, twenty-five screws along the top of the stabilizer were still visible, partly unscrewed. None of the screws along the bottom side were found. The screws along the top being no longer capable of restraining the leading edge during flight, it had separated from the stabilizer.

The crew at the MRO responsible for the work consisted of four mechanics, each man having more than fifteen years of experience replacing de-icing boots. They were expected to supervise four less-qualified mechanics who actually wielded the wrenches. A supervisor from a different crew inspected the work, followed by a ground run-up and test flight to determine proper functioning of the system. Everything checked out okay.

The MRO returned F-GTSH to the airline to begin transporting passengers again. But the leading edge was barely attached to the stabilizer.

The probable cause cited by the investigators in France was shockingly similar to what had happened at Continental Express.

> The incident resulted from incomplete and poorly performed maintenance work which was not detected during the ground check before approval for return to service. Thus, the progressive disappearance of the attaching screws was not noticed during the nineteen days of operation, which preceded the incident.[4]

Two unusually similar repair snafus involving Brasilia airplanes were enough to cause the FAA to inspect the maintenance and overhaul facilities of all airlines. Flight 2574 turned into a poster child for bringing attention to a declining safety culture at the nation's airlines.

Prompted by this and a series of other dangerous oversights, a suspected lack of corporate culture committed to safety moved to the forefront as the exclusive topic at the U.S. National Summit on Transportation Safety hosted by the NTSB in 1997. The move to improve air safety intensified on April 5, 2000, with the enactment of the Wendell H. Ford Aviation Investment and Reform Act for the Twenty-First Century, popularly known as AIR 21.[5]

As a law, AIR 21 mandated several changes to enhance aviation safety. One of them makes it unlawful to manufacture, distribute, or sell aircraft parts that are not FAA-approved. The sale and trade of bogus parts had long plagued the aircraft industry. Another provision involves closing a potential loophole in prosecuting criminal cases involving the transport of hazardous materials by air. The ValuJet disaster was the impetus for initiating this. But the part of the law of most interest to accident investigators involves providing whistleblower protection for airline employees. It calls for notifying authorities about employers who violate federal laws related to safety. In the past, few employees spoke up, believing they would be fired from their jobs.

Unfortunately, law or no law, many mechanics still face a hostile environment on the job. They are charged with keeping an airline's planes in the air, but it's the organizational environment they function in that determines their effectiveness. Executives set the strategic direction and tone at a company while shift supervisors delegate tasks to mechanics with the proviso that they adhere to an established culture—hopefully one emphasizing safety. That's how it's supposed to work.

In Texas, in France, and elsewhere, it is compliance with a safety-first culture that determines whether passengers arrive at their destinations alive.

Note: Many of the details presented in this chapter, such as dates, places, descriptions of events, conclusions, and quotes (unless otherwise attributed), were derived from National Transportation Safety Board, "Aircraft Accident Report, Britt Airways, Inc., d/b/a Continental Express Flight 2574, In-Flight Structural Breakup EMB-120RT, N33701 Eagle Lake, Texas, September 11, 1991, NTSB Identification AAR-92/04."

LOOSE NUTS

The accidents discussed in this book could be considered handpicked and not representative of aviation's overall safety record. The fact is that most people never hear about accidents caused by missing hardware and other small parts. No flying machine can function without them. And no aircraft is immune to becoming a victim of maintenance negligence. Such events occur with regularity, whether it's a sightseeing helicopter, a two-seat Piper Cub, or a 335-seat Boeing 787 Dreamliner.

Airliner accidents that result in fatalities become front-page news. Less prominent is a segment of aviation that seldom garners much publicity. It has to do with accidents involving the nation's enormous fleet of general aviation (GA) aircraft. The term "general aviation" encompasses a wide range of fixed- and rotary-wing aircraft—essentially everything other than the planes flown by scheduled airlines. The United States has more than twice as many GA aircraft as all other nations *combined*.

Excluding the recent MAX 8 accidents, the crash rate of scheduled airlines in the United States has fallen to near zero over the last decade, but the rate for GA aircraft remains the same as fifteen years ago. It is roughly *forty times higher* than at the airlines.[1] Accidents continue to kill thousands of private pilots, along with law enforcement and medical personnel, agricultural pilots, and executives flying aboard multi-million-dollar business jets.

"When you look at aviation, the place where people are getting killed is general aviation," said former NTSB chairwoman Deborah Hersman.[2]

Aircraft manufacturers and their lobbyists persuaded Congress in 1984 to limit injury and death claims caused by aircraft and parts more than eighteen years old. Approximately 75 percent of the 220,000 GA aircraft now registered in the United States, fall into that category.

Although many smaller aircraft were manufactured in the last century, there's a flurry of new aircraft being introduced. The Cirrus Vision SF50 is one of them. The SF50, known as the Vision Jet, is a lightweight airplane designed and produced by Cirrus Aircraft of Duluth, Minnesota. It's designed to be flown by a private pilot. Hardly a Piper Cub, the plane's $2.38 million price tag doesn't interest middle-class people living on a tight budget. A single Williams turbofan engine producing 1,900 pounds of thrust provides the power. What makes the plane unique is that it has only one engine and is built entirely of composite materials. Its success is impressive, the company posting an order backlog for six hundred planes, the first one delivered to a customer in December 2016. In 2018, Cirrus was awarded the prestigious Collier Trophy for the "greatest achievement in aeronautics or astronautics in America" during the preceding year, recognizing the SF50 as the first FAA-certificated single-engine civilian jet.

On April 18, 2019, enthusiasm surrounding the revolutionary plane mellowed. On that day, the FAA grounded all ninety-nine planes that had been delivered to customers in the United States. The reason: three of them had been involved in dangerous incidents between November 2018 and April 2019. The incidents had to do with the aircraft's stall warning and protection system (SWPS) and an electronic stability and protection system (ESP). In the three incidents, the systems moved the flight controls even though the planes were nowhere near a stall, flying with sufficient airspeed, and at a safe AOA. The systems were designed to protect pilots from crashing by shaking the control stick and pushing the stick forward. The plane then diving, the pilot had to quickly grab the stick to restore level flight. There were a few rattled nerves but fortunately no accidents resulted.

Unlike the mystifying events brought on by MCAS on the 737 MAX, it was clear what caused the SF50 to act in this frightening manner. An emergency airworthiness directive issued by the FAA spelled it out.

> Cirrus and Aerosonic [manufacturer of the AOA sensor] have identified the probable root cause as an AOA sensor malfunction due to a quality escape in the assembly of the AOA sensor at Aerosonic. Two set screws that secure the potentiometer shaft to the AOA vane shaft may have improper torqueing and no application of thread locker to secure the two set screws.[3]

The term "quality escape" means a lack of quality control at the sensor manufacturer.

The serious problems with the Cirrus and MAX centered on AOA sensor malfunctions. However, Collins Aerospace manufactured the sensors for the MAX. "The Cirrus ESP system is unrelated to the 737 MAX Maneuvering Characteristics Augmentation System," a representative from the FAA indicated during the height of the MAX crisis. "The ESP assists the pilots, but does not take control and can be overridden with control inputs."[4]

Two small screws installed incorrectly had risked people's lives and brought about the SF50 grounding by the FAA.

Of all the aircraft flying today, helicopters are the most accident-prone. They owe their existence to a unique ability to take off and land vertically. Their rotating wings are driven by a complex system of gears, shafts, and bearings. If a critical nut or bolt holding any of these parts together fails in flight, the result is an instant descent at high vertical speed followed by a "hard" landing or crash.

The number of accidents involving helicopters that fly sightseeing tours in the United States is disproportionately high compared to other segments of commercial aviation. One detailed maintenance safety study documented that improper maintenance was the "cause of malfunction in 32 percent of commercial helicopter crashes in Hawaii occurring between 1984 and 2008."[5] Hawaii has one of the largest fleets of sightseeing helicopters in the country.

On December 7, 2011, a Sundance Helicopters Eurocopter AS350 B2 crashed in the mountains outside Las Vegas, Nevada. The pilot and four passengers were killed and the aircraft destroyed. The helicopter was flying level at 3,500 feet, had climbed to 4,100 feet, turned 90 degrees to the left and slowed. It then plunged toward the ground as rapidly as 2,500 feet per minute. The wreckage of the helicopter was found in a ravine about fourteen miles east of Las Vegas. The NTSB's probable cause:

Inadequate maintenance of the helicopter, including the improper reuse of a degraded self-locking nut, the improper or lack of installation of a split pin and inadequate post-maintenance inspections, which resulted in the in-flight separation of the servo control input rod from the fore/aft servo and rendered the helicopter uncontrollable.

Adding her own comments, Deborah Hersman, former NTSB chairwoman said, "Inserting a small pin, smaller than a paper clip, and just one small step in a routine maintenance procedure was the necessary action; the omission of this action was the difference between an uneventful flight and tragedy."[6]

On June 27, 2017, a Eurocopter EC 130 B4 sightseeing helicopter, also operating out of Las Vegas, lost all engine power and made an emergency landing in mountainous terrain near Boulder City, Nevada. There were seven people aboard, and two of them suffered minor injuries. The tourist flight had been scheduled to take them over the Grand Canyon.

The helicopter's engine had failed because a mechanic working at its manufacturer had forgotten to reinstall the oil filter. The helicopter flew for 110 hours without the filter installed before its turboshaft engine finally seized from lack of lubrication. It was amazing that the engine ran for so long.

The NTSB's probable cause offered the technical details.

> A loss of engine power due to the failure of the manufacturer to reinstall the oil filter after it was removed for inspection, which led to coke pollution that obstructed the oil jet and resulted in the subsequent oil starvation of the axial compressor rear bearing oil and its subsequent failure.[7]

Near Rockville, Idaho, on May 26, 2017, a month before the June 27 accident in Nevada, the flight of a Bell 206B helicopter, modified to spray agricultural fields, came to an abrupt halt. Its engine failed while the helicopter was 50 feet above the ground. The pilot attempted a power-off autorotation, but the helicopter landed hard in a marshy field. The investigation pinpointed a crack in a driveshaft coupling that transferred power from the helicopter's engine to the transmission driving the rotor. A loose bolt whose washer had worn a depression in the coupling's outer surface was the root cause. Overstressed, the coupling had failed. The NTSB determined the probable cause of the accident was "the in-flight failure of the engine-to-transmission drive shaft due to a fatigue fracture of one of the KAflex flex frames caused by a loose bolt, which resulted in a total lose of engine power and a subsequent hard landing."[8]

On March 22, 2015, a Robinson R44 crashed after its pilot lost control of the four-seat, piston-powered helicopter. The pilot was killed and his two passengers injured. NTSB investigators determined the probable cause: "An inflight loss of control due to the likely detachment of the forward left servo control tube upper rod end attachment bolt." The helicopter came to rest on the top floor of a house about three miles northwest of Orlando, Florida. The mechanic who had performed the most recent maintenance on the helicopter's flight control system didn't complete the work. The chief mechanic was then called in to finish it. But the chief mechanic didn't make any entries in the aircraft's logbook because he "forgot." Because the missing bolt was not found, the reason why it was missing could not be conclusively determined. However, it was obvious that neither a nut nor a cotter pin had been installed to secure it.[9]

Helicopters aren't the only GA aircraft prone to maintenance mistakes. On February 13, 2008, a Piper PA-23-250 Aztec, a popular twin-engine airplane often used to transport businesspeople, crashed near Sterling, Kansas, killing the pilot, the sole occupant. The five-seat, piston-powered plane was in cruise flight at 6,000 feet when it suddenly entered an uncontrolled descent and slammed into the ground. It cartwheeled, hit a cow, and scattered debris over a distance of 668 feet. NTSB investigators discovered that the plane's stabilator trim pushrod was not attached. The nut and cotter pin used to secure it to a trim tab were missing. There was an indication that its securing nut had loosened during the flight. Disassembly of the pushrod showed elongation of its attach hole, confirming the maintenance oversight. [This looks Similar to Par 10 wayner A

GA aircraft suffer the vast majority of maintenance-caused accidents, but as we've seen, the scheduled airlines contribute their share. On August 27, 1990, a United Airlines Boeing 747-422 made a wheels-up landing at Los Angeles International Airport after completing a thirteen-hour flight from Australia. There were 323 passengers and a crew of 10 aboard. The pilots had noticed that a warning light for the nose and main body landing gear assemblies indicated that the wheels remained up and locked. The plane had to be landed with the landing gear retracted. Two-dozen passengers suffered minor injuries while exiting on emergency evacuation slides. Examination of the plane revealed that a bolt was missing that connected the arm of a hydraulic valve to the cockpit control that actuated the gear system. Another bolt was found partially screwed out with its nut and cotter pin missing. The plane was eight months old, and United Airlines had no responsibility for the accident, Boeing, as its manufacturer, took the blame. The NTSB's probable cause: "The failure of the manufacturer (Boeing) to ensure that the landing gear selector valves and their associated drum link assemblies were properly installed prior to delivery of the aircraft."[11]

United Airlines doesn't have a monopoly on accidents, but thirty-six years before the wheels-up landing of the 747 at Los Angeles International, another of its planes made a wheels-up landing, again with no fatalities. On January 19, 1955, a twin-engine, piston-powered Convair 340 operated by United made an emergency landing on a snow-covered cornfield six miles southeast of Dexter, Iowa. The airliner had experienced severe vibration, accompanied by a loss of elevator control. Almost stalling, the pilot was able to force the nose down into a steep dive and flare the plane for a landing before striking the ground in a flat attitude. The thirty-six passengers and crew of three were evacuated without injuries. "The vibration backed off a nut in the servo tab system that had been installed without a cotter pin securing it. This resulted in a sequence of failures that ended in almost complete loss of control of the aircraft elevators," the CAB accident investigation report said.

> The Board determines that the probable cause of this accident was a series of omissions made by maintenance personnel doing a scheduled inspection which resulted in the release of the aircraft in an unairworthy condition and an almost complete loss of elevator control during flight.[12]

Forty years later, on October 13, 1995, an Airborne Express McDonnell Douglas DC-9-31 was cruising at 13,000 feet when its pilots heard a loud bang. The plane began to shudder, and the pilots descended to make an emergency landing at Cedar Rapids, Iowa. During the landing roll, the engine thrust reversers were activated, but the left one failed to deploy. Later examination revealed that erratic movement of the reverser's top door had repeatedly struck the lower door, causing it to break. A closer look revealed that a bolt, washer, castellated nut, and cotter pin were missing. It appeared that they had never been installed.[13]

Airlines operating in other countries have their share of accidents as well. On March 13, 2007, an All Nippon Airways de Havilland Canada DHC-8-402Q Dash 8 crash-landed at Kochi Airport in Japan after a flight from Osaka-Itami Airport. As the pilots approached the airport, the plane's nose landing gear would not extend. After trying several techniques to lower it, all unsuccessful, the pilots made a landing with the nose gear retracted. There were fifty-six passengers and four crewmembers aboard. No injuries were reported. The doors for the nose gear were found in a closed position. An investigation determined that a spacer had migrated out of a hinge in the door linkage mechanism and had interfered with the airframe, preventing the door from functioning. The spacer came out because a bolt and its nut had not been installed. It was a near-new aircraft. The responsibility for the mistake fell on the manufacturer, not the airline.[14]

On January 31, 2005, a Danish Air Transport European-built ATR 42-320 crashed at Bergen-Flesland Airport in Norway. The plane was on a scheduled flight. During takeoff, the pilots encountered control problems with the elevator. There were twenty-two passengers and three crewmembers aboard, but no injuries were reported. The high-wing, twin-engine, turboprop-powered airliner was manufactured in 1986. The problem began when one of three hinge bolts attaching the right-hand elevator to the horizontal stabilizer loosened and separated. Because the center bolt had fallen out some time earlier without being discovered, the elevator was left hanging in place with only one remaining hinge.

The self-locking nuts holding the center and outboard hinge bolts in place had not been tightened to the required torque value, the investigators determined.[15]

No airliner, business jet, helicopter, or private plane is immune to ending up the victim of an accident. But it's unusual when an expensive, supposedly well-maintained racing plane crashes due to a couple of loose screws. On September 16, 2011, a horrific accident occurred at the National Championship Air Races in Reno, Nevada. A highly modified North American P-51D named *The Galloping Ghost* was flying the third lap of a race at over 500 mph when it abruptly pitched up, rolled inverted, and smashed into the ground in front of the grandstands. The pilot was killed along with ten spectators. Another sixty-nine people were injured. It was the deadliest air show disaster in U.S. history. Worn locknuts retaining screws that held an elevator trim tab had failed. The NTSB noted,

> The probable cause of this accident was the reduced stiffness of the elevator trim tab system that allowed aerodynamic flutter to occur at racing speeds. . . . The reduced stiffness was a result of deteriorated locknut inserts that allowed the trim tab attachment screws to become loose.[16]

As a final example, although the military services in the United States are reported to be exemplary in maintaining high-performance jets, mistakes still creep in. Take the case of what happened on September 14, 1997, when a U.S. Air Force Lockheed F-117A lost a wing during an air show near Baltimore, Maryland. According to witnesses, the plane's wing began to vibrate "like a flag whipped up by the wind" as the jet flew past a crowd of spectators. The wing then snapped off from the fuselage, the pilot ejecting safely. The $42-million plane crashed and burst into flames. No one on the ground was hurt, but a house was destroyed and several others damaged. An investigation disclosed that only one of five 1-inch fasteners that secured the wing had been reinstalled following repair work.[17]

Whether it's AOA sensors failing, nuts unscrewing from bolts, or other hardware missing, maintenance-related accidents continue to haunt the worlds of both civil and military aviation.

12

OUTSOURCED

The nation's airline industry has been profitable for ten years. Through deep fare cuts, continuous Internet marketing, and a never-ending demand from travelers, the carriers have conquered the boom-and-bust cycles that have affected them since the Great Recession. Airline CEOs are satisfied. But are their passengers?

The International Air Transport Association reports that airlines based in North America will post a $15 billion net profit in 2019. Up $500 million from 2018, that translates into a net profit of $14.77 per passenger. Seven years ago, the number was a paltry $2.30.

Investors who stuck it out owning airline stocks have done well. And most passengers are satisfied paying rock-bottom fares to fly wherever they want. What they hate are uncomfortable seats, crowded and dirty planes, and inattentive customer service. Take seating. The average width of seats has shrunk from 18 inches before airline deregulation to approximately 16.5 today. Even worse, the average amount of legroom between the rows of seats has dropped from 35 inches to about 31. In a nation with increased obesity, minimizing seat sizes is the wrong way to go for health and safety reasons. But installing miniscule seats is a simple way to boost profits.

As profits increase, it doesn't seem right that passenger comfort, health, and safety decline. A perennial quest to make ever more money causes airline CEOs to squeeze as many bodies as possible into their stretched aluminum tubes. The industry's unwillingness to widen seats and increase their spacing traps people in a stiff position for hours on end. Their fate has been compared to that of sardines sealed in a can.

While air carriers continue to profit from stuffing in passengers, they may end up paying in another way. The cramped, claustrophobic environment brings on leg cramps—and something more sinister. The hours of discontent spent aloft or stuck on the ground taxes the patience of passengers, causing some of them to overreact to small annoyances. The media regularly reports on drama escalating from such incidents.

In 2018, after years of prodding by consumer groups, Congress passed the Safe Egress in Air Travel (SEAT) Act to demand that the airlines provide a minimum width and distance between seats. The FAA has been charged with determining those dimensions and enforcing their implementation. Beside comfort, the rationale is to ensure that passengers can quickly evacuate a plane in the event of a crash.

Some of what passengers experience today can be traced to deregulation of the nation's airlines in 1978. Recognizing that event's fiftieth anniversary in 2018, Transportation Secretary Elaine Chao referred to deregulation as a "seminal event" that "democratized air travel for consumers." She noted that the average airfare is 42 percent lower today than it was in 1980. There are 27,000 flights taking off each day, carrying 2.3 million passengers. Chao went on to say that the demand for air travel "is exploding" and will double in the next twenty years.[1] She did not address the question of how enough employees will be found to fly and maintain the number of planes needed to handle the growth. Incoming president Donald Trump nominated Chao, former secretary of labor in the George W. Bush administration and wife of Senator Mitch McConnell, to head the Transportation Department. It has been during her tenure as secretary that the MAX crisis erupted and now awaits final resolution.

Beside a reasonable level of comfort, another concern of those who fly frequently is maintenance outsourcing. It may be a topic of little interest to most of the public, but it's a serious concern of consumer protection groups and politicians. The word itself conveys bad connotations to travelers, particularly those flying regularly for business. They may have read newspaper or magazine articles detailing how mechanical failures have occurred because airlines contract their maintenance to repair facilities in Central America or Asia. However, at Allegiant Air and Emery Worldwide, the opposite was true. The deficient work had been performed in Oklahoma and Tennessee.

The outsourcing of jobs to other countries has ignited a tinderbox of worry, especially among the thousands of FAA-licensed mechanics in the United States. Many of them have lost their jobs or fear they will in the future. They cite a lack of licensed personnel at foreign operations, poor supervision, lax security, no drug testing, sloppy work, erratic inspection, and the use of unapproved parts. They believe that such dangers will result in a chain of fatal accidents, sooner rather than later.

Outsourcing continues to persist as a political topic, its origin dating to the 2004 presidential election. At the time, a prolonged debate ensued about the effect of outsourcing on the nation's workforce. Corporations didn't view it as an issue, but Democratic candidate Senator John Kerry sharply criticized companies that outsourced jobs.[2] Today, a tremendous number of blue- and white-collar jobs previously filled by workers in the United States have moved to other countries—at a fraction of the cost of employing them stateside.

There is a considerable number of people who think the government should step in to impose restrictions on companies that routinely export jobs. Unionized employees consider outsourcing to be "union busting," causing them to lose bargaining power and making it easier for corporations to fire workers and ship their jobs elsewhere.

Not only have maintenance management philosophies changed over the years, but the kinds of planes the airlines buy and fly are different too. To gauge the current state of America's participation in building airliners, an imaginative visit to an airport of sixty years ago is in order. The airport ramp would be crowded with airliners built by Lockheed, Douglas, Boeing, Fairchild, Martin, and Convair. With the exception of Boeing, *none* of these American companies still produce commercial aircraft. Other than the planes built by Boeing, the only ones seen at airport gates today are made in Canada, France, Brazil, and soon Japan. U.S. airliner manufacturers other than Boeing are no longer in business or have merged with larger companies. For years, the airlines in the United States have "outsourced" airliner manufacturing to other countries. The same transition took place within the automotive industry in the 1970s. Inroads made by Honda, Toyota, Volkswagen, BMW, and other carmakers shifted production from America to foreign soil.

Next to automobiles, nowhere is globalization more evident than in commercial airliner manufacturing. The extent of this transition became evident when regional airliners were developed in the 1980s. Bombardier in Canada introduced the CRJ series, while Embraer in Brazil competed with its E-Jet series. On a larger scale, Airbus SE in Europe has nicked away at Boeing's market share for over a quarter-century after introducing its A320 series of jetliners.

In July 2018, Boeing announced a joint venture with Embraer. Boeing would own 80 percent of a newly formed company to manufacture Embraer's regional jets, the Brazilian plane maker retaining 20 percent. It cost Boeing $4.2 billion to close the deal, with government anti-trust approval expected by the end of

2019. Boeing wants to level the playing field with Airbus and that company's new A220 regional jet. The pattern of aircraft industry consolidation continues.

Soon after his election in 2016, President Trump visited Boeing's factory in North Charleston, South Carolina, where the latest version of Boeing's 787 Dreamliner was unveiled. During the visit, he praised Boeing and its employees, vowing to protect the nation's manufacturing jobs. "We want products made by our workers, in our factories, stamped with those four magnificent words: Made in the USA," Trump said during a speech there.[3]

It sounds simple, but it isn't. Although the 787 is assembled in the United States, its thousands of component parts are manufactured in dozens of other countries—the result of globalization. A principal reason for such "outsourcing" is that 70 percent of Boeing's customers happen to be airlines based in foreign countries. Offering economic opportunities to those nations makes sense. In today's integrated world economy, it's how business is done. Government intervention with the intent to modify carefully crafted trade agreements can prove destabilizing, particularly for the aviation industry.

If at some point in the future Boeing decides to exit the commercial aviation side of its business, as Lockheed did in the 1980s, the United States will be left with *no* manufacturer of commercial airliners.

The September 11, 2001, terrorist attacks transformed how the airlines operate their businesses along with the way their vendors supply planes, parts, and services. Owing to sharply reduced air travel following the attacks, every major airline in the nation slid into bankruptcy during the early 2000s. To survive, their CEOs felt it necessary to slash legacy costs, meaning employee salaries, benefits, and pensions. Pilots, flight attendants, and mechanics lucky enough to still be employed watched their compensation shrink up to 40 percent. Coping with a lackluster economy, the airlines found ways to survive and eventually prosper by taking a "lean and mean" approach to management.

Many other jobs disappeared when the major airlines contracted with regional carriers to provide less-expensive lift using fifty-seat regional jets. It's called "code sharing." To casual observers, the planes may appear to be "United" or "American" but they are flown by smaller airlines that few people have heard of.

There is little financial incentive for the airlines to change how they operate. Maintenance is not generally a profit center so they continue to reduce the ranks of licensed mechanics, shut down overhaul bases in the United States, and outsource more heavy maintenance to low-cost MROs. Doing so cuts costs in half or more and keeps shareholders happy by guaranteeing them large dividends.

There's plenty of research to justify why outsourcing, if carefully controlled and monitored, can benefit both the airlines and their passengers. The undisputed payoff for airlines is that they make more money. For passengers, an airline's ability to offer cheap fares by reducing operating costs is more than welcome. But if the airline-MRO relationship is handled in a slipshod manner and poorly monitored by the airline and the FAA, a breakdown in safety occurs.

As an example, the FAA's inspection of foreign repair facilities is sporadic. All mechanics in the United States are tested for substance abuse; at repair shops in other countries, they're not. The FAA doesn't make unannounced visits at those shops either. It never visits the vast majority of them. When errors affecting flight safety occur, it can't subpoena the records of a shop in another country as it can in the United States. And it can't revoke the license of careless mechanics there because the FAA doesn't license them. If there's criminal activity, it's unable to demand that the suspects be apprehended. There's no provision to slap civil penalties on workers or the shop owners. Because the workers aren't subject to background checks, the Transportation Security Administration has no authority over the workforce to prevent security lapses that could result in terrorist activity.

Passengers crowding into today's airliners have no idea where the planes they are boarding are maintained. All established airlines outsource some work regularly. They use FAA-approved MROs wherever they may be located. It doesn't matter to them where the work is performed, provided that its cost and the MRO's reputation for quality are acceptable to the airline.

There's been no lack of bad press concerning outsourcing. In January 2003, US Airways Express Flight 5481 crashed shortly after takeoff from Charlotte, North Carolina. All twenty-one people aboard were killed. Part of the responsibility for the accident was placed on an inexperienced MRO mechanic who assembled the flight controls incorrectly. The MRO was located in the United States.[4]

In 2005, the Immigration and Customs Enforcement agency arrested twenty-seven illegal immigrants working for Triad International Maintenance Corporation (TIMCO) in Greensboro, North Carolina, one of the nation's largest MROs. None of the workers, immigrants from Central and South America, Sudan, and the Philippines, had terrorist ties but the incident raised concerns about the hiring practices of MROs operating in the United States. Two of the former TIMCO employees were sentenced in U.S. District Court on charges related to document falsification. They had fake FAA mechanic licenses. "Having those with fraudulent identity documents working on or near critical aviation infrastructure is an unacceptable risk to public safety" noted a June 2005 report

from the Office of Inspector General for the Department of Transportation.[5]
TIMCO happened to be one of Allegiant Air's MROs.

Outsourcing has surged since the beginning of this century, with questions
arising about the experience level and background of mechanics working on
the complex avionic and propulsion systems of jetliners. While some domestic
airlines maintain their planes in places such as El Salvador, other airlines use
MROs located as far away as Hong Kong and Singapore. The repair bases may
be distant, but the costs of the services they dispense make sense to chief financial officers. To save time and fuel, other airlines send their planes to MROs in
the southern states and Midwest where labor costs are lower and unions aren't
much of an issue. While this is happening, longtime mechanics staffing in-house
maintenance facilities at the airlines keep thinning out.

Accusations have surfaced concerning the safety culture at foreign-based facilities, but these ignore problems at MROs in the United States. The problems
plaguing foreign operators such as mechanics having limited English reading
ability, insufficient training, or poor work skills is experienced by some of the
domestic MROs as well.

During June 2018, responding to the growing use of foreign-based MROs by
the nation's airlines, several members of Congress decided to tap the power of
consumerism. Sen. Claire McCaskill (D-MO), Rep. John Garamendi (D-CA),
and Rep. Dan Donovan (R-NY) introduced the Aircraft Maintenance Outsourcing Disclosure Act of 2018 (H.R. 6028 S. 3026).[6] The bipartisan legislation called for the airlines to disclose where the maintenance for a given plane
had been performed. The Transport Workers Union of America endorsed the
bill to protect the jobs of its members and increase their numbers.

In a June 28, 2018, letter sent from Rep. Peter DeFazio (D-OR), Rep. Rick
Larsen (D-WA), and ranking members of the House Committee on Transportation and Infrastructure to Transportation Secretary Chao, immediate action
was requested.

> In reports and Congressional testimony dating back to at least 2003, the In-
> spector General has found deficiency after deficiency in the FAA's oversight
> of foreign repair stations performing maintenance on US airline fleets. . . . The
> only thing consistent about the FAA's oversight of these FAA-certificated facili-
> ties—which number more than 700 abroad—is its inconsistency, leaving far too
> many stones unturned.[7]

Mechanics at the major airlines were steadfast against outsourcing any repair
work, with those at American Airlines among the most vocal in urging passage

of the bill. More support for their cause came after an April 17, 2018, accident involving Southwest Airlines Flight 1380. The Boeing 737NG experienced a catastrophic failure of its left engine. The plane had departed LaGuardia Airport in New York bound for Dallas when, at 31,000 feet over Pennsylvania, a loud noise was heard and the plane began to shudder.

A fatigue crack in a single blade of the engine's fan assembly caused it to separate from the disc that retained it. The defect had gone undetected during previous inspections. Fragments from the engine's inlet and cowling struck the wing and fuselage, breaking a window that caused the cabin to lose pressure. A passenger was partly sucked out a window and died of her injuries. Fortunately, no one else was killed among the other 148 passengers and crew on board. The pilot was proclaimed a hero at a White House ceremony for safely landing the heavily damaged jet.[8]

It was reported that the engine's manufacturer was responsible for maintaining the plane's CFM International CFM56-7BE engines at its MRO in Brazil. Southwest Airlines did not provide heavy maintenance support for the engines.

The accident represented the last straw for the Southwest mechanics' union. The union and the airline's management had been at odds for years. On September 20, 2017, an FAA investigative team had visited Southwest's maintenance facility at Los Angeles International Airport. The visit was in response to a whistleblower complaint filed by several mechanics working there. They cited abusive language, threats, and extreme pressure coming from their supervisors.

Completing the interviews of the complainants and their managers, the FAA offered its opinion.

> There seems to be a lack of an environment of trust, effective communication and the willingness for employees to share mistakes, concerns or failures without the fear of threats or reprisal. This ultimately leads to a degraded level of safety that the SMS (safety program) is trying to maintain at the highest possible level.

Although acknowledging the failures, the FAA did *not* order corrective action. "Evidence of a violation of a regulation, order or standard of the FAA related to air carrier safety is not substantiated," the FAA concluded.[9]

The bill in Congress would have changed the game by advising travelers where the maintenance for a plane is performed *before* they hand over a credit card number to buy a ticket. The bill required the airlines to list on their website the city and country where their planes have undergone their most-recent heavy maintenance check. The information would be passed along to consumers as they shop for flights. Even tickets and boarding passes would include the information.

"I believe travelers should have the right to know whether the planes they're flying on were serviced by qualified aviation mechanics in the United States," said Garamendi, "or whether maintenance was outsourced to foreign countries with lower labor, technical, and safety standards. . . . This legislation empowers consumers, prioritizes transparency and also offers an opportunity to bring back good-paying manufacturing jobs."[10]

In a rare show of bipartisanship, Donovan commented:

"No one should ever get onto a plane unsure of whether or not the aircraft they are boarding has met proper safety standards. Unfortunately, airlines have increasingly outsourced their maintenance practices to overseas facilities, which are not held to the same standards and oversight as U.S. repair shops. This bill is a strong step forward in protecting consumers, strengthening job opportunities for American workers, and creating much needed transparency."[11]

The urgency surrounding outsourcing issues caused the president of a major labor union to join the legislators in asking for a change. "The American public deserves truth when flying," said John Samuelsen, president of the Transport Workers of America.

When deciding which airline to fly or which flight to buy, it shouldn't be a privilege to know where airlines are maintaining their aircraft. This legislation allows the flying public to make informed purchasing decisions, while supporting regulators' efforts to ensure all aircraft maintenance work is held to a uniform high standard of safety and security. . . . When airlines offshore this work, they eliminate the jobs of qualified workers who comply with strict FAA and TSA regulations. . . . American families fly on these planes, and our families simply deserve better. The thousands of highly skilled American aviation mechanics who have been competing on this uneven playing field deserve better—and the working communities that are built on solid, blue-collar jobs like these deserve better.[12]

McCaskill appreciated the support of both her colleagues and the union:

Before someone buys a ticket or boards their flight, they ought to know when and where that plane was last serviced—and whether it was done here in this country by the finest mechanics in the world, or done abroad by foreign workers. . . . This is a commonsense step to give consumers some peace of mind.[13]

It was logical that the Aircraft Mechanics Fraternal Association would join the Transport Workers of America in supporting the bill. "Much of the safety-sensitive maintenance at foreign repair stations are performed by unlicensed workers who lack the knowledge, training, or ability to grasp the English language," noted a news release from the union. "AMFA has worked for years to combat outsourcing."[14]

As expected, lobbyists retained by the major airlines were busy during the fall of 2018, diverting the attention of lawmakers away from the bill. Their biggest argument for killing it had to do with consumers being expected to pay higher ticket prices due to a jump in maintenance costs brought on by pulling the work back from other countries and having to pay union-scale wages.

On Capitol Hill, forcing constituents to pay more for anything is generally considered political suicide. "Safety" is an intangible concept for most people, but higher prices for tickets would hit them in the wallet—and cost votes for their elected representatives. The 2018 bill failed to garner support and was supplanted in 2019 by the Safe Aircraft Maintenance Standards Act. It awaits full House approval.

Not surprisingly, the major airlines outsource more than maintenance. As noted, they outsource the manufacturing of their planes to other countries. They also contract with little-known carriers for planes and crews to fly their shorter routes via code sharing while making it appear to passengers that these flights are operated by a major airline.

Passengers are more concerned about the width of their seat than a cotter pin that could be missing in the tail of a plane. Few owners of cars will check the tread depth of a tire or peer under a hood to search for oil leaks. The same holds true for people traveling by air. They trust an airline's management and the FAA to protect them from mechanical failures.

The FAA has a colossal responsibility to ensure both the safety of passengers and the economic vitality of the nation's airlines. In many ways, these two responsibilities have spread the agency's resources too thin. Consider TWA Flight 529, when the FAA sided with the airlines and didn't recommend modifying the elevator boost shift mechanism of Constellations. It was fortunate that a similar accident didn't happen before the planes were retired. When it came to Allegiant Air's rejected takeoff and shoddy work at AAR, the FAA didn't discipline either of the companies. The Emery Worldwide DC-8 fiasco served as another example of an airline's license not being revoked. As for the renegade work culture at Continental Express, it went unchecked until a fatal crash put the FAA in the spotlight for its lack of oversight. These and other incidents point to a laissez-faire approach to monitoring the airlines and the hundreds of MROs operating in the United States and abroad.

Ultimately, it's all about money. The FAA's budget is strained, airlines continue to shave costs and pyramid profits, and waves of economy-minded passengers pursue the cheapest possible fares.

Maintenance chiefs at airlines and MROs relish the current FAA regulatory environment. They are empowered, in essence, to police their own maintenance facilities. FAA inspectors remain in the background. When it comes to labor-intensive heavy maintenance checks, the contracted MROs handle everything. Much as the FAA does, the airlines function as lesser participants in the process.[15]

In a world facing a shortage of licensed mechanics and an increased volume of business showing no sign of diminishing, MROs must employ thousands of mechanics to replace the mechanics who leave. Some are FAA-licensed; most are not. Workers move from one MRO to another as layoffs occur or when they can earn a higher wage working somewhere across town.

The FAA has argued that it doesn't have enough money to oversee at least seven hundred MROs operating in dozens of foreign countries. It allows the airlines to watch over their own heavy maintenance at those locations. The airlines assume responsibility for making sure that the repair work is done correctly. Similar to filing tax returns, it's an honor-based system.

As the FAA says when discussing its Compliance Philosophy program, "the FAA will not use enforcement as the first tool in the toolbox."[16]

The Office of Inspector General for the Department of Transportation has repeatedly called on the FAA to provide more stringent reporting from foreign MROs. Siding with members of Congress, the inspector general believes that the traveling public should be made aware of where the repair work on a given plane is performed. In 2003, it asked the FAA to require drug testing of workers at all foreign-based MROs as a condition of a facility's FAA certification.[17] Seventeen years later, the FAA has not expanded the testing. Apparently, expansion can't be accomplished without a sizable boost in the agency's budget.

Drug abuse decreased among aircraft mechanics in the United States after the FAA mandated a drug-testing program in 1991. Previously, drug usage in the aviation industry was in sync with that of the general population. Among the violators, substance abuse caused a variety of mistakes in maintenance and inspection work. Rivets weren't installed properly, wires and piping were incorrectly connected, and inspectors "pencil-whipped" items as completed when they weren't.

Each day, in hangars or on airport ramps around the world, mechanics are interrupted or distracted while working. It may result when someone walks over to ask for help. Perhaps a supervisor needs a mechanic to sign a piece of paper.

Or a fellow mechanic might stop by to borrow a tool. These short interruptions are commonplace and can lead to serious errors.

Maintenance errors rank as one of the top three causes of aircraft accidents. The reasons are many: lack of clear work processes; carelessness or poor decisions made by mechanics or inspectors; *and* a questionable corporate culture at the airlines and their MROs. Toxic work environments cause mechanics to lose motivation and suffer increased stress. They bring on fatigue as the result of excessive time pressure, rotating work shifts, too much overtime, and a misunderstanding of how a seemingly minor mechanical defect can end up becoming the initiator of a catastrophe.

Life as an aircraft mechanic isn't easy. A consummate interest in working around airplanes is what keeps many of them on the job. Unlike medical professionals, mechanics don't carry malpractice insurance for protection should they be accused of making mistakes. In 1978, the FAA made it a serious violation if a mechanic lied about a repair task by falsifying a logbook entry or signing a fraudulent maintenance release. If a mechanic says that a task has been completed and the FAA finds out it wasn't, this can mean losing FAA licensure and not working in the aviation industry again. An employee's airline can face fines up to $250,000 per violation and forfeit its FAA certification. Compared to those of the past, these are stiff penalties. The mechanic is often penalized more than his or her employer.

Mechanics accused of negligence can end up in court as defendants in a lawsuit. Tort law doesn't require proving that a mechanic has violated FAA regulations. To find a worker negligent, jurors only need to determine that a mechanic "failed to exercise such care as would be reasonably expected of a prudent person under similar circumstances."[18] If it's reasonable to conclude that the mechanic was negligent, the plaintiff wins. If fatalities are involved, the award determined by a jury can run into tens of millions of dollars.

The possibility of being fired or sued causes mechanics to be hesitant in discussing errors. Losing hard-earned FAA certification and a coveted aviation career is enough for them to exercise extreme caution by double-checking each maintenance step. To their credit, the majority of them do. But if something goes terribly wrong in spite of such attention, their defense in court may be something like "I don't remember."

There's a seldom-discussed national emergency firming up: a severe lack of mechanics to ensure that the thousands of new jetliners being delivered will be properly maintained. Many seasoned mechanics are being forced to retire or pursue different careers. This has created thousands of positions to fill with not enough applicants. Schools offering mechanic training are fewer than in the past. Worse, there's not much interest in an aircraft mechanic career on the part of students. Bringing mechanic jobs back to the United States from other countries won't help unless the nation acknowledges its role in training and nurturing young people to prepare for these essential occupations.

It's easy for politicians to suggest that schooling mechanics for FAA licenses or moving skilled worker jobs back to the United States from foreign MROs is a simple matter. The problem is to find enough qualified mechanics. Given a choice of blue-collar jobs, young Americans might opt for an interesting aviation career. The roadblock is that many of them lack the necessary aptitude, focus, and drive. Aircraft technicians need a high level of mechanical ability coupled with excellent critical thinking skills.

The FAA reauthorization bill passed in October 2018 included a $5 million grant program to help alleviate the mechanic shortage. It encourages recruitment and partly subsidizes training programs at trade schools. The Aeronautical Repair Station Association (ARSA) welcomed passage of the bill.

"We're extremely proud the bill includes the aviation maintenance technician grant program championed by an ARSA-led coalition of more that thirty-five aviation organizations," said Christian Klein, executive vice president of the association. "The bill's workforce title also includes important reforms to improve mechanic training and other initiatives to encourage more Americans to pursue aviation careers."[19]

For decades, the military services in the United States have faced a shortage of qualified personnel to maintain aircraft. The problem became acute for the U.S. Army when it transitioned to flying technically sophisticated attack and transport aircraft. When the Army's AH-64 attack helicopter was developed in the late 1970s, the reading ability of the average soldier was extremely low. Army planners mandated that a soldier having no better than a middle school reading ability be able to comprehend every step in technical manuals in order to maintain the aircraft. "Dumbing down" the manuals to feature more illustrations and less text became the solution.[20] Today, the military's concerns aren't as critical, but another dilemma has emerged: finding enough capable people to fill a multitude of vacant mechanic slots. The airlines and their MROs are stuck with the same recruiting shortfall.

In the United States during the next twenty years, it's estimated that 189,000 additional mechanics will be needed to maintain the nation's fleet of aircraft. Approximately 30 percent of the existing mechanic workforce is approaching retirement. But only 2 percent of that workforce is being replaced by newly hired mechanics.[21]

There's another aspect often overlooked. It's the creation of well-equipped maintenance facilities staffed by capable mechanics having a desire to move along a career path and not remain in relatively low-paying positions. In contrast to the galloping technology associated with the computer and automotive industries, the fascination that drew people into aviation a half-century ago has largely dissipated. Salaries, benefits, and job satisfaction rank higher in other industries, compared to the unstable work environment existing at airlines and MROs.

In 2017, the Aviation Technician Education Council reported that 20 percent of the students graduating from aircraft maintenance trade schools pursued a career in fields *other* than aviation.[22] This means that thousands of newly minted FAA-licensed technicians are choosing to work in industries such as automotive and high technology. It's reported that some of them maintain high-tech rides at amusement parks such as Disneyland. They have the technical skills, and although they would prefer to work around airplanes, many of them cite the industry's obsession with outsourcing and relentless cost cutting as a reason to stay away from the allure of aviation.

Aviation makes a vital contribution to America's prosperity. According to the FAA, it accounts for more than 5 percent of the nation's gross domestic product, providing $1.6 trillion in total economic activity and supporting 11 million jobs.[23] At the top of the job pyramid are corporate CEOs. Near the bottom of the pay scale are the aircraft mechanics who make the economic engine thrive. Without the men and women in the hangars, no airplanes would be flying. Despite the obvious need for safety to take precedence over profitability, mechanics are told to skip steps or perform only specific tasks assigned to them and ignore other issues.[24] They fear retribution or termination if they don't comply.

Preventing endless cycles of maintenance errors, with their origins rooted in a systemic way of doing business, calls for an unwavering commitment to a safety-first culture. This means spending money and time for training and monitoring. It's an annoying request for profit-driven CEOs, but considering that one fatal accident can reduce a corporation's reputation in the marketplace to rubble, it's an expense worth paying. The commitment must encompass every aspect of an airline's maintenance operations, large or small. Importantly, the same set of values must govern safety practices at its MROs, whether located in the United States or another country.

Above all, the FAA must ensure that this commitment is firmly institutionalized and in place every year. It must make certain that the private sector's commitment to safety, which the agency oversees and regulates, is never compromised.

It is not my intent to demonize the FAA in its efforts to enhance and enforce safe maintenance practices. But with Allegiant Air Flight 436 in 2015, Emery

Worldwide Flight 17 in 2000, Continental Express Flight 2574 in 1991, and today's problems with the MAX 8 at Boeing, a systemic pattern has emerged that's difficult to ignore. For a variety of reasons, it appears that the FAA has taken a back seat to enforcement.

In the eyes of the FAA inspector assigned to investigate Allegiant Air Flight 436, the FAA's Compliance Philosophy program (renamed the Compliance Program in 2018) did not fulfill its responsibility during the investigation of that incident because neither the airline nor its MRO was punished. The agency's current strategic plan provides for a continuance of this philosophy and does not offer stringent enforcement with "teeth" in it. The plan uses the word "voluntary" six times in two consecutive pages.[25]

"If you've made an honest mistake, a temporary lapse of judgment, or have let your skills become rusty, you may be able to 'fix' the problem without facing a violation," the FAA indicates in its discussion of enforcement. "However, an airman who indicates that he or she is unwilling or unable to comply, or shows evidence of intentional deviation, reckless or criminal behavior, or other significant safety risk, would be ineligible for a Compliance Action."[26]

It would appear, based on the foregoing, that Allegiant Air, Emery Worldwide, Continental Express, and others should have lost their FAA operating certificates as corporations. They did not. The foibles overseeing the certification of the MAX also come to mind.

A major initiative stated in the FAA Aviation Safety Strategic Plan for the years 2020 through 2024 is to "establish and expand voluntary safety programs." It calls for manufacturers and airlines to provide unprecedented initiative regarding matters of safety, with the FAA providing "regulatory oversight."[27] The plan further states that the outcome will result from "parties sharing an open, trusting culture characterized by a commitment to compliance, self-correction and voluntary disclosure and to operating with a safety-first mindset that enables greater autonomy." Again, the key word throughout is "voluntary."[28]

Safeguarding passengers requires the sustained effort of licensed mechanics and an FAA that truly monitors corporations, along with airline CEOs committed to maintaining a work culture that ranks safety above all else.

(30) 6/20/2022 A

THANK YOU GOD FOR KEEPING ME SAFE DURING MY FLYING CARRIER

NOTES

CHAPTER 1

1. Within a decade of the introduction of the first generation of jet transports, aircraft manufacturers began "stretching" the length of their fuselages to accommodate ever more passengers. The MAX series is an example of that philosophy.

2. LEAP is an abbreviation for Leading Edge Aviation Propulsion. CFM International, a joint venture of GE Aviation in the United States and Safran Aircraft Engines in France, manufactures the engine. According to CFM, it offers a 15 percent improvement in fuel consumption and emissions compared to CFM engines powering the 737NG.

3. Bjorn Fehrm, "Boeing's Automatic Trim for the 737 MAX Was Not Disclosed to the Pilots," www.leehamnews.com.

4. David Gelles, Natalie Kitroeff, Jack Nicas, and Rebecca R. Ruiz, "Boeing Was 'Go, Go, Go' to Beat Airbus with the 737 Max," *New York Times*, March 23, 2019.

5. Ibid.

6. The yoke is a double-handle control similar to a steering wheel for controlling a plane's pitch and roll.

7. Hannah Beech and Keith Bradsher, "At Doomed Lion Air Flight's Helm, Pilots May Have Been Overwhelmed in Seconds," *Economic Times*, November 8, 2018. Although the Lion Air crew was confronted with a false stall warning, other accidents have occurred when pilots ignored stall warnings. In 2009, Air France Flight 447, an Airbus A330 flying from Rio de Janeiro to Paris, plunged into the Atlantic Ocean during the dark, early morning hours. Ice had obstructed the holes in pitot tubes that fed airspeed signals to the autopilot, causing the autopilot to disconnect. A copilot quickly assumed manual control but for some reason ignored a continuous stall warning and pushed the plane's nose further up rather than down. The big jet, fully stalled, fell into the sea, killing on impact the 228 people aboard (Bureau of Enquiry and Analysis for Civil Aviation

Safety, "Safety Investigation into the Accident on 1 June 2009 to the Airbus A330-203, flight AF447," July 29, 2011).

8. Sean Broderick and Adrian Schofield, "Lion Air Interim Report Highlights Confusion and Dysfunction," *Aviation Week & Space Technology*, November 30, 2018.

9. Sean Broderick, "ALPA: Simulator Time Not Needed to Un-Ground 737 MAX," *Aviation Daily*, May 8, 2019.

10. James Glanz, Mika Grondahl, Allison McCann, and Jeremy White, "What the Lion Air Pilots May Have Needed to Do to Avoid a Crash," *New York Times*, November 16, 2018.

11. Gelles, Kitroeff, Nicas, and Ruiz, "Boeing Was 'Go, Go, Go.'"

12. Jeremy Bogaisky, "Crash of Lion Air 737 MAX Raises Questions about Autopilot and Pilot Skills," *Forbes*, November 8, 2018.

13. Federal Aviation Administration, Emergency Airworthiness Directive (AD) 2018-23-51, November 7, 2018.

14. Peter Robison and Margaret Newkirk, "Boeing Charted Own Safety Course for Years with FAA as Co-pilot," *Bloomberg*, March 23, 2019.

15. Aaron C. Davis and Marina Lopes, "How the FAA Allows Jetmakers to 'Self-Certify' That Planes Meet U.S. Safety Requirements," *Washington Post*, March 15, 2019.

16. Andy Pasztor and Andrew Tangel, "Boeing Withheld Crucial Safety Information on New 737 Models, Experts Say," *Wall Street Journal*, November 12, 2018.

17. Federal Democratic Republic of Ethiopia, Minister of Transport, Aircraft Accident Investigation Bureau, "Aircraft Accident Investigation Preliminary Report, Ethiopian Airlines Group, B737-8 (MAX) Registered ET-AVJ," March 2019.

18. Federal Aviation Administration, "Emergency Order of Prohibition, Operators of Boeing Company Model 737-8 and Boeing Company Model 737-9 Airplanes," March 13, 2019.

19. James E. Hall, "The 737 Max Is Grounded, No Thanks to the F.A.A.," *New York Times*, March 13, 2019.

20. Dominic Gates, "Flawed Analysis, Failed Oversight: How Boeing, FAA Certified the Suspect 737 MAX Flight Control System," *Seattle Times*, March 17, 2019.

21. Ibid.

22. Ibid.

23. Ibid.

24. Beechcraft Owners and Pilots Group, www.beechtalk.com.

25. Davis and Lopes, "How the FAA Allows Jetmakers to 'Self-Certify.'"

26. Robison and Newkirk, "Boeing Charted Own Safety Course."

27. Boeing 737 Max Aircraft Hearing, House Transportation and Infrastructure Aviation Subcommittee, C-SPAN, June 19, 2019, www.c-span.org/video/?461886-1/boeing-737-max-aircraft.

28. National Transportation Safety Board, "Auxiliary Power Unit Battery Fire, Japan Airlines Boeing 787-8, JA829J, Boston, Massachusetts, January 7, 2013, Report NTSB/AIR/14-01," Washington, DC, November 21, 2014.

29. James E. Hall, "A Back Seat for Safety at the F.A.A.," *New York Times*, April 25, 2013.

30. David Gelles, "A Top Executive at Boeing's Troubled South Carolina Plant Is Out," *New York Times*, May 22, 2019.

31. Hall, "A Back Seat for Safety."

32. Samme Chittum, *The Flight 981 Disaster* (Washington, DC: Smithsonian Books, 2017), 32.

33. National Transportation Safety Board, "American Airlines, McDonnell Douglas DC-10-10, N103AA, Near Windsor, Ontario, Canada, June 12, 1972, Aircraft Accident Report NTSB AAR-73-2," Washington, DC, February 28, 1973.

34. Chittum, *The Flight 981 Disaster*, 121.

35. French Secretariat of State for Transport, "Turkish Airlines DC-10 TC-JAV Report on the Accident in the Ermenonville Forest, France on 3 March 1974, Final Report, February 1976."

36. National Transportation Safety Board, "American Airlines, DC-10-10, N110AA, Chicago-O'Hare International Airport, Chicago, Illinois, May 25, 1979, Aircraft Accident Report NTSB-AAR-79-17," Washington, DC, December 21, 1979.

37. Sean Broderick, "Ethiopian MAX Crash Simulator Scenario Stuns Pilots," *Aviation Daily*, May 10, 2019.

38. Ibid.

39. Ibid.

40. Minda Zetlin, "Boeing CEO Says Safety Is Highest Priority: The Company's Pricing Says Something Different," *Inc.*, March 24, 2019.

41. Ibid.

42. Sean Broderick, "Boeing Did Not Fix MAX AOA Warning Issues Found in 2017," *Aviation Daily*, May 5, 2019.

43. Sam Mintz and Brianna Gurciullo, "FAA Faces Loss of Trust as Congress Digs Into Crash Probes," *Politico*, March 26, 2019.

44. Hall, "A Back Seat for Safety."

45. Commercial Airline Safety Hearing, Senate Commerce Subcommittee, C-SPAN, March 27, 2019, www.c-span.org/video/?459047-1/faa-ntsb-officials-testify-airline-safety-wake-boeing-737-crashes.

46. Boeing 737 Max Aircraft Safety Hearing, House Transportation and Infrastructure Aviation Subcommittee, C-SPAN, May 15, 2019, www.c-span.org/video/?460584-1/faa-ntsb-officials-testify-boeing-737-max-aircraft-safety.

47. Boeing 737 MAX Aircraft Hearing, House Transportation and Infrastructure Aviation Subcommittee, C-SPAN, June 19, 2019, www.c-span.org/video/?461886-1/boeing-737-max-aircraft.

48. Nicola Clark, "Jet Order by American Is a Coup for Boeing's Rival," *New York Times*, July 20, 2011.

49. Federal Aviation Administration, "FAA Revokes Repair Station Certificate of Xtra Aerospace of South Florida," October 25, 2019, www.faa.gov/news/press_releases/news_story.cfm?newsId=24314.

CHAPTER 2

1. Allegiant Air uses secondary, less active airports because their landing fees are lower than the fees of airports owned and operated by major cities.

2. According to Allegiant Air, ancillary fees must be paid for checking luggage, carry-on luggage (except something the size of a purse), food and drinks, advance seat assignments, and paying by credit card.

3. Peter Pae, "Allegiant Air's Prudent Ways Help It Soar Amid Slump in Travel," *Los Angeles Times*, May 13, 2009.

4. Allegiant Air planes aren't scheduled like those of other major airlines, whose jets are in the air up to thirteen hours a day, making as many as six to eight takeoffs and landings each day. Allegiant Air's jets fly only a few hours a day. On Tuesdays and Thursdays, much of the fleet is parked.

5. Phil Luciano, "Aborted Takeoff Shakes Peoria Passengers' Allegiance to Allegiant," *Journal Star*, August 31, 2015.

6. In 2015 I witnessed an incident involving an Allegiant Air MD-80 leaving the Monterey, California, airport for Las Vegas. The passengers had boarded and remained seated in the hot plane with both the plane's auxiliary power unit (APU) and airport ground power unit (GPU) inoperative. With no air conditioning, the crew opened the cabin doors and emergency exits over the wings to let in fresh air. A mechanic finally arrived to fix the GPU, and its hose was connected to the plane to bring air into the cabin and start the engines for the long-delayed flight. The passengers had sat inside sweltering for well over an hour.

7. Luciano, "Aborted Takeoff Shakes Peoria Passengers' Allegiance."

8. Allegiant Air did not disclose which pilot served as captain for this flight. Both men were reportedly approved as captains.

9. A small, hand-operated tiller, positioned along the left side of the captain's seat, is a standard feature for steering most airliners on the ground.

10. Luciano, "Aborted Takeoff Shakes Peoria Passengers' Allegiance."

11. Ibid.

12. Ibid.

13. Airline Pilot Central, August 27, 2015, www.airlinepilotforums.com.

14. Ibid.

15. Airline Professionals Association, Teamsters Local Union No. 1224, "Allegiant Air Pilots' Letter to Passengers," April 2015, www.apa1224.org/AllegiantAirPilot Letter.asp.

16. Airline Pilot Central, September 2, 2015, www.airlinepilotforums.com.

17. William R. Levesque, "Allegiant Air Aborts Flight during Takeoff at 138 MPH," *Tampa Bay Times*, August 28, 2015.

18. Airline Pilot Central, August 29, 2015, www.airlinepilotforums.

19. The MD-83 has two separate elevator control surfaces on its tail. The nut secured a hydraulic boost cylinder for moving the left elevator, which would force the

nose of the plane down should it encounter a stall. Because the nut was missing, the elevator pivoted into an unexpected "up" position, forcing the nose to rise while the main landing gear wheels were still on the ground but the jet was moving too slowly to take off safely.

20. By re-engineering the DC-9's Pratt & Whitney JT8D turbofan's noisy compressor and turbine sections, the engine manufacturer developed a new version of the engine called the JT8D-200 series. It offered more thrust with a substantial reduction in noise and fuel consumption.

21. Alan Levin and Mary Schlangenstein, "FAA Zeros In On Unsecured Tail Bolts; Risk Is Catastrophic," *Bloomberg*, October 27, 2015.

CHAPTER 3

1. AAR Aircraft Services, "AAR and Allegiant Commemorate 100th Aircraft Delivery," October 10, 2012.

2. AAR Aircraft Services, www.aarcorp.com/mro/.

3. Nathaniel Lash, William R. Levesque, and Anthony Cormier, "Breakdown at 30,000 Feet," *Tampa Bay Times*, November 2, 2016.

4. National Transportation Safety Board, "Aircraft Accident Report, Loss of Control and Impact with Pacific Ocean, Alaska Airlines Flight 261, McDonnell Douglas MD-83, N963AS, about 2.7 Miles North of Anacapa Island, California, January 31, 2000, NTSB Identification AAR-02-01," Washington, DC.

5. Associated Press, "FAA Investigates Safety Complaint against Alaska Airlines," *USA Today*, September 30, 2005.

6. Susan Simpson, "OKC Labor Market Tight for Aircraft Mechanics," *Oklahoman*, August 3, 2010.

7. Airline Pilot Central, www.airlinepilotforums.com, August 29, 2015.

8. Federal Aviation Administration, www.faa.gov/news/updates/?newsid=86688.

9. Airline Pilot Central, www.airlinepilotforums.com, September 1, 2015.

10. National Transportation Safety Board, "Aircraft Accident Report, Inflight Fire and Impact with Terrain, ValuJet Airlines Flight 592, DC-9-32, N904VJ, Everglades, near Miami, Florida, May 11, 1996, NTSB Identification AAR-97/06," Washington, DC.

11. Curt Anderson, "ValuJet Crash behind Air Safety Changes," Associated Press, May 10, 2006.

12. John McArdle, "Indicted in 1996 ValuJet Crash, Airline Mechanic Still on EPA's Most-Wanted List," *New York Times*, May 11, 2011.

13. Richard N. Velotta, "Unusual Incidents Rock Allegiant Air's Profitable Course," *Las Vegas Review-Journal*, August 29, 2015.

14. The Airbus series of jet transports are equipped with a diagnostic system to warn the flight crew and ground-based mechanics of aircraft faults. Two Electronic Centralized Aircraft Monitor (ECAM) displays provide information about many air-

craft systems. Sensors continually monitor those systems. If any one of the parameters monitored moves out of bounds, the crew is warned with an indication on the display. Messages from the ECAM system are also retained for later retrieval. The output can be sent to a printer or transmitted to maintenance control at the airline via an Aircraft Communications Addressing and Reporting System (ACARS).

15. LRUs are major assemblies such as pumps, valves, and avionic black boxes.

16. *Flight International*, "Maintenance Errors Cripple A320," February 1–7, 1995.

17. Teamsters Aviation Mechanics Coalition, http://teamsterair.org/tamc/about-tamc.

18. Teamsters Airline Division, "Avoidable Maintenance, Operational Issues Persist at Allegiant Air," March 8, 2016.

19. *CBS News*, "Allegiant Air Goes On Defensive After '60 Minutes' Report," April 16, 2018.

20. Jon Hemmerdinger, "DOT Reviewing FAA's Oversight of Allegiant and American Airlines," *Flight Global*, May 10, 2018.

21. *CBS News*, "Airline Mechanics Feel Pressured to Overlook Potential Safety Problems: 'Accident Waiting to Happen,'" February 4, 2019.

22. Senators Edward J. Markey and Richard Blumenthal to Daniel K. Elwell, acting FAA administrator, February 12, 2019.

23. Ibid.

24. Airline Pilot Central, www.airlinepilotforums.com, August 29, 2015.

CHAPTER 4

1. Civil Aeronautics Board, "Aircraft Accident Report, Trans World Airlines, Inc., Lockheed 1049A, N6902C, and United Airlines DC-7, N6324C, Grand Canyon, Arizona, June 30, 1956, SA-320," Washington, DC.

2. Robert Serling, *Howard Hughes' Airline: An Informal History of TWA* (New York: St. Martin's, 1983), 257.

3. *San Bernardino Sun*, "4 Major Airlines Slashing Operations," February 20, 1961.

4. TWA losses for the first quarter of 1961 reached nearly $10 million. By mid-year, the airline found itself in dire straights. It appeared that filing for bankruptcy might be the only option to save the company. Howard Hughes had committed to buying a large fleet of Boeing 707 and Convair 880 jets, running up huge debts. He had unwisely procrastinated in making the decision about their purchase, causing TWA to lose its competitive edge in the travel market. Pan American, American Airlines, and United Airlines were already flying jets on many of TWA's routes.

5. The vertical stabilizers improved directional control characteristics and reduced the plane's height so it could fit inside almost any airline hangar. The Douglas DC-6 and DC-7 could not fit in many hangars due to their taller single tails.

6. The engines produced 2,200 hp at 2,000 rpm for takeoff. They drove 15-ft, 3-blade, Hamilton Standard full-feathering, constant-speed propellers.

7. This Day in Aviation, "Important Dates in Aviation History: 5–6 February 1946," www.thisdayinaviation.com/6-february-1946/.

8. Ibid.

9. In 1956, ten years after TWA first introduced the Connies, the airline installed refrigerated air conditioning with individual "eyeball" outlets for passengers and crew at each seat. The system was installed at considerable expense in all L-049s, but its reliability didn't meet expectations.

10. *Portsmouth Herald*, "Carefree Vacationers Wiped Out in Air Crash," September 2, 1961.

11. An engine run-up is a standard preflight check for any aircraft powered by piston engines.

12. Chuck Feldman, "Sept. 1 marks 50th Anniversary of Deadly Plane Crash in Clarendon Hills," *Doings Clarendon Hills*, August 31, 2011.

13. Rudolph Unger, "After 30 Years, Few Traces of Air Crash That Killed 78," *Chicago Tribune*, August 28, 1991.

14. *Portsmouth Herald*, "Carefree Vacationers."

15. "Flight 529," WNBQ-TV Channel 5, September 1, 1961, www.fuzzymemories .tv/index.php?c=4118.

16. Thomas Powers, "Full Story of Air Crash," *Chicago Daily Tribune*, September 2, 1961.

17. *Portsmouth Herald*, "Carefree Vacationers."

18. Mike Ellis, "Clarendon Hills Part I: Reliving the 1961 TWA Airliner Crash," *Hinsdale Magazine*, April 2015.

19. Cathy Gordon, "TWA Flight 529," Facebook, www.facebook.com /groups/241582219245634/.

20. Rodger Morphett, "The Hand of God," *Contrails*, March 18, 2008, www.twa seniorsclub.org/memories/contrails/thehandofgod.html.

CHAPTER 5

1. Mike Ellis, "Clarendon Hills Part I: Reliving the 1961 TWA Airliner Crash," *Hinsdale Magazine*, April 2015.

2. *TWA Skyliner*, "CAB Inquiry Seeks Cause of CHI Crash," September 18, 1961.

3. The front and rear aluminum spars of the horizontal stabilizer were found cracked, most likely due to severe oscillatory forces. Before breaking free, the elevator control surface, hinged to the horizontal stabilizer, had oscillated in an unrestrained fashion. That violent motion, in all likelihood, is what tore the tail fin off.

4. The extreme accelerations experienced by the plane drove the spool even lower in the bore of the valve. This resulted in continuing the up-elevator pressure and, by creating a vicious cycle, increased the erratic acceleration forces causing the plane to be tossed about in the sky.

5. The bolt was intended for use where a tight fit was imperative, such as connecting the linkages of flight controls. AN-175 bolts are manufactured to such a high level of precision that they can only be inserted in a hole if tapped into place using a small hammer. A tight fit was required to prevent even slight vibrations from occurring in the control system. If the bolt were undersized by as little as a few thousandths of an inch, it wouldn't be able to carry the needed shear load. The periphery of the bolt also had to be snug with the surface of its hole. These threaded fasteners, including bolts, screws, nuts, and washers are identified by AN (Air Force-Navy), NAS (National Aircraft Standard), or MS (Military Standard) designations.

6. *TWA Skyliner*, "CAB Inquiry Seeks Cause."

7. TWA signed an agreement in 1954 to locate its maintenance shops at the airport. Owning the $18 million facility, the city leased it to TWA. During its peak usage in the 1960s the base was Kansas City's largest employer with approximately six thousand employees working in the hangars and shops.

8. A washer was used to prevent scuffing and gouging of the part, an important safety consideration.

9. The omission of the washers was a violation of approved maintenance practices but not considered a contributing factor that resulted in this accident.

10. The unique parallelogram-shaped linkage served as a vital component for integrating yoke movements from the cockpit with the force exerted by the boost cylinder to move the elevator. The linkage moved a tiny spool inside a valve. Its only function was to direct high-pressure hydraulic fluid to the cylinder. When each of the parts worked in unison, the elevator control surface would move up or down in response to what the pilots commanded it to do.

11. The de-boosting procedure was covered, but not stressed, as a part of the pilot training program at TWA and other air carriers because boost failures had been either rare or nonexistent.

12. Temco Overhaul and Aerosystems, "Report no. G8047.5, Evaluation of Elevator Control System C/RC-121 Aircraft, July 13, 1961."

13. David Kent, email to author, March 11, 2019.

14. *Skyliner*, "Missing Bolt May Be Clue to Crash," October 16, 1961.

15. Georg Kohne et al., "Lufthansa Super Star," position paper, January 18, 2019.

16. All twenty-five remaining L-049 Constellations were sold to California Airmotive Corporation in March 1962 for a total of $700,000. The company was a buyer and seller of old airline transports. TWA had once paid Lockheed more than this for a single L-049.

17. The explosion's probable cause was a short circuit resulting from frayed wiring that ignited vapors in the jet's center fuel tank (National Transportation Safety Board, "Aircraft Accident Report, Inflight Breakup over the Atlantic Ocean, Trans World Airlines Flight 800, Boeing 747-131, N93119, Near East Moriches, New York, July 17, 1996, AAR-00/03").

18. Civil Aeronautics Board, "Aircraft Accident Report, Northwest Orient Airlines, Inc., Lockheed Electra, L-188C, N 137US, O'Hare International Airport, Chicago, Illinois, September 17, 1961, SA-364," Washington, DC.

19. Ibid.

20. Robert Serling, *The Electra Story: Aviation's Greatest Mystery* (New York: Bantam Books, 1991), 106–7.

21. Kent, email to author.

CHAPTER 6

1. The name of the airport is attributed to Carl Mather, a teenage second lieutenant in the Army Signal Corps during World War I. As a pilot trainee, he was killed in an accident on the field. Mather's classmates requested that the facility be renamed in his honor. During World War II Mather Field became a major player in training pilots, navigators, observers, and bombardiers for deployment to the war front.

2. Denise Gellene, "Consolidated Freightways to Buy Emery, Creating U.S.' Biggest Heavy Cargo Shipper," *Los Angeles Times*, February 14, 1989.

3. Ibid.

4. By the end of the 1970s, airlines operating so-called Stretch Eight versions of the DC-8 were considering upgrading their aging jets rather than buying newer and quieter planes. In April 1979, United Airlines began upgrading thirty of its DC-8-61s with efficient CFM56-2-C1 fanjets.

5. National Transportation Safety Board, "Aircraft Accident Report, Uncontrolled Impact with Terrain, Fine Airlines Flight 101 Douglas DC-8-61, N27UA, Miami, Florida, August 7, 1997, NTSB Identification AAR-98-02," Washington, DC.

6. Christopher Heredia and Michael Taylor, "Cargo Shift Worried Crew in Crash," *San Francisco Chronicle*, February 18, 2000.

7. National Transportation Safety Board, "Aircraft Accident Report, Trans International Airlines Corp. Ferry Flight 863, Douglas DC-8-63F, N4863T, J. F. Kennedy International Airport, September 8, 1970, NTSB Identification AAR-71-12," Washington, DC.

8. The takeoff weight was calculated to be 279,231 pounds, including 63,764 pounds of cargo and 66,700 pounds of fuel. The maximum allowable takeoff weight for this version of the DC-8 was 322,000 pounds.

9. Miles Corwin and Jenifer Warren, "Cargo Plane Crashes outside Sacramento, Killing 3," *Los Angeles Times*, February 17, 2000.

CHAPTER 7

1. On January 31, 2000, Alaska Airlines Flight 261, a McDonnell Douglas MD-83, had plunged into the Pacific Ocean off the Ventura County coast. All eighty-eight passengers and the crew aboard the jet were killed when it impacted the water. A scheduled flight, it had departed Puerto Vallarta, Mexico, for the Seattle-Tacoma International Airport. The accident's cause was later attributed to a total loss of aircraft pitch control caused by the excessively worn threads of a jackscrew that moved the horizontal stabilizer. Failure to properly lubricate the threads was determined to be the fault of Alaska Airlines. Records provided by Alaska Airlines indicated that proper lubrication had been accomplished, whereas it had not been (National Transportation Safety Board, "Aircraft Accident Report, Loss of Control and Impact with Pacific Ocean, Alaska Airlines Flight 261, McDonnell Douglas MD-83, N963AS, about 2.7 Miles North of Anacapa Island, California January 31, 2000, NTSB Identification AAR-02-01," Washington, DC). At the time of the Emery accident, the NTSB could offer no conclusions as to why Flight 261 had crashed. This lack of a cause intensified the public's concern; seasoned air travelers were antsy, while others simply took the family car to go places.

2. Emery's in-house maintenance capabilities were limited, opening the door to MROs like TTS to bid on the airline's heavy maintenance requirements. It is assumed that TTS was the low bidder for such work.

3. Andy Pasztor and Rick Brooks, "Emery Suffered from Safety Issues Long Before It Faced FAA Grounding," *Wall Street Journal*, August 24, 2001.

4. *KIRO-TV Eyewitness News*, "Pilots Warned FAA Prior to Fatal Crash, Said Crews Living on 'Borrowed Time,'" April 13, 2002.

5. *Gainesville Sun*, "Air Cargo Dangers Fly Under the Radar," July 9, 2006.

6. *Los Angeles Times*, "Emery Pilots OK Strike in Bid for 1st Contract," July 25, 2000.

7. Pasztor and Brooks, "Emery Suffered from Safety Issues."

8. Steve Scott, "Missing Retention Bolt in Elevator Actuator Mechanism Led to Crash of Emery Jet," *Defense Daily*, August 11, 2003.

9. Ibid.

10. *Gainesville Sun*, "Air Cargo Dangers."

11. Scott, "Missing Retention Bolt."

CHAPTER 8

1. Simon Hradecky, "China Airlines B738 at Okinawa on Aug. 20th 2007, Airplane in Flames at Stand," *Aviation Herald*, August 20, 2007.

2. During the 1980s, I was a project engineer at a major aircraft manufacturer undertaking a research study to implement an automatic aircraft inspection, diagnostic, and prognostic system.

3. Because helicopter engines, transmissions, and rotors depend entirely on rotating mechanisms to create aerodynamic lift, the hardware used to attach them endures severe stress.

4. *Chicago Tribune*, "Resort Airlines Awarded Safety Citation for '52," August 9, 1953.

5. United Press International, "Plane Carrying 38 Soldiers Crashes at Louisville Airport; 22 Persons Killed, 19 Hurt," *Middlesboro Daily News*, September 29, 1953.

6. Western Airlines merged with Delta Air Lines in 1986, becoming a wholly owned subsidiary of the Atlanta-based carrier and losing its corporate identity as an independent airline.

7. It was three years before Western and other airlines serving Los Angeles would move their operations and gates into newly constructed satellite buildings on World Way West, along the west side of Sepulveda Boulevard. To this day, an iconic circular-theme building identifies the futuristic airport.

8. The aerodynamic lift of a wing or control surface increases with the square of the velocity. If a plane flies twice as fast, four times more lift force is generated.

CHAPTER 9

1. www.smartcockpit.com, "Embraer EMB 120."

2. At the time of the accident flight, N33701 had accumulated 7,210 hours along with 10,009 takeoff and landing cycles. The cabin was configured with ten rows of double passenger seats along the right side and ten rows of single seats on the left. The total number of Brasilia airplanes flying for U.S.-based airlines then being 150, Continental Express operated 34 of them.

3. Airline policies and Federal Air Regulations didn't mandate that flight crews be notified of such repairs.

4. Elizabeth Hudson, "14 Killed in Commuter Plane Crash," *Washington Post*, September 12, 1991.

5. Ibid.

6. Ibid.

7. As with other airplanes, the horizontal stabilizer provides lift to balance the pitch of the wings. Deflecting the elevator attached to the rear of the stabilizer changes the pitch attitude. The lift force needed to establish trimmed flight depends on many factors such as the plane's center of gravity, engine thrust, airspeed, and how the plane is configured.

8. When ice builds up on leading edges, a de-icing system pumps air into flexible boots fitted along the leading edges to inflate and deflate the boots in cycles. As the boots inflate, the ice on them cracks and is swept away.

9. National Transportation Safety Board, "Aircraft Accident Report, Atlantic Southeast Airlines, Inc., Flight 2311, Uncontrolled Collision with Terrain, an EMB-

120, N270AS, Brunswick, Georgia, April 5, 1991, NTSB Identification AAR-92-03," Washington, DC.

CHAPTER 10

1. The airline had a written policy governing disciplinary action, including the following forms of progressive discipline: verbal counseling or reprimand; formal counseling and written warning; probation; suspension; dismissal; and immediate dismissal without notice.

2. Associated Press, "Airline Is Faulted in '91 Plane Crash," *New York Times*, July 22, 1992.

3. Federal Aviation Administration, "Aviation Incident Final Report: Embraer EMB-120RT, Incident Number FTW931A048, December 9, 1992," Washington, DC.

4. Bureau of Enquiry and Analysis for Civil Aviation Safety, "Serious Incident on 29 September 1998 at Clermont Ferrand (63) to the Embraer 120 'Brasilia' Registered F-GTSH Operated by Regional Airlines," Report f-sh980529a."

5. *Wendell H. Ford Aviation Investment and Reform Act for the 21st Century*, Public Law 106-181, 106th Cong.

CHAPTER 11

1. Thomas Frank, "Safety Last: Lies and Coverups Mask Roots of Small-Plane Carnage," *USA Today*, June 17, 2014.

2. Ibid.

3. Federal Aviation Administration, "Emergency Airworthiness Directive, April 18, 2019, Cirrus Design Corporation (Cirrus) Model SF50 Airplanes, AD # 2019-08-51," Washington, DC.

4. Woodrow Bellamy III, "FAA Grounds Cirrus Vision Jet after Angle of Attack Incidents," *Avionics International*, April 19, 2019.

5. Sarah-Blythe Ballard, "The U.S. Commercial Air Tour Industry: A Review of Aviation Safety Concerns," *Aviation Space and Environmental Medicine* 85, no. 2 (February 2014):160–66.

6. Linda Werfelman, "Inadequate Maintenance," *AeroSafety World*, March 29, 2018.

7. National Transportation Safety Board, "Aviation Accident Final Report, Eurocopter EC 130 B4, Loss of Engine Power (Total), N151GC, Boulder City, Nevada, June 27, 2017, Accident Number WPR17LA133," Washington, DC.

8. National Transportation Safety Board, "Aviation Accident Final Report, Bell 206B, System/Component Malfunction/Failure (Non-Power), N24FS, Rockville, Idaho, May 26, 2017, Accident Number WPR17LA113," Washington, DC.

9. National Transportation Safety Board, "Aviation Accident Final Report, Robinson Helicopter Company R44 II, Registration N30242; Orlando, Florida, March 22, 2015, Accident Number ERA15FA164," Washington, DC.

10. Aviation Safety Network, "ASN Wikibase Occurrence # 14661," https://aviation-safety.net/wikibase/14661.

11. National Transportation Safety Board, "Aviation Incident Final Report: Boeing 747-422, Los Angeles, California, Incident LAX901A305," Washington, DC.

12. Civil Aeronautics Board, "Accident Investigation Report, United Air Lines, Inc., Convair 340, N 73154, Dexter, Iowa, January 19, 1955, SA-302," Washington, DC.

13. National Transportation Safety Board, "Aviation Accident Final Report, Airborne Express McDonnell Douglas DC-9-11, Registration N945AX; Cedar Rapids, Iowa, October 13, 1995, Accident number: CHI96LA011," Washington, DC.

14. Aviation Safety Network, https://aviation-safety.net/database/record.php?id=20070313-0.

15. Aviation Safety Network, https://aviation-safety.net/database/record.php?id=20050131-1.

16. National Transportation Safety Board, "Aviation Accident Brief, Pilot/Race 177, The Galloping Ghost, North American P-51D, N7911, Reno, Nevada, September 16, 2011, NTSB Identification: NTSB/AAB-12/01," Washington, DC.

17. *Los Angeles Times*, "Air Force Says Stealth Fighter Crash Is Due to Missing Bolts," December 13, 1997.

CHAPTER 12

1. Kerry Lynch, "A4A Urges FAA Funding Plan," *Aviation International News*, October 2018.

2. Edmund L. Andrews and Jodi Wilgoren, "Kerry to Propose Eliminating a Tax Break on U.S. Companies' Overseas Profits," *New York Times*, March 26, 2004.

3. Benjamin Zhang, "Trump Just Used Boeing's New Global Airliner to Attack Globalization," *Business Insider*, February 17, 2017.

4. National Transportation Safety Board, "Aircraft Accident Report, Loss of Pitch Control during Takeoff, Air Midwest Flight 5481, Raytheon, Beechcraft) 1900D, N233YV, Charlotte, North Carolina, January 8, 2003, NTSB Identification AAR-0401," Washington, DC.

5. Office of the Inspector General, U.S. Department of Transportation, "Two Former Repair Station Mechanics Sentenced and to Be Deported in Undocumented Alien Case," June 27, 2005.

6. *Aircraft Maintenance Outsourcing Disclosure Act of 2018*, H.R. 6028—115th Congress, 2nd Session, 2017–2018.

7. Peter DeFazio and Rick Larsen, letter to Transportation Secretary Elaine Chao urging action to improve oversight of overseas repair stations, June 28, 2018.

8. National Transportation Safety Board, "Southwest Airlines Flight 1380 Engine Failure, Investigative Update," www.ntsb.gov/investigations/pages/dca18ma142.aspx.

9. Federal Aviation Administration "Whistleblower Complaint EWB17634, Southwest Airlines," November 16, 2017.

10. John Garamendi, "Congressman John Garamendi Introduces the Aircraft Maintenance Outsourcing Disclosure Act," June 7, 2018, https://garamendi.house.gov media/press-releases/congressman-john-garamendi-introduces-aircraft-maintenance -outsourcing.

11. Transport Workers Union of America, "Aircraft Maintenance Outsourcing Disclosure Act of 2018 Prioritizes Safety, American Jobs," June 7, 2018, www.twu.org /aircraft-maintenance-outsourcing-disclosure-act-of-2018-prioritizes-safety-american -jobs/.

12. Ibid.

13. Ibid.

14. Aircraft Mechanics Fraternal Association, "AMFA Supports Aircraft Maintenance Outsourcing Disclosure Act," June 16, 2018, www.amfanational.org/?zone= /unionactive/view_article.cfm&HomeID=708554&page=Test.

15. Under Federal Air Regulation Part 121 governing the operation and maintenance of regularly scheduled major air carriers, an airline is responsible for the upkeep and safety of its planes whether its own mechanics maintain them or the work is outsourced to an MRO.

16. Federal Aviation Administration, "Compliance Philosophy," www.faa.gov/news /safety_briefing/2016/media/SE_Topic_16-10.pdf.

17. At the time of Allegiant Air's rejected takeoff in Las Vegas, there was no requirement to perform drug testing at foreign MROs. However, AAR and the airline were in full compliance with the testing regulations, as were other MROs located in the United States.

18. Mike Busch, "The Savvy Aviator #51: A Mechanic's Liability," *Avweb*, November 22, 2007, www.faalawdefense.com/pf/a&p_liability.pdf.

19. Aircraft Repair Station Association, "ARSA's Klein Hails FAA Bill as 'Historic Victory,'" October 3, 2018, http://arsa.org/faa-reauthorization-2018/.

20. Donald J. Porter, *Howard's Whirlybirds: Howard Hughes' Amazing Pioneering Helicopter Exploits* (London: Fonthill Media, 2013), 168.

21. Kerry Lynch, "AAR Points to Prospects to Fill Labor Pipeline," AINonline, February 1, 2019, www.ainonline.com/aviation-news/business-aviation/2019-02-01 /aar-points-prospects-fill-labor-pipeline.

22. Aviation Technician Education Council, "ATEC Pipeline Report," December 2018.

23. Federal Aviation Administration, "The Economic Impact of Civil Aviation on the U.S. Economy," November 2016, www.faa.gov/air_traffic/publications/media/2016 -economic-impact-report_FINAL.pdf.

24. *CBS News*, "Airline Mechanics Feel Pressured to Overlook Potential Safety Problems: 'Accident Waiting to Happen,'" February 4, 2019.

25. Federal Aviation Administration, "Aviation Safety Strategic Plan, FY20–FY24," April 2019, www.faa.gov/about/office_org/headquarters_offices/avs/media/avs_strategy_508_final.pdf.

26. Federal Aviation Administration, "Compliance Philosophy."

27. Federal Aviation Administration, "Aviation Safety Strategic Plan."

28. Ibid.

INDEX